(ORLO MILLER)

THIS WAS
LONDON

THE FIRST TWO CENTURIES

Butternut Press Inc. Westport, Ontario, 1988

Canadian Cataloguing in Publication Data

Miller, Orlo, 1911–
    This was London

Includes bibliographical references and index.
ISBN 0–921575–07–6 (bound)

1. London (Ont.) – History.   I. Title.

FC3099.L65M54 1988   971.3'26   C88–093835–0
F1059.5.L6M54 1988

ISBN 0–921575–07–6
Printed and bound in Canada

Butternut Press Inc.
P.O. Box 166, Westport
Ontario, K0G 1X0

Editor: Peter Smith
Graphic Design: Peter Dorn

For
Ann and David Lindsay

PREFACE

I take pleasure in extending warm greetings to the citizens of the city of London through the pages of this special book on the history of our community.

This Was London tells the story of our origin and development as a municipality. It serves as a reminder of the role played by our forebears in making our hometown a great place to live, work, and play.

The city of London has contributed immeasurably to the life of southwestern Ontario and, indeed, the province as a whole. May this book instill in each of you a sense of pride in our rich civic heritage.

David Peterson
Premier of Ontario

CONTENTS

FOREWORD

The Reverend Orlo Miller has written a history of London that is eminently readable and enlightening. He brings his life-long experience and affection for the city to bear in describing the events, people, and organizations that have shaped the community since Peter MacGregor built the first house near the forks of the Thames in 1826. His credentials for this task are well-founded, as evidenced by the fact that he, together with Fred Landon and Edwin Seaborn, reorganized and revitalized the London and Middlesex Historical Society in 1936. For more than fifty years, then, Orlo Miller has been an acute observer of the City's history – its successes and failures.

Several great themes thread through the pages of *This Was London*. These include the seminal influence of the army, the railways, the University, the business community, and the Churches.

It is easily forgotten that the British Army was the principal source of social and economic activity from 1837, when the Garrison was established on eight square blocks bounded by Dufferin, the present CPR tracks, and Clarence and Waterloo streets. Two sets of buildings erected at a cost of $400,000, an enormous sum in those days, ushered in the first of a number of economic stimuli that have shaped London – climaxing during the First World War, when 16,000 troops were trained at Wolseley Barracks.

Since 1845, when the London and Gore Railroad Company (1834) was revived and renamed the Great Western Railroad Company, the influence of the railroads has had a lasting influence on London's preeminence as the "capital" of Western Ontario. Mr Miller describes the first train from Hamilton in 1853 (which comprised a wood-burning locomotive and two coaches), a trip that took six hours.

The evolution of the University of Western Ontario, from its founding as Huron College by Bishop Isaac Hellmuth in 1863, is told in detail and substantiates the claim that UWO has been a most important influence in the growth and maturing of the city. It is difficult to realize that while the University library housed only two hundred volumes in 1908, it has more than two *million* today.

The business community is personified by well-known London families including the McClarys, the Bechers, the Leonards, the Hymans, and the Blackburns whose ownership of the London *Free Press* goes back to its purchase by Josiah Blackburn in 1852.

The long-lived influence of London's church leaders dates from the arrival of the Reverend William Proudfoot (Presbyterian), the Reverend James Jackson (Methodist), and the Reverend Benjamin Cronyn (Anglican) in 1832. Notable dates include Bishop Cronyn's election in 1857 and the first Canadian Salvation Army meeting in 1882.

But this summary of Orlo Miller's entrancing history must not obscure the charming descriptions of the progress and misadventures of London's rollicking early years. Anecdotes describe Francis Evans Cornish, a four-term mayor of the mid-nineteenth century whose misdemeanours embraced public assaults, drunkenness, bigamy, and divorce, and the colourful career of Mayor George Wenige, the first of whose nine terms dated from 1923.

Not overlooked either are famous criminal cases like the trial and hanging of Henry Sovereign for the murder of his wife and seven of his eleven children, or the weekly break-and-enters of "Slippery Jack," a young army officer who won a bet by entering a house every week for a year – where he tickled the feet of the occupants and left without being apprehended or identified.

Noteworthy events enrich the narrative – the great fire of 1845, which left 200 buildings in ashes and resulted in a by-law banning frame buildings; the capsizing of the SS *Victoria* in 1881, with a loss of as many as 230 lives; and the Labatt kidnapping of 1934.

Mr Miller makes it clear that London did not exist in isolation. World events like wars, depressions, royal visits, Asiatic cholera, and typhoid epidemics punctuated London's development. The author has cleverly framed local events with international landmarks by adding notes at the bottom of each page describing developments in other countries year by year, to put London's history in context.

Not neglected are the city's cultural and social history, ranging from the beginning of London's strong theatre tradition, which originated with an amateur performance led by Dr O'Flarity in 1840.

One event might be illuminated by my own family tradition. The author states that because of their opposition to the Rebellion Losses Bill signed by Lord Elgin in 1849, Irish toughs and Tories destroyed a series of ever-green arches erected on Hamilton Road to welcome that gentleman to this city. My great-great-grandfather Benjamin Higgins recounted in *his* version that Orangemen (of whom he was one) levelled the arches because "They were glad to walk over the green, but were damned if they would walk under it."

We who love London and its history are indebted to Orlo Miller for *This Was London* because its scholarship is made enjoyable and informative by the inclusion of dozens of anecdotes, often amusing, sometimes tragic, which carry the reader from page to page. His final chapter, entitled "City for Sale," is a strong plea for preserving heritage buildings and neigh-bourhoods. One hopes that Mr Miller's heritage concerns will influence London's councillors and citizens to save the historic Talbot Block of commercial buildings between King and Dundas streets, which includes London's first town hall, dated 1842. If this endeavour succeeds, the Talbot Block will be a lasting memorial to the Rev. Orlo Miller, an outstanding Londoner and engaging historian.

John White

PREFACE

This is a social history of a middle-sized Canadian city.

It covers a period of 195 years, from the time it emerged as a concept in the mind of John Graves Simcoe, the first lieutenant-governor of Upper Canada, to the present year.

It may justifiably be called an "anecdotal history." It is meant to be read, not grappled with. There are no obtrusive footnotes to dull the appetite of the general reader. For those who wish to know more, the Bibliography and Notes at the end of the book may provide some answers.

No city, not even one as prideful and insular as London, Ontario, exists in a vacuum. Inevitably its history is influenced by events occurring far outside its boundaries. Marshall McLuhan did not invent the global village. He merely gave it definition.

To demonstrate this linkage between *urbs et orbis,* a timetable is appended at the bottom of each page, in the space normally occupied by footnotes. These entries illustrate what events were taking place in the contemporary world outside the Forks.

An attempt has been made in this history to present as fair a picture as possible of the various strata of London society over the 162 years of its official existence.

Much space has been devoted in the past to the story of London's Establishment – the community leaders, the wealthy and the influential.

The middle classes – the artisans, the small merchant and businessmen, the professionals – have received a lesser amount of attention.

The poor, the disadvantaged, the visible and invisible minorities have been very largely ignored. What is here written about them can in no sense be construed as the last word on the subject. One can only hope it may be the first.

Finally, I would ask the reader to remember that the people who inhabit these pages were real people. They were not statistics or mere dates on cemetery headstones. They did brave things. They did stupid things, just like us.

However, it must always be remembered that they obeyed standards and reacted to stimuli that were much different from ours.

Failure to recognize this basic fact has resulted in much distortion of historical evidence. As the American writer Gerald W. Johnson wrote in 1943:

Nothing changes more constantly than the past; for the past that influences our lives does not consist of what actually happened but of what men believe happened.

This present book purports to be a record of *some* of the things that actually happened in London, Canada, between 1793 and 1988.

Orlo Miller
London, Ontario
March 1988

ACKNOWLEDGEMENTS

It was Major Hume Blake Cronyn who first aroused my interest in the general subject of history, It was Dr Fred Landon who directed my attention to the history of my own community. It was Dr Edwin Seaborn who helped me unearth previously unknown collections of original source material. It was Dr Richard E. Crouch who provided me with quarters to use as a centre for historical and genealogical research. I am deeply indebted to the memory of these dear friends of many years ago.

Since 1926, the year of the centennial of London's founding, I have relied heavily on the resources and assistance of the London Public Library and the library of the University of Western Ontario.

Over the years the staff of the municipally-operated library have given me generous help under a succession of librarians, beginning with Fred Landon and continuing with his successors, Richard Crouch, Deane Kent, Stanley Beacock, and the present director, Reid Osborne. Staff members to whom I am especially obliged include Miss Eleanor Shaw, Miss Elizabeth Spicer, and the present custodian of the London Room, Glen Curnoe.

At the University of Western Ontario I have long enjoyed the academic assistance and personal friendship of Dr James J. Talman, Dr Landon's successor as Librarian. I owe an enormous debt of gratitude and affection to the indefatigable director of the Regional Collection, Edward Phelps, whose skill in finding and annexing source material is legendary. I am grateful to many of his colleagues at the D.B. Weldon Library, including John Lutman, Guy St Denis, Stephen Harding, and Alan Noon.

Many individuals have provided help. Martha Blackburn who, like her late father, Walter J. Blackburn, is a good friend, has graciously given permission for the use of material from *A Century of Western Ontario*, a history of the London *Free Press*. Janet Hunten has brought many pictures and articles to my attention. Nancy Poole, director of the London Regional Art Gallery, has always been a tower of strength, academically and personally.

I am fortunate in the friendship of the city's booksellers. Especial thanks must be given to Gerald Klein, who pressured me for years to write this history; to Roberts Holmes, who showed me how to sell books once they are written, and to Robert Pittam, who shares my love for trees and the Baconian Club.

Above and beyond all these friends of history, I submit my heartfelt thanks to my wife, collaborator, editor, critic, and CEO (Chief Encouraging Officer) Maridon, who has shared in, and suffered from, my obsession with the past.

Finally I must acknowledge the City of London itself, my joy and my despair.

May it someday grow up and take its place among other gracious cities of the world.

History is philosophy teaching by examples.   Dionysius of Halicarnassus (*c.* 40–8 BC)

If men could learn from history, what lessons it might teach us! But passion and party blind our eyes, and the light which experience gives is a lantern on the stern, which shines only on the waves behind us!   Samuel Taylor Coleridge (1772–1834)

Titus Antoninus Pius ... His reign is marked by the rare advantage of furnishing very few materials for history; which is, indeed, little more than the register of the crimes, follies and misfortunes of mankind.   Edward Gibbon (1737–1794)

Mad from life's history,
Glad to death's mystery,
Swift to be hurl'd
Anywhere, anywhere,
Out of the world!
Thomas Hood (1799–1845)

History is bunk.   Henry Ford (1863–1947)

Nearly all our best men are dead! Carlyle, Tennyson, Browning, George Eliot! – I'm not feeling very well myself.   *Punch,* 104 (1893), 210

PROLEGOMENA

Take a map of North America.

In the heart of the continent, due south of James Bay, which hangs like an udder from the full belly of Hudson Bay, fixed on the criss-cross lines of latitude and longitude like a cluster of grapes on a trellis – the Great Lakes.

Take a map of Canada.

Water-locked, in the heart of the lake system, like a broad arrow pointed at the Mississippi – a huge triangle. Its base, Lakes Erie and Ontario and the St Lawrence River; its eastern angle, the junction of the St Lawrence and Ottawa rivers; its western angle, the mouth of the Detroit River where it empties into Lake Erie; its northern apex, Lake Nipissing.

This is Southern Ontario.

Take a map of Ontario.

In the southwestern angle of the mother triangle of Southern Ontario, a second, smaller triangle. Its base is Lake Erie; its northern apex the long, bony finger of the Bruce Peninsula, pointing north-northwest to Tuktoyatuk on the Arctic Ocean.

This is Southwestern Ontario.

Take a map of Southwestern Ontario.

In the heart of the triangle, equidistant from Toronto on the east, Windsor and Detroit on the west, and Owen Sound on the north, is the City of London.

What follows is its story.

John Graves Simcoe (1752–1806), first lieutenant-governor of Upper Canada. Simcoe wanted London as his capital. From *London, Middlesex Historical Society* (1917). UWO

CHAPTER ONE

BEGINNINGS

MONDAY, 4 FEBRUARY 1793

The Gov. set off from hence [Niagara-on-the-Lake] in a sleigh with 6 officers & 20 soldiers for the Mohawk Village on the Grand River where Capt. Brant & 20 Indianz are to join him & guide him by the La Tranche River to Detroit, no European having gone that track & the Indians are to carry Provisions.

The Gov. wore a fur Cap tippet & Gloves & maucassins but no Great Coat. His servant carried two Blankets & linen. The other Gentlemen carried their Blankets in a pack on their Back.

Mrs Simcoe's Diary, ed. Mary Quayle Innis (Toronto: Macmillan of Canada, 1965).

SATURDAY, 2 MARCH 1793

By an act of the Parliament of Great Britain, the western portion of the old Province of Quebec, from the Ottawa River to the Detroit, has been set up as a separate British colony under the name Upper Canada. The appointee of King George III to the governorship of the new province is Lieutenant-Colonel John Graves Simcoe, a veteran of the late war with the rebellious American colonies, which have now been erected into a republic under the presidency of General George Washington.

Along the banks of the St Lawrence and Niagara rivers and the north shore of Lake Ontario, smoke rises from the chimneys of the log-cabin homes of thousands of dispossessed persons made homeless by revolution, heroes by act of parliament. The United Empire Loyalists are settling into their new homes, preparing to establish a tradition, a way of life, a national mythology.

Westward of these pioneer encroachments, there is little but wilderness and wolves. Here and there along the waterways – at Brantford on the

---

1793 Claude Joseph Rouget de l'Isle, *La Marseillaise.*

Grand River, at Delaware on what is now the Thames, and at Sandwich on the Detroit River – an occasional plume of smoke unfurls in the damp spring air from the clearing of a solitary settler. Between these lonely shielings, nothing but the leafy hush of the nearly impenetrable forest. This is the Western District of the Province of Upper Canada. Its southern limit is Lake Erie, its northern (by statute), the North Pole.

In the heart of this huge administrative district, the capital of which is Detroit, on a high, pine-crowned bluff overlooking the confluence of the two branches of the river known to the coureur de bois as "La Tranche," a group of men in military uniforms stands surveying the scene. The envoy of King George III is inspecting his royal master's western dominion.

Accompanying Simcoe are his aides-de-camp, Lieutenants Thomas Talbot, Thomas Grey, and James Givins. The governor's secretary Major Edward Baker Littlehales is taking careful notes, for this is a special stop on the vice-regal tour. He notes the reason later, in his journal:

We struck the Thames at one end of a low, flat island enveloped with shrubs and trees. The rapidity and strength of the current were such as to have forced a channel through the mainland, being a peninsula, and formed this island. We walked over a rich meadow and at its extremity came to the forks of the river.

The Governor wished to examine this situation and its environs, therefore we remained here all the day. He judged it to be a situation eminently calculated for the metropolis of all Canada. ...

In this manner a dream was born. Say, rather, still-born, for Simcoe's plan was not viewed with favour in the places where such decisions were made, in Quebec City or London, England. A site known by the Indians and the French as Toronto was renamed York and established by Simcoe, however reluctantly, as the capital of the province.

From the coming of the Loyalists in 1784 until the War of 1812, immigration into Upper Canada flowed from south to north – from the New England states, New York, and the adjacent Northwest Territory into the Canadas. After the war the direction changed. The next great tide of immigration flowed from east to west. Building to a crest in 1832, the year that saw 92,000 migrants reach British North America, this movement originated in the United Kingdom. Dispossessed Scottish crofters, famine-weakened Irish peasants, land-hungry English tenant farmers – all saw Canada as a land of promise, a new Canaan overflowing with milk and honey. Land in this new dominion of trees was free for the asking.

1793 Alexander Mackenzie reaches the Pacific Ocean from Montreal, by land.

Every man could become a land-owner in his own right. In the Old Country a single freehold acre made a man a proprietor. Here, every Tom O'Brien, Dick Jones, and Harry MacKenzie could have a fifty-, one-hundred-, or two-hundred-acre *estate,* by simply asking for it.

Thus, in the course of a single generation, from this tattered collection of beggars, thieves, rogues, failed merchants, tax-evaders, shepherds, and little people, there emerged a Canadian middle class.

TUESDAY, 21 MARCH 1826

In hundreds of clearings throughout the length and breadth of the peninsula, smoke is rising from settlers' chimneys. In the last thirty years the population of the western section of the province has increased tenfold. From the older settled areas in the east the tide of immigration has been flowing steadily westward. A decade ago, in 1816, the vanguard had surged to and past the Long Point district on Lake Erie. The high-water mark of this period was the little village of Vittoria. As a centre of population, it became the administrative capital of the huge District of London. A courthouse was built here that also housed the District grammar school.

Now, in 1826, the centre of population has shifted. It may now be placed at the geographical centre of the district that bears the name placed upon it by the late Governor Simcoe – London – at approximately the forks of the River Thames. North and south of the Forks are two rapidly growing settlements.

South, in the Township of Westminster, a mix of Scots and New Englanders, with the Americans predominating numerically. North, in the Township of London, a growing settlement of Tipperary Irish Protestants, awaiting the arrival of their Roman Catholic compatriots to renew old feuds and shed new blood.

Squarely between these two thriving groups, at the Forks itself – nothing. From time to time, since 1800, land in the vicinity has been involved in paper transactions, squatters have squatted, shacks have been built and fallen down, speculators have gambled, lost, and moved on. But at Simcoe's chosen dream-city, not a house, not a smoking chimney, not a garden patch. Nothing.

The governor's phantom community is still part of the twilight zone, even though it appears, firmly marked in its proper place, in a geography textbook printed in England, in 1824.

Why?

How is it that with settlements springing up on all sides, with the stra-

---

1826 First railroad tunnel built on the Liverpool-Manchester line, in England.

tegic location of the site so apparent, how is it that this splendid, pine-crowned bluff overlooking the fertile valley of the Thames stands bare and lifeless?

Let us look at the site more closely. For clarity, we will use the modern street grid. First, the bluff itself, an elevation that falls steeply from its crest to the west and north. The pitch is still evident today from the west, but the declivity to the north is camouflaged by 150 years of road-building. The original surface of the ground at the corner of Dundas and Ridout streets is nearly twenty feet below the modern roadway.

Directly to the east of the bluff is a swamp that covers half the area of a city block, fed by a meandering, marshy stream. Tradition claims that an early resident lost a wagon to the gluey depths of the bog, which was apparently filled in by the 1840s. Southward, a second creek, its bed marked by two more miasmic marshes, wanders down to the south branch of the Thames, in the general vicinity of the former Hay Stationery building on York Street. Nearly a kilometer to the north, a third stream, much larger than the other two, but just as swampy, feeds into the north branch of the Thames, south of Oxford Street.

Between the two southern streams and the northern watercourse there is a tall gravelly knoll, roughly located on the present street allowance between St Paul's Cathedral and the London Club. At the foot of this knoll, extending from Queens Avenue to Dundas Street, a quicksand bog. The Dominion Public Building at the corner of Queens Avenue and Richmond Street, the former press room of the London *Free Press* on the east side of Richmond Street, and the Canadian Imperial Bank of Commerce building at the northeast corner of Dundas and Richmond streets – all have their footings in this ancient Ice Age bog.

South of the quicksand trap there is another gravelly knoll. Where this hillock was, on the east side of Richmond Street, between Dundas and King streets, there stands today one half of a major commercial building erected in the year London became a city. The fire that destroyed part of the structure left the datestone intact – The Victoria Block 1855. In clearing this site for the building the contractors of 130 years ago found the grave of an unknown French gentleman, dress-sword by his side.

This then was the site of London in the year 1826 – sand, gravel, trees, marshy streams, the debris of the great glaciers of the Ice Age.

To Simcoe's military mind, the physical conditions of the site in no way detracted from its strategic importance. However, those same conditions rendered it inappropriate for farming and so the Forks remained unoccupied.

1826 Benjamin Disraeli publishes, anonymously, his first novel, *Vivian Grey*.

Now, a generation after the governor's visit, Simcoe's dream-capital has been given a second chance. In November 1825, the London District courthouse and gaol at Vittoria were heavily damaged by fire. This gave the authorities an opportunity to choose a more central location for the administrative capital. A principal factor in the eventual choice of the Forks of the Thames was undoubtedly the influence of Simcoe's former aide-de-camp Thomas Talbot on the members of the commission appointed to determine where the new courthouse was to be built.

It has fallen to Talbot's right-hand supporter, the dour New Englander Colonel Mahlon Burwell, to lay out the new town-site. Among his helpers, all anxious to pick up a few much-needed government shillings, is a local tavern-keeper, a Highlander named Peter MacGregor, who is serving as a chain-bearer.

By late summer, the plan of the new town is complete – on paper.

The plan is much more modest than the sketched outline of Simcoe's city, which is to be found in the Public Archives at Ottawa. As defined in Burwell's work the site was bounded on the south and west by the Thames River. The northern boundary is a street allowance appropriately called North Street. This street jogs to the south around the southern boundary of the farm owned by John Kent since 1821. The jogged portion of the street is now called Carling, the eastern section is Queens Avenue.

The eastern border of the town plot is a street named in honour of Thomas Talbot's boyhood friend, Arthur Wellesley, Duke of Wellington. Between Wellington Street and the Forks, one north-south thoroughfare is named for the Duke of Clarence, card-playing regal roisterer, third son of the third George and drinking companion in the days of the Regency of the same Thomas Talbot. Another street bears the name of the Duke of Richmond, governor-general of Canada, which country he made famous in 1819 by dying of hydrophobia in what were then its western wilds. One is named for Talbot himself and one for Thomas Ridout, surveyor-general of Upper Canada, to whom presumably Mahlon Burwell was indebted for this and other surveying commissions. Ridout Street, following an ancient Indian trail, is the community's principal north-south artery.

The major east-west street is Dundas, a road built by order of Governor Simcoe to connect the village of Dundas, on Lake Ontario, with his phantom city of London. Both the road and the village were named for the Right Honourable Henry Dundas, secretary of state for the Home Department from 1791 to 1801. Another east-west street is named after His Majesty King George IV (King Street); another for Frederick Augustus, Duke of York, second son of George III, who was Thomas Talbot's

---

1826 James Fenimore Cooper, *The Last of the Mohicans.*

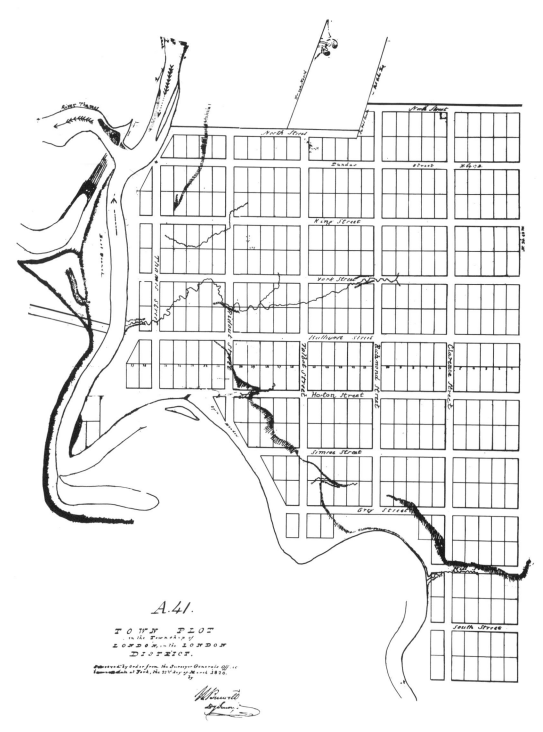

Map of the London townsite by Thomas Ridout, surveyor-general of Upper Canada, after the 1826 survey by Col. Mahlon Burwell. AO

The Reverend Doctor Thomas Webster (1809–1901), while still a boy, saw Peter MacGregor establish the first residence and business on the London townsite in 1826. From F.T. Rosser, *London Township Pioneers* (Belleville: Mika Publishing, Inc.)

commander in the ill-fated invasion of Holland by the British Army in 1799; one bears the name of Wilmot Horton, under-secretary of state for the colonies, and the last honours Henry, third Earl of Bathurst, colonial secretary and secretary for war from 1812 to 1827.

The names are grandiose. The markers are wooden stakes pounded into gravel, sand, and mud.

MONDAY, 2 OCTOBER 1826

In the bogs, the bullfrogs are croaking. Overhead, a flock of geese honks mournfully, southbound over the scarlet and yellow forest.

On the main branch of the Thames, below the Forks, a river ferryman, pole poised in midstream, stops. Struck by something unusual in the well-known scene, he looks upriver. With his ague-stricken forefinger he draws his passengers' attention to a slow streamer of smoke, crawling into the upper air from a hidden chimney behind the bluff that crowns the Forks.

It's the smoke of London's *first* chimney.

Eastward of the site, a seventeen-year-old resident of London Township, on his way to the grist mill at Byron, also notices the the rising signal of human habitation. Many years later, when he is an internationally-

---

1826 Felix Mendelssohn, *Overture to A Midsummer Night's Dream.*

renowned Methodist minister, author, and supporter of women's rights, the Reverend Doctor Thomas Webster will recall that autumn evening and identify the two participants in the domestic drama at the Forks. They were, according to him, Peter MacGregor and his friend John Woods.

The following morning, by the simple process of hanging a tin cup on the doorjamb, first settler Peter MacGregor becomes London's first hotel- and tavern-keeper, its first businessman. He is soon joined by others. Abraham Carroll, a United Empire Loyalist from Westminster Township, opens a second hotel, grandly christened the Mansion House, on Dundas Street. Work is begun on a pretentious, Gothic-style courthouse, designed more or less in the fashion of Thomas Talbot's birthplace, Malahide Castle, Dublin, Ireland. Tall, cold-eyed George Jervis Goodhue, a Yankee pedlar, opens the town's first store, sells his first stock over a board suspended between two kegs, and clears 500 per cent profit. The Church of England sends a missionary priest, the Reverend Edward Jukes Boswell, to found a congregation and to build a church.

Meanwhile the tide of immigration continues to flow steadily westward; Highland Scots for Lobo Township, Tipperary Irish for Biddulph, Pennsylvania Dutch for Yarmouth. For Kent County, French Canadians, English, Irish, Scots, and refugee black slaves from the United States of America. Onward the tide sweeps, into Lambton and Essex counties, until it washes up in a polyglot surf on the east shores of the Detroit and St Clair rivers' meeting, for the moment at least in amity, the almost forgotten backwater of the Sandwich settlement, established by the French nineteen years before the Battle of the Plains of Abraham.

From York to Sandwich – 250 miles by the military highway, rough-hewn from the dense forest in 1811. From it, extending off in a dozen directions, new roads, new trails, leading into scores of new settlements.

Everywhere the "plock-plock" of the settler's axe, ripping into the thousand-year-old woody bulwark, tearing the roots from the yielding earth, building gigantic bonfires of walnut, oak, and hickory, whose smoke can be seen as far away as Chicago. The Western Ontario pioneer labours from dawn to dusk, industriously laying the groundwork for the twentieth century's ecological cataclysm.

Like a dissolving view in a motion picture, the trees are going, revealing the bare, rich soil beneath. In the next stage the pioneer, scratching the stump-strewn ground with a pine branch, will give way to the wheat farmer, roiling the soil with his iron plough, stripping it of its laboriously-accumulated humus, in a mad race for the gold in bread-hungry England's bulging coffers.

1826 Stamford Raffles founds the Royal Zoological Society, London, England.

Almost imperceptibly, pre-history has become history.

TUESDAY, 9 JANUARY 1827

The first business of the new capital of the huge District of London is the law; the second is the lodging and entertainment of those whose business brings them to the courts.

The first court to meet in London is the court of general quarter sessions of the peace. This bench of magistrates combines to some degree the functions of a modern grand jury and a county council. Serious criminal charges like murder, manslaughter, and grand larceny are brought here first. If the magistrates, after due consideration, bring in a true bill, the case is passed on to the court of assizes for trial. In its civil capacity the bench is responsible for naming road overseers, fence viewers, assessors, and pound-keepers. It also allots licenses for "houses of entertainment," taverns that have some rooms available for travellers.

Today's sessions are being held in a two-storey frame building standing on the southwest corner of Ridout and Dundas streets, on the public square. It is meant to serve as a temporary courthouse, gaol, and school, pending the construction of the permanent courthouse. Its timbers are still fresh from the axe and adze, for the building has been rushed to completion in time for the sittings of the hamlet's first court.

Almost the entire population took part in the erection of this structure. The contractor – if such a grand term may be used for a functionary more accurately described as an amateur foreman – was Peter MacGregor. Since there were prisoners who had to be housed during the pleasure of the magistrates, someone had to look after them. The most suitable person to do this was also the most conveniently located for the purpose – Peter MacGregor, host of the village's first inn.

Since many of the magistrates came from remote regions of the District, accommodation had to be provided for them. For the first session, that meant Peter's so-far-unnamed hostelry.

Finally, both the visiting magistrates and the prisoners had to be fed. The obvious person to look after this responsibility was also, naturally, Peter MacGregor. Here then, was a classic case of conflict of interest. In the result, Peter chose to feed the prisoners first, in order to get them out of the way. This led to vociferous complaints by the hungry magistrates, some of whom remembered a similar incident some three years previously.

It had happened at a banquet of the Fourth Militia Regiment following Militia Training Day, regularly held annually on the birthday of King

---

1827 John James Audubon, *Birds of North America.*

George III, 4 June. The affair, in 1824, was being held at Peter MacGregor's inn at Byron. As the party was about to be seated, an officer announced:

"I do not want any common men, but we officers, to sit at this table."

The "common men" responded to the challenge by attacking indiscriminately the food and their officers. The incident was in no way Peter's fault; but it, and his tender treatment of the London prisoners, gave additional emphasis to his reputation as a democrat.

Such clashes between classes were perhaps amusing at the time, but there was a darker side to them; in another ten years such differences would lead to bloodshed. In January 1827 MacGregor's error of judgment was not seen as a serious threat to civil order, but certainly as injurious to the dignity of the law, of which the magistrates, regardless of background, were very conscious.

These justices of the peace were all men of substance. Some of them had had considerable experience in the development of the area. As instance, the chairman, Joseph Ryerse, was the son of a United Empire Loyalist who had settled in Norfolk County, in the eastern reaches of the District, in the late 1790s.

The most distinguished member of the bench was Edward Allen Talbot, aged thirty-two, a native of Tipperary County, Ireland. Talbot and his father Richard S. Talbot were co-founders of an Irish settlement north of the Forks, in London Township, in 1818. E.A. Talbot was the author of *Five Years' Residence in the Canadas,* published in England in 1824. The book was subsequently translated into two or three European languages (without the author's permission) and had a perceptibly negative effect on emigration from the United Kingdom.

Talbot was not popular with the other magistrates; he was considered a radical in politics and a visionary in everything else. Within the next handful of years he busied himself establishing London's first newspaper, designing a locomotive, promoting a railway to link London and Hamilton, proposing the building of a canal from Goderich on Lake Huron to Port Stanley on Lake Erie, urging a flood-control project at the Forks of the Thames, painting (and later destroying) a portrait of himself, and obtaining letters patent for an "Atmospheric Propelling Engine"!

Such protean characters arise seldom in the life of any community, indeed of any nation or generation. They are often admired by their posterity but distrusted by their contemporaries.

The agenda for this first London session of the court was heavily engaged with housekeeping matters. Among other items, Stephen Van Every was appointed gaoler, thus relieving Peter MacGregor of one of his constel-

---

1827 The United States tries to buy Texas from Mexico.

lation of functions. A rash of minor assault cases followed, after which the court stood adjourned.

SATURDAY, 24 NOVEMBER 1827

News of the new community on the Thames has reached the people of Ancaster, Dundas, and Hamilton through the medium of the Gore *Gazette*. There was an advertisement and what in modern newspaper parlance would be termed "reader copy" – a sort of bonus to the advertiser, who in this instance was Peter MacGregor's principal rival, Abraham Carroll:

HOTEL in the New Town of LONDON. – The subscriber having erected, and licensed as an INN, a commodious two-story Frame Building, on Dundas Street, in the Town or Village of LONDON, commonly called the Forks of the Thames, begs leave to apprise the Public thereof. The Hotel is within a few rods of the superb Building now erecting in the Town as a Jail & Court-house for the LONDON DISTRICT, has the best stabling accommodations, and is, in every respect, well qualified to afford comfort and convenience to the Public who may have occasion to resort to the County Town of the London District.

London, Nov. 24, 1827   ABRAHAM CARROLL

The accompanying news story is one of the earliest extant accounts of the infant community. It is generous in its description, which includes a subtle reference to the paper's new client, obviously the proprietor of the "very respectable Tavern."

NEW TOWN OF LONDON. Almost as long ago as we can remember, a Town of the above name was laid down on the Map of Upper Canada – and the people of Britain – with the exception of the very few, to whom actual observation had taught the fallacy of such an idea – were thence induced to believe that a young Metropolis was growing up on the banks of the Upper Canadian Thames. It will, therefore, be a matter of surprise to many, when they are informed that, until the last eighteen months, this Town had only an ideal existence, and that the spot upon which it was marked, was in the centre of an uncultivated forest. Within the period above mentioned, however, the spot in question has been fixed upon by the Legislature, as the scite for the District Town, and in consequence where lately not a tree was felled all has now become bustle and activity. A considerable tract of country has been cleared – roads laid out – bridges built – and between 20 and 30 buildings, about half of Frame, have been erected – including a temporary Jail and Court House – a

1827 The New York State Legislature abolishes slavery.

Capt. Thomas Fallon came to London
in 1827. He later became an officer in
the US Army and mayor of San José,
California. From *California Cavalier*
(Innishfallen Enterprises Inc.).

very respectable Tavern – a Blacksmith's Shop – a Brewery (erecting) – one or
two small Merchants' Shops and some very good Dwelling Houses. The scite is
a very handsome one, at the Forks of the Thames, on an elevated piece of table
land, commanding an extensive view of Forests and cultivated Farms on the
opposite banks of the River, to the South & the west, & thro' a fine avenue of
trees on Dundas street, which has been opened from the Town for several
miles. The Court House, which will be one of the most magnificent buildings
of its kind in Upper Canada, is commenced, under the superintendance of a
most respectable architect (Mr Ewart) a great proportion of the bricks have
already been made, the foundation dug, and preparations for actively carrying
on the work, are in a forward state. The Town is favourably situated, and but
for the state of the roads in its neighbourhood, which are at this time, scarcely
passable, might soon become a place of some importance.

The correspondent for the *Gazette* gave the town "between 20 and 30
buildings." Another authority allots to these buildings a total population
of 133. Some of them were destined to become permanent residents;
others were just passing through.

Among the latter were adventurers like Thomas Fallon, a young Irish-
man who later recalled arriving in the village with a number of Irish
families in this year of 1827:

We were settled in London with about twenty other families by 1827. London

---

1827 Karl Baedeker begins publishing his travel guides.

was founded in that year in the crook in the river where the branches of the
Thames meet, an east-facing "U" with the main buildings at its bottom. In
those days the forest enclosed the village. ... Our home was a quarter mile
down Rideout street and slightly east on the South Branch of the river. We had
good land, and although we were in modest straits, my father took great
consolation that we were "founders" of this place.

Some of those who arrived during London's first twelve months bore
names that have become community fixtures. In the van were the
merchants, ready and eager to take advantage of a new and promising
market. That is to say, they *became* merchants when they set up shop in
the village. Previously most of them had been pedlars and tinkers, carrying
their stock-in-trade or the tools of their profession on their backs, like
George Jervis Goodhue, a pedlar, and the brothers John and Oliver
McClary, who were tinkers. Most of them did very well indeed. When
George Goodhue died a half-century after his arrival he was the richest
man in the western portion of the province.

The McClary brothers did at least as well. They were New Englanders,
sons of a former lumber merchant who had been bankrupted by the War
of 1812-1814, subsequently settling in Westminster Township south of
London. The brothers McClary were well-connected in the United States,
being cousins of two presidents of the republic – John Adams (1735–
1826), the second president, and John Quincy Adams (1767–1848), the
sixth – a fact proudly proclaimed on a towering memorial in London's
Mount Pleasant Cemetery. The brothers parlayed their tiny enterprise
into one of the largest manufacturing concerns on the continent. The
stoves fashioned by the McClarys became famous throughout the British
Empire. Today the memorial in the cemetery, a city street, and a magnificent house at the southwest corner of McClary Avenue and High Street
recall the name of the presidents' distant kin.

TUESDAY, 21 OCTOBER 1828

Under overcast skies, the tall, unsmiling, cold-eyed Yankee merchant
George Jervis Goodhue follows the coffin of his beloved wife Maria Fullarton to her grave in the glebe land belonging to the Church of England
at the northwest corner of Ridout and Dundas streets. The words of the
Anglican service are spoken by the Reverend Alexander Macintosh, who
has come up from his church at St Thomas for the occasion. Most of
London's population has turned out for the simple funeral and interment.

1828 Catholic Emancipation Act allows Roman Catholics in Great Britain to sit in Parliament.

"Almighty God, with whom do live the spirits of those who depart hence in the Lord, and with whom the souls of the faithful are in joy and felicity. ..."

As the ancient words fall damply in the malarial mist arising from the river, the eyes of all turn on Goodhue. He has not many friends in this group; in the years to come he will have even fewer. How will he take the death of the girl he is said to have loved? His face tells nothing; it is not a face that speaks of what is behind it.

As the words of the final blessing fade away, Goodhue's principal rival, the Irish merchant Dennis O'Brien, daring the wrath of his Catholic God to be present at the burial of an infidel, steps forward to express his personal sorrow and regrets; but the Yankee, seeing nothing but his own grief, has already turned away to make his sad journey to his solitary bed.

"Unto Almighty God we commend the soul of our sister here departed. ..."

Seven years later, when the boundaries of the town are extended northward, the first of the new east-west streets is named Fullarton.

THURSDAY, 19 AUGUST 1830

They had been streaming into the village ever since the judge had spoken those awful words "and may God have mercy on your soul. ..."

It had been only three days since the verdict was delivered. Pioneer justice is swift. By the hour appointed the population of London had swollen temporarily to ten times its normal 300 souls. They came from all the surrounding townships; from Westminster, London, Lobo, Caradoc, North Dorchester, Yarmouth, Bayham (where Constable Timothy Conklin Pomeroy had been shot and killed), Malahide, Southwold, Delaware, Nissouri, Zorra, and Oxford. They came from outside the sprawling District of London, from York (né Toronto) and Hamilton. There was even at least one visitor from the United States, Orson Squire Fowler, a young student from Yale University.

The attraction?

It is Con Burleigh's hanging day.

The sordid little story began on the morning of 16 September 1829. Constable Pomeroy, pursuing a suspect on a charge of "theft, burning property, destroying cattle, etc.," was ambushed by someone and fatally shot. A cap found at the scene was identified as belonging to the person Pomeroy was pursuing – Cornelius Alverson Burleigh (sometimes spelled Burley). A reward of one hundred pounds offered by the District author-

---

1830 Oliver Wendell Holmes' poem, "Old Ironsides", saved U.S.S. Constitution.

ities speedily resulted in Burleigh's capture and confinement in the rude cells of the temporary courthouse.

Many people had doubts about Con's guilt, fuelled by his odd behaviour during a jail-break in the long winter of his incarceration. Escaping from the primitive accommodations was no big deal. All the prisoners took advantage of the break for freedom, except Cornelius Burleigh. He, being certain, he said, of his own innocence, remained behind to await his acquittal.

Whatever the true facts of the case were, Burleigh's conviction of his innocence was not shared by others, including the witnesses who testified against him, the jury that found him guilty, and the judge who sentenced him.

Three men – two clergymen and a vacationing undergraduate – played leading roles in the last act of Con Burleigh's pathetic little tragedy. The Reverend James Jackson, a Methodist circuit-rider said to have been distantly related to Andrew Jackson (1767–1845), seventh president of the United States, made Con his particular charge, although "target" might have been a more accurate description of the object of his daily attendance. He was determined to elicit a confession; but due to the "obduracy and insensibility" of the condemned man, it was not until forty-one hours before his execution that Burleigh "burst into a flood of tears" and "in the presence of the Revd. Messrs. Boswell, Smith and Jackson" made his "Dying Confession."

The wording of the confession, subsequently printed in handbill form at Hamilton, owes little to the prisoner and a great deal to his confessor-tormenter. Cornelius Burleigh could neither read nor write, yet in the confession this educational failure is acknowledged in these words:

I was left to wander through the world, under the influence of depravity, without the advantages of education, or religious instruction, to counterbalance the influence of my natural propensities to evil, of various kinds, particularly that of frequenting all places of profane resort. I was often found in the merry dance, and lost no opportunity of inducing thoughtless and unguarded females to leave the paths of innocence and virtue. ...

These, of course, are the words and sentiments of a fundamentalist Methodist, not those of an uneducated farmer's son. The printed copy of this bogus production carried as well a multiple-verse piece of doggerel, also obviously the work of Mr Jackson, based at least in part on a Methodist

---

1830 Ladies' skirts, stiff collars become part of men's dress.

hymn dating from the early 1820s. The scansion is marvellously primitive.

The three ecclesiastical corbies, Jackson, Boswell, and Smith, are to share the religious functions surrounding the public death of Cornelius Burleigh. Jackson has top billing. He reads the "Dying Confession" from the scaffold "by Burley's request"; Mr Smith, apparently a Baptist minister, gives the homily before the 3,000 witnesses, and the closing prayer; Edward Boswell, the Anglican missionary, has a less obvious role – he baptizes the young man "aged as he supposed about 26 or 27" and gives him Holy Communion.

Now at last it is time. In the presence of the multitude Cornelius is cast into eternity.

His time, however, is not yet. The official rope cannot bear the condemned man's weight. It snaps and he is deposited on the ground, dazed but alive. Someone is sent to fetch a new rope from Goodhue's store across the street. Burleigh's conversion is complete. He walks among the crowd with the tag-end of the broken rope dangling from his neck, his whole mind devoted to "prayer, praise, singing and thanksgiving."

Once more the condemned man is led on to the scaffold. The rope is adjusted and the trap sprung, to the sound of that peculiar and terrifying exhalation of breath from the crowd that seems to have been a feature of all public executions – a sound composed in part of civilized compassion, in part of savage delight.

Some members of the crowd leave at this point, but most remain for the second act of the drama. The sentence of the court has only been half carried out; the corpse, by law, must now be "delivered to the Surgeons for dissection." This is the moment eagerly anticipated by the medical professionals of the District of London and their private students. Legally, the only corpses available for teaching purposes are those of condemned criminals. The British tradition said nothing about the place where the dissection was to be carried out. In Canada, lacking hospitals and operating theatres, it is carried out in public, in the open.

Scalpels at the ready, the physicians and their pupils crowd around the body, with the heavily-breathing audience peering over their shoulders. In short order, poor Con's body is reduced to its basic components, some of which will find their way into specimen jars for later study.

A choice portion of the remains has been spoken for and promised to a lay student of another discipline: the pseudo-science of phrenology. Burleigh's skull, its contents removed, is cleaned, cured, and presented to Orson Squire Fowler.

Fowler had been one of the many curious persons who had been allowed

---

1831 Great pandemic of Asiatic cholera reaches Central Europe.

to visit Burleigh in his cell. There he had run his practised hands over the condemned man's cranium, indicating on a chart where the walls of the skull were thin, and where they were thick, and connecting these features with aspects, often of a contradictory nature, of Burleigh's personality.

After a short, indecent interval following the execution, Fowler conducted a lecture in a darkened hall, using the skull and a candle to prove the truth of his assertions. Sure enough, the geography of Burleigh's cranium bore out Fowler's predictions. Where he had said the skull walls were thin, the candlelight shone through; in other areas Con's thick-headedness allowed no light to emerge.

How these facts could be said to "prove" the scientific accuracy of phrenology is difficult now to determine, but they actually did set the young man's feet on the road to phenomenal popular success and great riches.

In the 1880s, on a farewell lecture tour, Fowler returned to London and here left a portion of Cornelius Burleigh's skull with the Harris family of Eldon House, where it remains on public view to this day.

THURSDAY, 7 JULY 1831

The first issue of London's first newspaper, the London *Sun,* has appeared on the streets of the village. Its editor is Edward Allen Talbot. Much of the journal's four pages is given over to a description of the new District capital and the two adjacent townships of London and Westminster. Praise is heaped on the courthouse, just completed at a cost of £4,000 Provincial Currency, equivalent to 16,000 American dollars:

The Court House, which is allowed by strangers to be the finest building in the Province, stands within about twenty yards of the brink of the hill, which may be said to be the bank of the river. It is 100 feet long, 50 feet wide and 50 feet high. The building, although not strictly Gothic, is in that style, and with its Octagon towers has much the appearance of the ancient castles, so much admired in Great Britain and Ireland. ... The Court room is finished in a very superior manner. ... The prisoners are admitted into the dock from the jail beneath, by means of a trap door. ... The debtors prisons are in the upper part of the house, and are finished in a neat, convenient and comfortable manner. There has, however, been one great error committed in the erection of this building; it fronts the river instead of the town ... and exposes to the view of every person who enters the town the windows of the criminal cells; a sight at all times the least pleasing to the stranger or the citizen. ...

1831 Population of Great Britain, 13.9 million; United States of America, 12.8 million.

THURSDAY, 1 SEPTEMBER 1831

Edward Allen Talbot, London's chief and most eloquent promoter, continues his non-stop panegyric on the new village:

As the rapid increase of this town is a subject which seems to excite very general astonishment, we shall from time to time lay before our readers, a brief statement of its population and improvements. About three months ago, we, in company with the Editor of the Western Mercury, counted the houses then built and building; the number was then about 70. To-day we again counted the number; and find it to be 96, viz: 22 two-story framed houses, 59 one and a half stories, also framed, and 15 hewd and other log houses one story high. ... In enumerating the houses we do not include the Court-house or places of public worship. There are building in the town a Protestant Episcopal Church, 80 by 40; a Methodist meeting house, and a Roman Catholic Chapel; and we understand the members of the Kirk of Scotland, residing in the town and its vicinity, have it in contemplation to build a Church so soon as they can obtain a Clergyman from Scotland.

As a further inducement to genteel settlement, the Irish statistician informs the world that males in the village outnumber females four to three. The precise figures are: twenty-six bachelors and fourteen spinsters. "It must therefore," says Mr Talbot, "be a desirable situation for ladies of enterprise."

MONDAY, 23 JANUARY 1832

Dr John Becker Crouse of Colborne, near Simcoe, Norfolk County, conducts an inquest on the bodies of Polly Sovereign (or Sovereen), wife of Henry Sovereign, and seven of their eleven children. The verdict is murder. Henry Sovereign is charged with the crime and committed to trial at the London assizes. The new year has begun badly. Worse is to come.

SATURDAY, 28 APRIL 1832

The *Constantine,* carrying Irish immigrants, docks at the quarantine station on Grosse Isle, near Quebec City. Of 179 passengers, twenty-nine have already died, the result of an epidemic of Asiatic cholera brought into England by refugees from the Polish rebellion of 1830–1831 and thence into Ireland, where it spread rapidly among the peasantry.

1832 Asiatic cholera, introduced by Irish immigrants into Canada, filters southward into the United States; reaches Mexico in 1833.

Dr John Patrick Donnelly (1779–1832). A retired Royal Navy surgeon, Donnelly died attending victims of Asiatic cholera at London. Sketch by Stanley Dale, from Edwin Seaborn, *The March of Medicine in Western Ontario* (Toronto: Ryerson, 1944).

SUNDAY, 3 JUNE 1832

The *Carricks* from Ireland puts in at Grosse Isle; 145 passengers, forty-five deaths.

THURSDAY, 7 JUNE 1832

The *Voyageur,* a steamer plying the St Lawrence River, makes an illegal stop at Grosse Isle, takes off some of the passengers from the *Carricks,* and lands some of them at Quebec.

SUNDAY, 10 JUNE 1832

At Quebec, fifty-five cases of Asiatic cholera are reported, of whom forty-five have died.

FRIDAY, 15 JUNE 1832

The plague has reached York, following outbreaks in Montreal and Kingston. The lieutenant-governor of Upper Canada, Sir John Colborne, orders hospitals set up in the District of London at Turkey Point, Port Stanley, and London itself for the reception of sick immigrants.

SATURDAY, 30 JUNE 1832

Dr John Patrick Donnelly, a retired Royal Navy surgeon, arrives in London on his way to the St Clair River, where he intends taking up land. He

---

1832 Asiatic cholera appears in England; in February, quarantine station established at Grosse Île, below Quebec City.

appears before the board of health to offer his services, if needed. The board waives the rules governing the medical profession in the province, grants him an immediate licence to practise medicine, and asks him to assume charge of the cholera hospital on the Hamilton Road, some distance out of town. Later that night Donnelly writes to his family at St-Roch, Lower Canada:

London, U.C. 30th June, 1832.

My dear Marie and little Family,

I arrived here at 5 o'clock in good health, thank God, as I left you. It is now ½ past 6, I can say very little as I am in a hurry to post this, the post goes out tomorrow at 4 a.m. I'm certain you have been very anxious to hear an account of the ravages the cholera morbus made. Just as I was happening on my way through York, in this town, I attended two cases myself. I saved one by God's help. It happened in a home I lodged in. ... I am extremely anxious to hear from Edmund as he was in the scene of the cholera. There is nothing of the kind here yet. ... I will go and see about my crown lands on Monday 2nd, July, God willing. ...

THURSDAY, 12 JULY 1832

The London *Sun* reports that seven cases of cholera have been reported in the village; of these, three persons had died and one had recovered.

THURSDAY, 2 AUGUST 1832

The London *Sun* announces that the board of health has recorded forty-seven cases of cholera and thirteen deaths. The first victim of the disease was Eliza MacGregor, a sister of Peter MacGregor. Mrs MacGregor, mother of Peter and Eliza, prostrated herself on the damp earth of her daughter's grave and died the next morning. That was on 15 July. The following day, her son-in-law Mr Pullen, a coach-maker, died. Dr John Patrick Donnelly died on 30 July. The wife of his colleague Dr Elam Stimson died on 20 July, and their infant son five days later. The *Sun*'s account concludes:

The town is literally deserted by the inhabitants, there being now only about 27 men with their families remaining in it, there are on Dundas street alone upwards of 20 houses wholly shut up.

SATURDAY, 11 AUGUST 1832

Publication of the weekly newspaper, the London *Sun*, has been delayed two days in order to bring its readers the following report:

1832 Massachusetts legalizes the dissection of cadavers in medical schools.

Our Assizes which commenced on Tuesday morning, terminated at 11 o'clock today. And it is with ineffable pleasure that we announce the total disappearance of the Cholera in this town. On Tuesday morning such was the effect of public alarm that little hope was entertained that a sufficient number of Jurors, Grand or Petit, could be obtained to enable the Court to deliver the Gaol, but to the credit of the District a sense of public duty raised those called upon to perform it ... superior to personal fears. ... There were very few civil cases tried and those of an unimportant character. The following are the convictions which have taken place:

Henry Sovereign for the murder of his wife and 6 children. Sentenced to be hung on Friday, since reprieved until 11 o'clock on Monday.

Michael Robins, horse stealing. Sentence of death recorded.

Alexander Root, Petit Larceny, Banished for 7 years.

Andrew Root, Petit Larceny, Banished for 7 years.

John White, Grand Larceny, Banished for 7 years.

Daniel Kemp, Stealing a yoke of oxen, sentence of death recorded.

The harsh sentences handed down by Judge James Buchanan Macaulay were mandatory under the old British criminal code, which decreed the death penalty for several hundred crimes, many of them having to do with offences against property. By the early nineteenth century a popular reform movement had resulted in the commutation of most of these archaic sentences. Michael Robins and Daniel Kemp were not hanged at London; Henry Sovereign was. It was Sovereign's second date with the hangman. In 1828 he had appeared before the same Judge Macaulay charged with horse-stealing and had received the mandatory sentence of death. Executive clemency spared his life on that occasion. This time, no single voice was raised in protest. The evidence presented at his trial was overwhelming. By his wife, the long-suffering Polly, he had had eleven children. The youngest, Anna, aged two, somehow survived the savage blood-bath in the isolated cabin in Windham Township and died eighty-two years later, in 1914, "a tall, stately woman with beautiful white wavy hair." Three other children escaped the carnage by being away from home at the time.

The maniacal rage that had authored this tragedy filled the spectators at the trial with an almost supernatural dread, which was felt even by as sophisticated an observer as Edward Allen Talbot, who visited Sovereign's dungeon cell under the London courthouse on Sunday, 12 August 1832:

I visited him, at his own request, on Sunday morning. ... he was confined in a cell about 10 feet square, perfectly dark and completely sheeted, floor, walls

---

1832 Augustus Montague Toplady and Thomas Hastings, "Rock of Ages" (hymn).

and ceiling with iron. As we entered this dark abode we found him reading the Church of England Litany. He sat on a rush bottomed chair holding the book in one hand and a candle in the other – and as the Gaoler departed drawing upon us the massive door, I felt an indescribeable thrill of horror pervade my whole frame. ... His beard, which was closely shaved the day of his trial, had grown considerably, and with the faint light which a single candle afforded in so black an abode, his countenance assumed the most terrific appearance.

If Talbot expected to elicit a confession from a convicted murderer, as the Reverend James Jackson had two years earlier, he was disappointed. Henry Sovereign continued to protest his innocence until the instant his body plunged through the trap in the presence of a mere three hundred spectators who had dared the pestilence of cholera to see justice done.

SUNDAY, 11 NOVEMBER 1832

A visiting Presbyterian missionary, the Reverend William Proudfoot, preaches in the temporary courthouse, which has now become a school-house, on the morning of this day. The Methodist circuit-rider, the Reverend James Jackson, speaks in the building during the noon hour. At four o'clock a Church of England missionary, the Reverend Benjamin Cronyn, who arrived from Ireland the day before, conducts the Anglican service of Evensong. A delegation of local members of the Church of England appeals to Cronyn to remain in London instead of proceeding to his planned destination in the recently-settled Township of Adelaide. He will remain.

MONDAY, 31 DECEMBER 1832

"The Forks" has now been settled for a little more than six years. The population has grown to some 500, in spite of the ravages of the cholera epidemic. Few who passed through that terrifying time will ever forget it. London's first resident, Peter MacGregor, has sold out to Dr Hiram Davis Lee, and left for a farm in Westminster Township, heartbroken at the loss of three members of his immediate family circle to the disease that cost so many lives. Dr Elam Stimson, similarly mourning his losses, has set off for Connecticut to find a new wife to mother his orphaned brood. He will not return to the village at the Forks. Nor will the Reverend Edward Jukes Boswell, off to a new charge in eastern Upper Canada, leaving the gaunt frame of an uncompleted church to his successor, young Benjamin Cronyn. Boswell will live on in local folklore as the minister who mounted guard at the northern entrance to London, at Blackfriars

---

1832 *Ann McKim,* the first clipper ship for the China trade, is launched.

Eldon House, residence built in 1834 by Capt. John Harris, Royal Navy (ret.), treasurer of the District of London. Sketch by Bill McGrath, from *London Heritage* – second edition (London: Phelps Publishing, 1979)

Bridge, during the plague, warning travellers against entering the stricken town. He has sold his property to the treasurer of the District of London, Captain John Harris, RN, who has plans to build upon it a home that he will call Eldon House.

Of the physical aspects of the village of 1832, little will survive the next 150 years – a part of the foundation of Eldon House and some unmarked graves on the courthouse square.

The courthouse, in spite of its ambiguous siting with its back to its constituents, is the most noteworthy feature of the village, commented upon by all visitors to the area. Otherwise, there is nothing to see; simply a straggling collection of log and frame buildings bordering the imaginary street allowances on which the major traffic is pedestrian, with an occasional ox-cart or even a patrician horseman. All, without exception, are obliged to weave their way in and out and around the ubiquitous tree stumps.

The little village has survived its first great test. It has beaten back the first of the many waves of pestilence to be brought by the European immigrants who will become its citizens. Still to come before its place in history is assured – rebellion, civic disorder, fire, financial panic, and poverty.

1832 Andrew Jackson re-elected President of the United States.

CHAPTER TWO

REBELLION

To add some of my more personal recollections of these times. I will begin with the year of the Rebellion, 1837. I was then in my fifth year. We resided on Lot 15, in the third concession of London, on the brow of the hill, over the north branch of the Thames. All male adults had been summoned to serve in the militia, and all firearms requisitioned for their use. My father was absent in Ireland, on urgent family affairs. My mother surrendered to the militia all firearms in her possession, with many musket bullets cast by herself. We lived in hourly apprehension of invasion, for rumours were rife of approaching bands of rebels, and it was thought that any night we might be burned in our beds.

Verschoyle Cronyn, *The First Bishop of Huron*, Transactions of the London and Middlesex Historical Society, Part III, 1911.

By 1836 the population of London had reached 1,246, according to Edward Allen Talbot. Of his fellow-townsfolk Talbot had this to say:

Taking a view of the very great improvements made in this town and vicinity during the short period of settlement ... we think we may safely say that no town in British North America has advanced so rapidly, or can boast of a greater number of respectable families. ...

Many of the "respectable families" Talbot referred to were, like his own, parishioners of the Reverend Benjamin Cronyn, rector of the new frame church of St Paul on North Street (Queens Avenue). There were four other churches in the village, again according to Talbot, but they counted for little. The Church of England represented the Tory Establishment. All others were "Dissenters" and therefore presumably Reform-minded.

The Anglican Establishment in London included such exotic figures as the landlord of Talbot's little printing office, the Earl of Mount-Cashell;

1836 Adelaide, Australia, founded.

Captain Joseph Cowley, a relative of the Duke of Wellington; Henry Corry Rowley Becher, member of an old established Yorkshire family; Captain John Harris, Royal Navy (retired); Dr John Salter, a former Navy surgeon, apothecary, and social reformer; Hamilton Hartley Killaly, an engineer, graduate of Trinity College, Dublin, and the Royal Academy of Science; and George Washington Busteed, former secretary to the governor of the West Indian island of St Lucia.

The Episcopalians controlled to a large degree the economy and the society of the village. A similar but more powerful group presided over the life of the provincial capital, Toronto, né York. Because of the many interrelationships among the Toronto proprietors, their enemies referred to them as the Family Compact. Although there was no such intimate bond among the members of the London Establishment, they came to be looked upon as a junior Family Compact.

It was easy to identify the members of the Establishment. They announced their affiliation every time they went to church. Their opponents were "chapel folk" – Methodists, a sect characterized by one writer as consisting of "The ignorant and uneducated; their adherents are principally the natives of the country, settlers from the United States, and emigrants from England." Worse still, they were staunch advocates of temperance, which brought down upon them the wrath of Colonel Thomas Talbot, who named them as members of "Damned Cold Water Drinking Societies."

In the hyperbole of the hustings, therefore, the equations were simple: Church of England = Tory; Methodism = Reformer. In reality, of course, the distinctions were much more subtle and complex.

Consider some instances.

Dr Charles Duncombe of St Thomas and Norwich, who was, next to William Lyon Mackenzie, the chief activist of the Reform movement, was a direct descendant of King James II of England through his mother Rhoda Tyrell.

The two Talbot brothers, Edward Allen and John, both prominent Anglicans, edited newspapers in London and St Thomas devoted to the Reform cause.

Charles Latimer, an English attorney barred from practice in Upper Canada because of rules inspired by the Family Compact, became a London merchant and ammunition-supplier to the Reform guerrillas.

Elijah Leonard, an ironmonger from New York State, member of a family that had engaged in that trade since 1637, made no secret of his Reform sympathies, meanwhile buying surplus cannonballs from the Brit-

---

1836 Texas becomes an independent republic, with Samuel Houston as president.

ish Army for eventual manufacture into stoves.

The Reverend William Proudfoot, minister of a schismatic Presbyterian church, was an intellectual radical whose congregation were, almost by definition, Reformers.

The movement for political reform was gathering strength everywhere in North America and Europe in the 1830s and resulted, in 1834, in the election of a Reform majority in the lower house of the Legislature of Upper Canada. It is a coincidence worth nothing that in that same year six farm labourers in the Devonshire village of Tolpuddle in England were sentenced to seven years' imprisonment in an Australian penal colony for organizing a farmers' union. Five of the six later settled in the London (Canada) area after their release.

In Devonshire and in Toronto the conservative Establishment was shocked, indignant, and frightened by these evidences of the spread of "revolutionary" sentiment. There had been rebellions in France and Poland in the 1830s; a slave revolt in Virginia and civil uprisings in Switzerland and Brazil in 1831, in Germany in 1832, and in Mexico in 1833. In such an atmosphere political rhetoric soon leaped the bounds of good taste and even reason, to become boldly inflammatory and irresponsible. A Conservative broadside printed at St Thomas called for volunteers to attack a meeting of local Reformers:

NOTICE

The Ripstavers, Gallbursters, etc., with their friends, are requested to meet at St Thomas, on the 17th of January, at 12 o'clock, as there will be more work for them to do on that day. The Doctors are requested to be in readiness to heal the sick and cure the broken headed. Let no rotten eggs be wanting. As the Unionists are all Yankees, a few pieces of pumpkin will not be amiss.

Whatever Unions may be in England, it must be remembered that in this country with Republicans at their head, they are the next step to Rebellion. ... Therefore, most noble Ripstavers, check the evil, in the beginning, that is, hoe them out – sugar them off – in short sew them up. The Dastards may think to screen themselves from the public fury by holding their meeting at a private house: but public or private put yourselves in the midst of them. You have a right to be there. It is a public meeting.

Whoever the "Gallbursters and Ripstavers" were, they turned out in force to do the Establishment's bidding, as Colonel Talbot, the local auto-crat, gleefully reported a few days later:

1836 Nikolai Gogol, *The Government Inspector.*

My rebels endeavoured to hold a meeting at St Thomas on the 17th,
Dr Franklin's birthday ... but in which they were frustrated by my royal guards,
who routed the rascals at all points and drove them out of the village like
sheep, members with broken heads leaving their hats behind them – the
glorious work of old Colonel Hickory. In short, it was a most splendid victory.

The pot finally boiled over with the unfortunate appointment of a political incompetent, Sir Francis Bond Head, as lieutenant-governor of Upper
Canada. Head called a new election in which he himself played a leading
role, informing the voters that unless they returned a Tory government,
Britain would disown the province.

London, with its population of 1,246, was now entitled to a seat in the
Legislature. The Family Compact candidate was London's godfather,
Colonel Mahlon Burwell. The Reformers put up John Scatcherd, a justice
of the peace from Nissouri Township, a Reformer so radical in his views
that he had termed King George IV a "Public Calumniator."

The election campaign of the summer of 1836 was short, sharp, and
vicious. The London Establishment followed its parson into battle:

The Rev. Mr Cronyn is rendering himself as obnoxious to the farmers of this
country as he was once to the people of Ireland. He is here as he was there, a
busy meddler in the affairs of State; and a violent stickler for the domination
of his church, and the exclusive privileges of his order. He went along with the
Tory candidates throughout the Township of London, soliciting votes.

SATURDAY, 2 JULY 1836

It's evening on the second and last day of balloting in London's first and
most disgraceful election. By now nearly everyone entitled to vote has
stepped up to the hustings and declared his choice, verbally. Only those
who meet the stiff property qualifications may vote; the secret ballot is a
generation in the future, and universal suffrage is a fragile dream in the
minds of a few "radical" thinkers.

The town's in an uproar. Gangs of Tory bullies have been roaming the
streets all day, hunting down known Reformers and Reform sympathizers,
announcing (on whose authority no one knows) an award of five pounds
for every cracked Liberal skull.

All day Tory Orangemen from the back concessions of London Township have been streaming into town on horseback, by cart, wagon, and
buggy. Now, with the polls about to close, comes the final attack on the
democratic process.

1836 Michael William Balfe, *The Maid of Artois* (opera).

SONG,
For the LONDON ELECTION.

LEGAL DEPARTMENT.

There came to our Town a poor Native of Erin,
The coat that he wore was a wild monster's skin,
The Limbs of the Law were quite persevering,
So Wilson and Becher declared he'd run in.
John Harris, that *Hero* that fought on the Ocean,
Agreed to buy Votes and to pay by PROMOTION;
Killaly declared 'twas a most pious notion,
  And sung Hallelujah to *Sydenham's Lord*.

MEDICAL DEPARTMENT.

He employed Esculapius to find him in Physic,
So Anderson's Cough Drops were bro't to his aid,
LEE brought in his *Pils* as a cure for the *Phthisic*,
  And Moore mixed a cordial that's called Lemonade,
Each day as it passes this Bright Constellation,
Assemble together to hold consultation,
Disdaining of course any remuneration,
  But to sing Hallelujah to Sydenham's Lord.

MERCANTILE DEPARTMENT.

The Merchants were then called forth to convention,
  And ask'd what they'd do for *Lord Sydenham's Man,*
Mr. Smith said to office he ne'er had pretension,
  However, he'd give his support to the plan.
Then Goodhue, O'Brien, and Claris and Farley,
Tho' always divided, came forward to parley,
Determined to kneel at the shrine of GREAT CHARLIE,
  And sing Hallelujah to Sydenham's Lord;

BOARD OF WORKS.

A mere remnant of Genius was next brought in action,
  To vote for their Sage with the spectacled Eyes,
They counted the Profits complete to a Fraction,
  And were fully persuaded their *Wages would Rise.*
Then Matthews and Ellis, and Cardon and Pringle,
A strange combination in common to mingle,
But knowing that money was certain to jingle,
  They sung Hallelujah to Sydenham's Lord.

I'M SURE OF SUCCESS.

Says Hamilton now I am sure of Election,
  For men of all nations and parties agree,
I find that in money a man has protection,
  So money I'll spend, it costs nothing to me.
When first I came up, I felt like repining,
I thought that my Friends were to Douglas inclining,
But I *Whispered a Story* about Jonny's resigning,
  And sung Hallelujah to *Sydenham's Lord.*

32D REGIMENT.

Hark! Hark!!—what a change, my death bell is tolling,
  The Tories have brought in the Troops to their aid;
There is Stansfield & Westy & Dixon & Colerick,
  Who fought once before at *St. Denis* 'tis said;
Oh! hard is my fate, I must now lose my station,
Lord Sydenham looks for a quick resignation,
Having met with the People's dire disapprobation,
  There is no use in singing to Sydenham's *Lord.*

PERJURY AND IMPRISONMENT.

Says Gibbins if swearing can yet beat the Tories,
  My service is ready I'm good at an OATH,
Old Cornish and Colleague in such matters glories,
  FIVE DOLLARS IN CASH will secure us them both.
There are ten honest men that I'll keep from Election,
I'll *swear out a Writ* that will cause their detection,
Our Counsellor says there is no imperfection,
  In any who sings unto Sydenham's *Lord.*

FINAL RESULT.

I have now given a fair statement of matters,
  Beginning at A, I've come down to Z.*
So let Doctors and Lawyers and Merchants & Hatters
  Be ready for office, we've nothing to dread.
Happy the man with a pulse of ambition,
Blessed be the day I received your petition,
There's many will envy my happy condition,
  But I will sing praises to Sydenham's Lord.

See Mr. Killaly's speech on private correspondence.

London election song. UWO

It's a ragged, loud, torch-lit parade, led by a gigantic black man. It piles up in a disorderly rout on the courthouse square. A drunken Reformer is perched precariously on the roof of George Goodhue's general store, reciting the Liberal hymn, which is, fortunately for him, audible only to those nearest to him:

Up then, for Liberty, for Right,   Our king, our government and laws,
Strike home, the tyrants falter,   While just, we shall obey 'em,
Be firm, be brave, let all unite,   But Freedom's Heaven-born, holier cause
And despots' schemes must alter.   We hold supreme above 'em!

Suddenly the mob, many of its members armed with clubs and stones, advances on the hustings where the candidates and their supporters are gathered. The main target is John Talbot, whose editorials in the St Thomas *Liberal* have roused the wrath of the Family Compact supporters. As stones begin to rain on the wooden platform, Talbot finds himself in very real danger. He and his friends take shelter in the courthouse. The mob follows. Talbot goes to ground in the nearby home of his brother Edward Allen. This is a mistake; it's an obvious bolt-hole. As the first stone crashes through the front window, John dives out of a back window and claims a last-hope refuge in the home of the government's returning officer, the lawyer John Wilson, who escorts him out of the village to safety.

When the dust clears and the broken heads are bandaged, the results are announced. Colonel Talbot's right-hand man, Mahlon Burwell, has ten votes more than the Reform man, John Scatcherd.

The Tories celebrate their triumph; tomorrow morning St Paul's Church will be packed with hangovers. The Reformers go off to lick their wounds and plot revolution.

By the fall of 1837 armed rebellion seemed inevitable, but its causes were only partly political. A poor harvest in 1836, followed by a late spring and a disordered growing season — rain when rain was not needed, drought when it was — early frosts, and a second scanty harvest brought severe suffering to a farm population largely dependent on a one-crop economy — wheat for export, mainly to the United States. In that country similar weather conditions had depressed farm incomes and wrought havoc on the nation's financial institutions. Hundreds of private banks were forced to suspend specie payments. On Wall Street the financial heart of North America suffered cardiac arrest:

1836 The first of William Holmes McGuffey's *Eclectic Readers* is published.

New York, April 27, 1837. ... Matters very bad. ... Confidence annihilated; the whole community, big and little, traveling to ruin in a body. Strong fears entertained for the banks, and if they go, God only knows what the consequences will be.

George Templeton Strong was a student at Columbia University in New York City. His diary records what was very nearly a complete collapse of the financial structure of the American republic:

May 2 – Matters worse and worse in Wall Street. Workmen thrown out of employ by the hundred daily. Business at a stand. ...

May 4 – ... Fears entertained that tomorrow the attack will be general on all the banks; if so, they'll go down and then all the banks from Maine to Louisiana must follow – universal ruin. People talk ominously about rebellions and revolutions on this side of the Atlantic. ...

May 9 – ... As I expected, there's a run on all the banks, the depositors drawing out the specie as fast as the tellers can count it. They are in a dangerous situation ... and if they break, we shall have a revolution here. ...

The panic peaked the following day, 10 May, when all the banks in New York stopped payment and closed their doors. Troops were called out to maintain order.

The effect on the farmers of British North America was harsh and immediate. Wheat for export to the United States had been paid for in American bank-notes; those notes were now worthless.

By mid-year the banks of Upper Canada were threatening to close their doors too; thousands of farmers were sinking into abject poverty; the civil courts were awash with suits for debt; and the few men with "safe" money were making a killing in the mortgage market.

Economic distress combined with political discontent produced the right recipe for rebellion. As has been said before, revolutions are caused by empty bellies, not by political slogans.

When rebellion finally came to Upper Canada, in December 1837, it was pathetically mismanaged. The two military leaders, Mackenzie in the Home District (Toronto) and Duncombe in the London District, proved to have been more effective on the hustings than on the battlefield. The battle at Montgomery's Tavern in Toronto lasted less than half an hour. The force under Dr Duncombe's command assembled at the village of Scotland, in Oakland Township, listened to a speech, and disbanded without firing a shot.

1836 Charles Dickens, *Pickwick Papers*.

The people of London, deprived of facts, existed on rumour. Toronto was distant three days' travel from the Forks. It was nearly a week after Mackenzie's defeat before accurate information reached the village. On Christmas Day, Mrs M.A. Seabrook wrote to her mother in Buckinghamshire, England:

We did not know the extent of our danger until it was over. ... London was appraised of her danger about ten o'clock at night. The specie was taken from the bank and put into the court house and guarded. The town militia paraded several nights. Our magistrates became very active in raising militia. An order went out that everyone between sixteen and sixty was to meet armed, and constables were sworn in. We were guarded all night, no one being suffered to pass without being inquired into. Many were taken prisoner. ...

The aftermath of the loyalist triumph was the inevitable witch-hunt. Before the end of the year, sixty-one men had been arrested and squeezed into the dungeon cells below the courthouse. Few if any of them had been taken in arms. They were picked up because they were known Reformers, they had voted Reform, they had spoken in favour of political reform, they had attended public gatherings where Reform was mentioned – or they were strangers, like the two Mormon missionaries who were accused of spreading "seditious doctrine."

Conditions in the dungeons rapidly became intolerable. As Edward Allen Talbot had discovered when he visited the condemned murderer Henry Sovereign five years earlier, no daylight reached these appalling cubicles, the walls dripped, a single daily bucket served for drinking water, bathing, the washing of clothing, and the elimination of body wastes, and the infrequent meals were pushed through a small square opening, which also provided the only source of air from the outside.

Soon the authorities had to deal with an outbreak of typhoid fever as well as a rash of other complaints. At least two prisoners died as a result, one of them being John Grieve, a member of one of the Reverend William Proudfoot's congregations.

Meanwhile the British government had acted swiftly to contain the insurrection. Elements of the 32nd Regiment of Foot under the command of Lieutenant-Colonel John Maitland were despatched to London. A little ten-year-old girl who lived with her parents in the eighteenth house to be built in London, recalled the coming of the regiment:

The regulars were sent for at the first outbreak, but it took them so long to travel the distance (the 32nd came the whole way from Halifax on sleighs) that

---

1837 Chicago incorporated as a city. Area, 10 square miles. Population, 3,297.

View of London and Westminster Bridge, 1842. UWO

things had pretty well quieted down before they arrived. I remember being so disappointed when I saw them march through the town, that their coats were not red; but a big soldier threw open his grey overcoat, and my small woman's eyes were delighted with the sight of the red coat, which afterward seemed to take possession of the town. We had five of them billeted on us. Every resident was obliged to accommodate a certain number till the Government secured Dennis O'Brien's new block for a barracks.

That was in January 1838. The O'Brien Block, said to have been the first brick building erected in London, stood on the northwest corner of

1838 British-Afghan War begins; lasts until 1842.

Ridout and Dundas streets, across from the courthouse. It served for a time not only as a barracks but as a prison for the overflow from the courthouse cells. When the political crisis continued to cause concern, a decision was made to construct more permanent facilities. Before the year was out, ground had been secured, a contract granted, and work begun on a large barracks complex north and east of St Paul's Church.

Scarcely had work begun on clearing the site of its forest cover when the troops were called out. The military actions along the border of Upper Canada in 1838 could hardly qualify as more than skirmishes in the context of European warfare, yet in the popular histories of the United States of America they are elevated to partisan glory as the "Patriot Wars." In a 1984 novel by Joyce Carol Oates a character is identified as "the distinguished General Whimbrel of the Patriots' War of 1837."

Here's how all these things came about.

When Mackenzie, Duncombe, and other rebel leaders escaped to the United States, they found many sympathizers among the tens of thousands of drifters thrown out of work by the great economic depression. A secret society known as the Hunters' Lodges was formed, dedicated to the task of "freeing" the Canadian colonies from Britain and turning them into independant republics; these would of course join the union of American states. The altruistic cast of this noble adventure is somewhat tarnished when one learns that Mackenzie and his colleagues promised their supporters – 80,000 of them at the height of the movement's success – handsome salaries, land grants, and high positions in the new republics.

Under pressure from Britain, President Martin Van Buren publicly declared the Lodges and their invasion goal to be illegal. This did not dampen the ardour of the majority of American politicians and their constituents who had envied the British possessions to the north ever since Britain conquered New France in 1759.

In the result the adventure failed, as had those abortive invasions of 1775 and 1812. Raiding parties landed near Prescott in eastern Upper Canada (November 1838) and at Windsor in the west (December 1838). Both attacks were tragically unsuccessful. The rebels captured at Windsor were brought to London to stand trial. A court-martial convened by the tough-minded lieutenant-governor of Upper Canada, Sir George Arthur, found forty of the raiders guilty of treason; all were sentenced to hang. Two of them were from the village of London: Elijah C. Woodman, a relative by marriage of the pioneer iron-founder Elijah Leonard; and James Milne Aitchison, nephew of the wife of the Reverend William Proudfoot.

1838 Queen Victoria's coronation.

Letter from exile in Van Diemen's Land (now Tasmania) in 1844, by Elijah Crocker
Woodman, a rebel captured in the raid on Windsor, on 4 December 1838. Released
in 1847, Woodman died on his way home to London UWO

1839 Boundary dispute between the state of Maine and the province of New Brunswick
      threatens war between the United States and Great Britain.

Arthur had made his reputation by putting down "native revolts" in Honduras and Tasmania, with great severity. He must have been aware that the same methods would not work with the "natives" of Upper Canada. He probably did not intend that all forty rebels should hang, but he was determined that the disaffected should be taught a stern lesson.

The gallows were erected at the front of the courthouse, which now faced the village instead of the river. It was built against the building, with the trap swinging inward. It was there that on 7 January 1839, Hiram B. Lynn, aged twenty-six, of Ann Arbor, Michigan, paid the supreme penalty for his political error. The Reverend Benjamin Cronyn attended the condemned man. As the trap fell, it crashed against the side of the courthouse. The reverberating vibration conveyed its message to those awaiting their death date in the dungeons below.

On 11 January it was the turn of Daniel Bedford, aged twenty-seven, a native of Upper Canada, a married innkeeper from the village of Norwich.

On that same date, *The Freeman's Advocate,* a weekly newspaper published in Lockport, New York, recorded the death of one of the most distinguished victims of that most unhappy time:

DIED – On Monday last, Edward Allen Talbot, late Editor of The Lewiston Telegraph, and one of the Refugees from Canada. He was formerly the editor of The Freeman's Journal in London, U.C., and has sustained for years both in England and Canada a high literary reputation, and was respected as a gentleman of high and honorable feeling by all who knew him.

At the outbreak in Canada he was compelled to fly to this country to avoid the penalty of his liberal opinions. Since leaving Canada, his health has been gradually declining, and on Monday last, far from his friends and among strangers, he breathed his last.

A funeral sermon was preached on Tuesday, by the Rev. Dr. Kent, of the Methodist Church, and his remains were deposited in the Cold Springs cemetery. We understand that he has left a large family in Canada to regret his loss, as another victim to Colonial tyranny.

Albert Clark, a twenty-one-year-old drifter from New Hampshire, was hanged on 14 January. After that, there was a three-week break in the chain of executions. One reason for this may have been the disappointing results achieved by Sir George Arthur's stern punitive policy. Considering popular interest in the public executions of the times, the Tory authorities had expected an attendance of at least three thousand at each of the hangings. Lynn's execution drew only two hundred. It was a subtle but effective rebuke.

1839 Louis Daguerre invents the daguerrotype process.

Lewis Adelbert Norton, jailed as a rebel in London in December 1837, was released in August 1838 and banished from the province for life. Settled in California. From *Life and Adventures of Col. L.A. Norton* (Oakland, Cal., 1887).

On the other hand, the funeral of the commandant of the British garrison attracted a full house in holiday mood. Lieutenant-Colonel John Maitland, commanding officer of the 32nd Regiment, a half-mad little martinet noted for meting out harsh punishment for minor infractions of military discipline, had earned the dislike of all during his brief residence in London. Local tradition reports that his sudden death in January 1839 was greeted with general satisfaction.

The hangings resumed on 4 February, when Cornelius Cunningham, aged thirty-two, from Beachville, in Oxford County, dropped through the trap. Feelings in London were running high; the mood was becoming dangerous. Even among the most partisan Tories there was a growing feeling of revulsion at this sacrifice of young lives. It was time to cry quits. There were two final executions, both on 6 February; after that the sentences of the remaining rebels were commuted to exile to Van Diemen's Land.

The memory of that last, double hanging remained green from many years. Both men who met death in one of its most ugly manifestations that bitter February day were well known in the District of London. Joshua Gillam Doan, member of a Quaker family established at Sparta in what is now Elgin County, had been with Duncombe in the abortive 1837 uprising and had then fled the country with a price of £100 on his head; he was among those captured at the Battle of Windsor. He was twenty-six

---

1839 Charles Goodyear, a Connecticut inventor, produces vulcanized rubber.

years old, married, the father of one child. Amos Perley was a native of New Brunswick; his residence was given as Burford, in Oxford County. His case was especially sad; one of the military judges who condemned him to the gallows was his cousin Captain Charles Strange Perley, also of Burford.

On Sunday, 27 January 1839, as the carefully-preserved candle flame wavered in the foul air of his dungeon cell, Joshua Doan wrote his last letter to his wife:

I am at this moment confined in the call from which I am to go to the Scaffold. I received my sentence to-day, and am to be executed on February 6th. I am permitted to see you to-morrow, any time after 10 o'clock in the morning, as may suit you best. I wish you to think of such questions as you wish to ask me, as I do not know how long you will be permitted to stay. Think as little of my unhappy fate as you can; as from the love you bear me, I know too well how it must affect you. I wish you to inform my father and brother of my sentence as soon as possible. I must say good-bye for the night, and may God protect you and my dear child, and give you fortitude to meet that coming event with the Christian grace and fortitude which is the gift of Him, our Lord, who created us. That this may be the case, is the prayer of your affectionate husband.

His simple personal arrangements made, Joshua Doan turned his mind toward his duties as a citizen of Upper Canada. On 4 February he gave a voluntary statement in the presence of John Douglas, a justice of the peace, and Lieutenant John Grogan, 32nd Regiment, commanding the gaol guard. After clarifying certain points raised at his trial, refuting some, endorsing others, he gave startling evidence concerning the collusion of American authorities in the attempted invasion of Upper Canada:

I do further say that there are a number of leading men in the United States, who hold high offices under the American Government, that do, to this day, mislead my countrymen, as well as they have misled me, by trying to facilitate the Rebel party in getting munitions of war, to carry on the expedition against the Canadas. I also saw a number of new United States rifles at Detroit, which were given out to the rebel party by one of the Captains, whose name is Fuller, from Ohio, who had command of a company of riflemen, and had drawn the rifles from the United States government, for their use, and gave his receipt for the return of which he is responsible; which trust he betrayed, in the appropriating them to the use of the Rebels, in invading Canada. ... I further state, that I was armed with a cartridge-box, and a musket, by the Captain of

---

1839 Josephine Amelia Perkins is the first lady horse-thief of record.

Grand Military Steeplechase, London, Upper Canada, 9 May 1843. The first stee-plechase held in North America. Painting by Eveline-Marie Alexander, wife of Sir James Alexander. UWO

my company. ... The rifles were all marked with the United States Government mark, which is U.S., and I believe they were from Ohio. ...

It is a custom, honoured by tradition, that men condemned by the state to die upon the gallows are expected to confer some "last words" upon posterity. We are not told if Joshua Doan availed himself of the oppor-tunity. Amos Perley did. His words set out with crystal clarity the Canadian policy of reform-by-consensus that is the despair of our young and the envy of our wise European contemporaries:

1839 12,000 Mormons found the city of Nauvoo on the banks of the Mississippi River in
        Illinois.

The Cause that led me to my present unhappy fate was the false and wicked misrepresentations of your own citizens. ... To such I would say, you can accomplish the object for which you are contending much sooner by reform than by revolution, and correct the abuses of which you complain by petitioning, and through the ballot-box, and restore peace once more to your now unhappy country, with all its attendant blessings and ever-varying charms.

The universal extension of human liberty and religious freedom is a object that has brought the mind and talent of the great and good of all ages to its aid and defence, and its consummation is a thing to be devoutly hoped for. By pursuing such a course as humanity and charity may point out to you, you may expect to enjoy all the blessings of freedom. ... by pursuing a mild and persuasive course, you will soon see the olive branch of Peace flourishing in your soil and the Tree of Liberty taking root therein. ...

1839 The Central American Federation breaks up into the separate states of Guatemala, Honduras, Nicaragua, El Salvador, and Costa Rica.

CHAPTER THREE

VILLAGE

*Caesar, when he went first into Gaul, made no scruple to profess 'That he had rather be
first in a village than second at Rome.'*
Francis Bacon, *The Advancement of Learning.*

The Rebellion brought about many changes. London became a police
village and George Jervis Goodhue was elected the first president of the
board. Only a few of the older settlers called it "The Forks" any more.
The British soldiers, in their letters home, usually referred to it as "New
London," and amused themselves comparing the Canadian Bond Street,
a lane between stumps, with its English namesake.

Prior to the Rebellion the commonest accent heard in London was
Yankee. Even some of the leading figures of the Anglican Establishment
read the Prayer Book responses with a New England twang. Now, quite
suddenly, the voices reading the lessons had the plummy accents of Oxford
or Cambridge, while on the streets one commonly heard the grating conso-
nants and the fluting vowels of a dozen different English counties.

One change that affected everyone was – money. Up until now, barter
had been the principal medium for the exchange of goods. Upper Canada
had no official currency. To meet the needs of commerce, the Legislature
had authorized the use of many European and New World coins for legal
tender. The commonest coin in actual use was the Spanish eight-*real* piece,
minted in Mexico. This was the "piece of eight" dear to all readers of
Robert Louis Stevenson's classic *Treasure Island.* The Spanish "piece of
eight" was not four dollars, but was one American dollar. This was a coin
similar in size and value to the English crown. To simplify calculations in
Upper Canada, the piece was valued at one pound, "Provincial Currency."
The system worked reasonably well in practice. Account books were ruled
in four columns, reading (from the left) pounds, dollars, shillings, and
pence.

1840 – Upper and Lower Canada united under one government by the Act of Union.

The arrival of the garrison added an element of joyous confusion. This was called Sterling. The British Army didn't deal in barter, United States banknotes, or Spanish pieces of eight. The troops were paid in cash, good British copper, silver, and gold. A tuppenny piece was a great chunky hunk of copper and a sovereign was real gold. With one ecstatic leap, London merchants jumped into the money. The British Army became the source of all good things. Not only were the soldiers paid in specie; so too were the artisans employed by the contractor for the building of the extensive barracks. This fortunate entrepreneur was Edward Matthews, an Englishman who had arrived in London in 1835.

The military reserve on which the barracks were erected occupied roughly eight square blocks, extending from what is now Dufferin Avenue north to the right-of-way of the Canadian Pacific Railway and eastward from Clarence Street to Waterloo Street. Two sets of buildings enclosed the parade square. The first, built in 1838–1839, consisted of thirty-six buildings, constructed of hand-hewn logs. The second set, built of sawn lumber and generally referred to as the "Framed Barracks," was completed sometime before 1843. Altogether the complex cost the British Government about one hundred thousand pounds ($400,000) – a truly enormous sum for the time and the place.

Inevitably the life of the village began to revolve around the huge reserve on its northern limits. Officers and enlisted men had needs, which the host community made haste to fill. The requirements of the men, being simpler, were probably the first to be met. Very soon, a row of grog shops and whorehouses sprang up along that portion of the present Richmond Street, then known as Sarnia Street, opposite the reserve.

The officers, many of them scions of old established English families, had physical needs too, but they exercised them in less overt ways, sublimating their sexual drive in sports. A section of the parade square became a cricket ground. Over the years cricket was gradually superseded by the North American game known as baseball (first introduced in the Oxford County community of Beachville in 1838). Other officers went in for the more exciting sports of horse-racing and the steeplechase.

Brawn was more easily satisfied than brain. For the intellectual, New London offered little. It was obvious that if the military required stimulation in this area, it would have to provide its own:

The residence of the military in our midst, the contract for the barracks, and the start given to building generally, made life easier. ... As Dr O'Flarity, of the 83rd Regiment, lived quite near us on the southeast corner of Richmond and

1840 – Last convicts landed in New South Wales, Australia.

THEATRE ROYAL,
LONDON.

The Gentlemen Amateurs

BEG TO ANNOUNCE THAT ON

Wednesday Evening, the 17th of January, 1844,

By permission of the Officers of the Garrison, who have granted the use of the Theatre,
they will have the honour to make their first appearance.

AN ORIGINAL PROLOGUE,

Written for the occasion, will be spoken by the Manager.

After which will be presented, Colman's much admired Play of the

Heir at Law.

DANIEL DOWLAS, (Baron Duberly,)	MR. STREET,
DICK DOWLAS,	MR. A. KEIR,
HENRY MORLAND,	MR. DIXIE WATSON,
STEDFAST,	MR. LUNDY,
DOCTOR PANGLOSS,	MR. JAS. SHANLY,
ZEKIEL HOMESPUN,	MR. HERBERT DIXON,
KENRICK,	MR. WILSON MILLS,
JOHN,	MR. GORDON,
WAITER,	MR. JOHN ASKIN,
LADY DUBERLY,	MR. CHARLES MOORE,
CAROLINE DORMER,	MR. BECHER,
CICELY HOMESPUN,	MR. FRANK COOK.

SONG,

"THE WIDOW MALONE,"
MR. COOTE SHANLY.

SONG,
"HARRY BLUFF,"
MR. HERBERT DIXON.

To coclude with the laughable Farce of

High Life below Stairs

LOVEL,	MR. BECHER,
FREEMAN,	MR. DIXIE WATSON,
PHILIP,	MR. CLEVERLY,
DUKE'S SERVANT,	MR. STREET,
SIR HARRY'S SERVANT,	MR. A. KEIR,
TOM,	MR. LUNDY,
ROBERT,	MR. ALLEN,
COACHMAN,	MR. GORDON,
KINGSTON,	MR. JOHN ASKIN,
KITTY,	MR. FRANK COOK,
LADY BAB'S MAID,	MR. CHARLES LEONARD,
LADY CHARLOTTE'S MAID,	MR. GILL,
COOK,	MR. WILSON MILLS,
CHLOE,	MR. SIMCOE LEE.

DOORS to open at half past seven o'clock ; Performance to commence at eight o'clock, *precisely.*
BOXES 2s. 6d.   PIT 1s. 3d.   Tickets to be had at the Stores of Messrs. CLARIS or DEASE.
☞ N. B.   No money taken at the Doors.

Vivat Regina.

Playbill for a performance by a civilian theatre company, 1844. All the female
roles were played by men, one of whom was Graves Simcoe Lee (see fig. 30). UWO

Horton streets, we saw a good deal of what was going on, and were once allowed to attend an amateur performance at a theatre on Wellington street, where the public library now stands. Standing trees supported the board roof and stumps, sawed off pretty evenly, supported the rough board seats. We went in a dark passageway by a door on North street. Dr O'Flarity acted the part of a ghost; so I suppose the play was Hamlet, but that I don't remember.

The building recalled so vividly more than sixty years later by Mrs Gilbert Porte was known as the Theatre Royal. It was a half-completed, abandoned Methodist chapel that stood on the southwest corner of Wellington Street and Queens Avenue. Ownership of the building had been casually and ruthlessly transferred by the local land baron, Colonel Thomas Talbot, by simply erasing from his land map the pencilled name of the church society and replacing it with the name of commandant of the London garrison.

The military theatricals were greeted with great enthusiasm by the townsfolk who until now had to content themselves with such entertainment as the occasional public hanging or the exhibition of an educated pig.

These early performances created a theatrical tradition in London that has been maintained up to the present. From time to time London amateur players have achieved notable success on the professional stage. The first to do so was Graves Simcoe Lee, a son of the innkeeper-physician Hiram Davis Lee. An early member of a civilian drama club, Lee turned professional and established his name as a Shakespearean actor in New York and elsewhere.

While some played cricket and others played Portia or Macbeth, still others painted. Many of the officers had received instructions in water-colour at the Royal Military Academy at Woolwich, England, under the great Paul Sandby or his son and successor Thomas Paul Sandby. Thanks to this group we have an excellent idea of how London looked in its village days.

It was an attractive village.

There is a pleasing symmetry to the view painted by a succession of artists from a favourite spot, a hill on Wortley Road, south and west of the Forks. From that distance the mud, the dust, the untidy ranks of stumps, the ash pits, and the malodorous ditches were mercifully invisible. The scene, in fact, could be that of a prosperous English village.

Close to, the reality was quite different.

1840 – Queen Victoria marries Prince Albert of Saxe-Coburg-Gotha.

At the top of the social pyramid, life was very good, if occasionally boring. The round of parties, balls, teas, *conversaziones,* gaming, and visiting differed little from what one might find in an English garrison town of two thousand inhabitants. The daughters of John and Amelia Harris lived a life remarkably free of restriction. If they danced until the small hours with a retinue of army officers and then slipped off for a moonlight sail across Lake Erie to Cleveland – what then?

An unknown writer of the period captured something of the essence of those carefree days – and nights:

> Sing the delights of London society –
> > Epaulette, sabretache, sword-knot and plume;
> Always enchanting, yet knows no variety –
> > Scarlet alone can embellish a room.
> While spurs are clattering,
> Flirting and chattering,
> > Bend the proud heroes that fight for the crown;
> Dancing cotillions,
> Cutting civilians,
> > These are the joys of a garrison town.
>
> Little reck we of you black coated laity;
> > Forty to one upon *rouge* against *noir;*
> On soldiers we lavish our favors and gaiety,
> > For the rest we leave them to feel *desepoir.*
> Odious vulgarity,
> Reckless barbarity,
> > We have for such *canaille* as these but a frown;
> While flirting with fusiliers,
> Smiling on Grenadiers –
> > These are the joys of a garrison town.

London's own social nucleus consisted of a very few families. Among these must be considered the Harris, Becher, Killaly, and Cronyn families. Some had money, all had position. Others had money, but no position. Money was acceptable, but only if a sufficient distance could be established between it and the means by which it was accumulated. Thus, George J. Goodhue, who in 1840 was elected first president of the village board of police, was acceptable because his funds came from usury, which leaves the hands physically clean. Dealers in wood ashes (from which soap was

---

1840 – Penny postage established in Great Britain.

manufactured) and similar products might bear on their persons embarrassing olfactory evidence of that abomination of nineteenth-century upper society – *trade!* For witness, the following anecdote:

Society began to assert itself in 1841, when the line was drawn pretty tight to preserve intact a select few of the better class of business men as being the only ones qualified for admission to the drawing rooms, which were always open to military tinsel, from colonel to captain. Upon a certain occasion an assembly was invited which admitted none of the citizens proper, but such as had (or were supposed to have) a good bank account. All right so far, but when the cards of admission were collected and it was discovered that one of them smelled very strongly of soap or fish oil, it raised a tempest in a tea pot, which nearly upset the whole affair.

While there were members of the "codfish aristocracy" (as the social climbers were known) who would have done almost anything for a card of admission to one of these gatherings, there were other men who would have spurned an invitation. Men like Simeon Morrill, the tanner, and Elijah Leonard, the foundry-owner, belonged to churches that opposed drinking, dancing, and gaming. While the Church of England did not encourage these practices, it carried out no active campaign against them. It is true, however, that on one occasion, after a particularly lavish affair given by George Goodhue at his home on Bathurst Street, Benjamin Cronyn preached a rather pointed sermon on the theme of Belshazzar's feast and its unfortunate consequences.

Then, of course, there were the politicians. Some of those who apprenticed in the rough-and-tumble of local politics went on to compete in larger, if no less noisy, arenas. They were the professionals. Others engaged in the electoral battles more as a kind of sport. They were the amateurs. They had more fun.

London's first municipal elections were held on Monday, 2 March 1840. The four wards of the village were named for the patron saints of the United Kingdom; St George's for England, St Andrew's for Scotland, St Patrick's for Ireland, and St David's for Wales. Each ward elected one councillor to sit on the village board of police. A fifth councillor was elected by the electorate at large.

In this initial election the Yankee storekeeper George J. Goodhue became councillor for St George's; Dennis O'Brien, his Irish business rival, was appropriately named to represent St Patrick's; Simeon Morrill represented St Andrew's; and John Balkwill, the brewer, was returned for St

---

1841 – Great Britain proclaims sovereignty over Hong Kong.

David's. The fifth member was the lawyer James Givens, son of the Lieutenant James Givens who had accompanied Lieutenant-Governor Simcoe on his 1793 reconnaissance of the forks of the Thames.

At the first meeting of the village board, the members elected Goodhue as president – another step in his inexorable rise to political patronage and financial power. It was a time for the establishment of community reputations. Dennis O'Brien, London's Number One Roman Catholic layman, came out of the experience with his prestige enhanced. He seems to have had few detractors, even fewer enemies.

The member for St David's was of a different sort. He had founded, in 1828, the brewery that became Labatt's. He was apparently an enthusiastic consumer of his own product. In witness there are two surviving notations concerning a council meeting of Monday, 23 October 1843:

John Balkwill, Esq., having attended the Board in a state of intoxication: ordered that the constable do remove him; he having done everything in his power to impede the proceedings of the Board. Carried. ...

John Balkwill, Esq., one of the members of the Board, having broken the windows of the office, or instigated the same to be done: ordered, that the Board adjourn till to-morrow morning.

It was further noted that Dr William King Cornish, clerk of the board, submitted his intention to resign, "owing to Balkwill's conduct." It so happened that the building in which the board held its meetings was owned by Cornish, who then turfed out the board and demanded the arrears of rent, amounting to £10 ($40) for three years' use. The building, which was London's first "town hall," was described by the late Dr Cl. T. Campbell:

The first "City Hall" was a small frame building plastered on the outside, situated on the corner of Fullarton and Talbot Streets. ... It remained there for many years. ... When I first knew it, Dr Jas. Lee occupied it as his office. It was a little one-storey building, with a verandah – the platform of which was level with the street. It was a very unpretentious affair; but the municipal authorities found it sufficient for their purposes.

Dr Cornish was an English lawyer who emigrated to Canada and, finding he could not practise law here, turned to the study of medicine under Dr Charles Duncombe. He came to London in 1831, in which year his

---

1843 Edgar Allan Poe, *The Pit and the Pendulum.*

son Francis Evans Cornish was born. He became successively (and sometimes concurrently) surgeon to the gaol, district coroner, justice of the peace, surveyor, road overseer, and land agent – a man for all seasons.

Deprived of their former meeting place, the village solons decided to build. A two-storey frame building was erected on what was to become London's Covent Garden Market. Later it was moved across the street to the northwest corner of King and Talbot streets and bricked over. At the time of writing (1988) it is one of a row of nineteenth-century structures threatened with demolition. Soon it may be that the only surviving relic of London's town hall will be its silver-toned bell, now enshrined in a memorial in London Township's "ghost village," Carlisle.

Before the bell was installed, village emergencies were signalled by means of a trumpet or bugle sounded by some designated individual. For less emergent occasions Londoners had three means of communication. Gossip was conveyed by word of mouth, commercial news by an officially-appointed town crier, and political intelligence by the weekly newspaper press.

London has always been a good town for gossip. Reputations by the hundreds have been made, broken, or enhanced over the tea pot or the coffee urn. The decade of the 1840s was a particularly juicy period:

Which young officer was currently courting which daughter of John and Amelia Harris?

What public official was said to be dipping into which public fund?

Was it true that the lady wife of Casimir Gzowski, the Polish engineer-in-exile, was in the family way again?

Some bits of gossip found their way into the official records.

In November 1843, Father Patrick O'Dwyer, pastor of the Roman Catholic log church at the southwest corner of Richmond and Maple streets, was arrested and fined for riding his horse on the downtown sidewalks. There was no way of keeping that quiet.

Then, of course, there was the scandalous case of Four-Eyed Stuart and the British officer.

In 1834 John Stuart, an attorney, married Miss Elizabeth Van Rensalaer Powell, daughter of Dr Grant Powell and grand-daughter of the Honourable William Dummer Powell, chief justice of Upper Canada. Soon afterward, the couple moved from Toronto to London, where Stuart entered into the practice of law. Three daughters were born to the couple in the ensuing five years. All was apparently well with them until 1839.

1843 United States newspapers begin use of word "millionaire."

In 1838, as we have seen, the 32nd Regiment of Foot was moved to London as a consequence of the Upper Canada rebellion. One of its officers was Lieutenant John Grogan. In the tight little society of "New London" it was inevitable that John Grogan and Elizabeth Stuart should meet. When they did, something happened. They soon became lovers. Then, in 1840, the regiment was moved to Toronto. Mrs Stuart informed her husband that she was going to visit her mother, about whose health she was concerned. Once in Toronto, Elizabeth Stuart left mother, husband, and daughters to live with the handsome British lieutenant. As soon as he heard of this, Stuart hopped a stagecoach, called on Grogan, and demanded satisfaction, according to the ancient code of the duel.

The two men met, on a misty morning in June 1840, on Toronto Island. Stuart fired first – and missed. Grogan then fired into the air. Satisfaction had been demanded and given.

Stuart, however, was not finished. He sued Grogan for "alienation of his wife's affections," won, and was awarded the astounding sum of £671 14s 3d Provincial Currency ($2,686.85 US) – a very large amount in those days.

Finally, Stuart took a step that made legal history. He petitioned the Parliament of Canada for a divorce from his erring spouse. The Act of Divorce (3d Victoria, Chapter 72), passed on 18 June 1841, was the first of its kind ever enacted by a Canadian parliament.

The Stuart-Grogan affair must have awakened unhappy memories in a second London household. On another June day, seven years earlier, John Wilson had shot and killed a fellow-law-student, Robert Lyon, in the last fatal duel ever fought in Canada. The meeting took place on the banks of the River Tay, at Perth, Ontario, on Thursday, 13 June 1833. In his subsequent trial on the mandatory charge of murder, Wilson defended himself and won acquittal. The following year he moved to London and established a law practice. In 1835 he married Miss Elizabeth Hughes, the young lady whose honour he had defended in the field.

It would take an Edward Gorey suitably to illustrate these two early-Victorian dramas. In the American artist's inimitable style we would see the adulterous couple in the Stuart-Grogan affair merrily dancing their way from one mess dinner to another, living happily ever after while the cuckolded husband takes to drink and totters off down the road to ruin and obscurity.

In the Wilson matter we would see the virtuous John Wilson and the virtuous Miss Hughes plighting their virtuous troth and proceeding on their virtuous path, she to raise a brood in the fear of God, he to rise step

---

1843 B'nai Brith, a Jewish fraternal organization, founded in New York.

by step to national prominence as lawyer, judge, and successful politician. Not exactly in the true Gorey tradition, one must admit, but in the final panels Gorey's Gothic magic could work its fey wonder, as we see John Wilson in his annual commemoration of the fatal duel, brooding, close-closeted in his private chambers, seeing no one, speaking to no one, the albatross of memory peering bleakly down on him from the bookcase. ...

Say what you will, the Victorians knew how to live, how to drink from the cup of life, from the bubbles winking at the brim to the dregs lurking at the bottom!

In a society such as this, gossip became almost an art form, tea-pot fiction in many cases being overtaken by courtroom fact.

Information of a more serious nature was conveyed by the town crier. The first two men named to this position were blacks, of whom the better-remembered was "General" George Washington Brown. Brown dressed in cast-off military uniforms, gleefully provided by young officers at the garrison. When Brown died in May 1845, his passing was marked by an eleven-stanza piece of doggerel verse in the London *Times*, of which the following is a sample:

> What man is there, who claims the rank
> Of "Londoner" who will not own
> How much he feels the common blank
> Made by the death of Gen'ral Brown!

In later years a white man, William Williams, was named to the position by the town council and served under a variety of administrations until the 1860s, when the city's daily newspapers made the job obsolete.

For many years the town crier and the weekly newspapers were competitors in the field of advertising. The crier had the obvious advantage of immediacy. A merchant-client could have him "cry" a sale as soon as he decided upon it, instead of waiting for the next publication day of the local weeklies, among which were the *Times*, the *Western Globe*, the *Inquirer*, the *Herald*, and the *Gazette*. The advertisements in these journals tended in consequence to be of an institutional nature. The first of the standard four pages was usually given over to "business cards," announcing services offered on a continuing basis by the advertisers. The third page usually contained such current advertisements as municipal announcements, coach and ship schedules, real-estate notices, and birth, marriage, and death announcements. A regular feature of the inside pages was a list, often a column in length, of letters being held at the post office awaiting their

1844 Alexandre Dumas, père, *The Three Musketeers*.

intended recipients. Sometimes the letters were prepaid, while others had to be paid for by those to whom they were addressed. (Postage stamps were not introduced into the Canada until 1851.)

Local news in the weeklies was usually reduced to a few skimpy paragraphs. Most of the information contained therein was already known to the readers either by word of mouth or from the town crier. Political news – local, regional, and national – took up most of what space was left. Partisanship was boldly and baldly displayed, often in language that would today be considered libellous, slanderous, or even criminal. The issue of the legal parameters of press freedom was yet to be decided. When it was, it was decided in London.

Meanwhile, there was another side to the society of London in the 1840s that has seldom been touched upon, either in contemporary records or in the selective memories of those who lived through the events.

There were poor people in London from the very beginning, and they had no protection against poverty and hunger except the sometimes chilly charity of the churches and church people. There was no official structure in place to answer the needs of those whom we today refer to in our oblique way as "the disadvantaged."

Only a few years earlier indigent widows were auctioned off to the highest bidder. Quite often the unfortunate females stepped from the auction block into that form of unpaid servitude called Christian marriage; but marriage was not a condition of sale. If the buyer didn't choose to formalize his relationship to his chattel – well, that was a matter between him and his conscience.

Nor was there any provision in the community's budget for the care of orphan children. No matter how blameless before the law, they went to prison – unless some person could be induced to come forward to adopt the orphan or apprentice him to a trade. The male pronoun is used because there were no trades open to females.

The imprisoned orphans shared what accommodation the gaol afforded with the debtors. These were men found without sufficient assets to discharge a debt of as little as ten shillings Provincial Currency ($2 US). A sad story that had currency many years ago told of a local doctor, imprisoned for debt, who had to sell his medical library, his instruments, and other possessions to get money with which – not to pay his debt, but to buy *food*. In Canada as in England at this time, felons were fed at the public expense, but the debtors were on their own.

At the very bottom of the social order were the new Irish immigrants and the blacks. Each group had its own ghetto – although of course the

1844 James Knox Polk (Democrat) elected 11th president of the United States.

The District of London courthouse, built 1827–1831, and the gaol, built 1844. Sketch by Reta O'Brien, from *London Heritage* – second edition (London: Phelps Publishing 1979).

term was unknown in Canada at that time. The "new" Irish, refugees from the latest famine and disease in that unhappy land, were located at the north end of the town, in an area north of Victoria Street and west of Richmond Street. This district was known as "Tipperary Flats" until well into the present century. Many of the blacks lived in a section of town south of York Street and west of Ridout. This was known for many years as "Nigger Hollow."

On the whole, the blacks were better off than the Irish. Many of them were escaped slaves, flying from bondage in the United States. This gave them a sort of romantic aura denied the ragged Irish. Some blacks arrived quite early in the late 1820s. There does not seem to have been any active prejudice directed against them. Alfred T. Jones, who came to London about 1833 and became a respected and successful apothecary, said the biggest problem for them were newcomers from England:

The people from the old country, being many of them unaccustomed to
colored people, have some strange ideas respecting us; a sort of "second-hand
prejudice". ...

Among the newcomers Jones referred to could have been the soldiers of the London garrison. These men must have been the envy of the town's poor, living as they did, in the care of the Queen, clothed, fed, bedded, and even paid. However, the private soldier of the Imperial Army in the 1840s had his own personal version of hell. Minor infractions of inflexible rules brought major penalties. The cat-o'-nine-tails saw frequent employment. A sentry who left his post for a moment to answer the call of nature was given a hundred lashes and branded with the letter D as a deserter.

Living conditions in the huge barracks complex left much to be desired. A report on sanitary arrangements made to the inspector-general of hospitals on 16 July 1840 is shocking in its details:

Besides that the use of Urine tubs for personal washing is most filthy, and must
engender other habits incompatible with personal cleanliness, it is positively
and highly injurious, aggravating a tendency to diseases of the Eyes
particularly; which are becoming increasingly prevalent in the Command. ...

While this state of affairs occurred elsewhere, subsequent reports to the inspector-general indicated that diseases of the eyes, caused by the practice outlined in the 1840 report, were four times as common in Canadian

---

1845 Richard Wagner, *Tannhäuser* (opera).

Dundas Street, 1842, looking west from a point near Waterloo Street. The church on the right is the first St Paul's, destroyed by fire on Ash Wednesday, 1844. Painting by Lady Eveline-Marie Alexander, from Alexander *L'Acadie* (London 1849).

military establishments as in England, and that the situation was worst of all in London, Upper Canada.

Despite these pockets of poverty and disease, London was, in its village days, a reasonably attractive, reasonably happy, and prosperous community, its rough-and-tumble pioneer days behind it, and a settled and serene Victorian afternoon ahead of it. The commandant of the British garrison had cooperated with village officials in removing the unsightly stumps on the main streets, to which travellers had referred in unflattering terms. They were used to make a picturesque fence around the military grounds. The lumber from the vanished trees had gone into the building of houses and stores. Like most Upper Canadian communities, London was a town of frame and log buildings. For a time the only brick structure in town was Dennis O'Brien's block opposite the courthouse square on Ridout Street, which had been used as a temporary barracks in 1838.

Such towns have always been susceptible to fire damage. Between 1837 and 1841, Saint John, New Brunswick, suffered three disastrous fires that, between them, destroyed two hundred buildings and almost wiped out the business section.

1845 Edgar Allan Poe, "The Raven."

London's turn came in 1844 and 1845.

On 21 February 1844, which was, ironically, Ash Wednesday, the wooden church of St Paul's caught fire and burned to the ground. A new organ, laboriously constructed by a talented cabinet-maker named Pringle, and installed in the church only a few weeks before, was consumed by the flames that spread south to Dundas Street, destroying several buildings there.

A bad fire in October 1844, demolished more than thirty buildings for a total loss of £15,000 ($60,000 U.S.), a very large sum for the times. Only two buildings survived in an area of almost three acres in the heart of the town.

These two fires were merely prelude to the main drama.

SUNDAY, 13 APRIL 1845

The congregation of St Paul's Church is at worship in the auditorium of the Mechanics' Institute on the courthouse square. Their new church is rapidly nearing completion, but it will be many months yet before they can take possession of the handsome brick structure.

The third Sunday after Easter.

It's the service of Matins, which in this low-church congregation is better known as Morning Prayer. The Lord has opened reluctant lips and his praise has been said, not sung. The service proceeds at its accustomed ponderous pace, while outside on the streets of London, life moves in solemn somnolence.

A newcomer to the village stops to admire the classic architecture of the Institute, set over against the neo-Gothic courthouse, the two together serving to crown London's Acropolis.

The pedestrian is Marcus Gunn, a Scot recently arrived from New Brunswick. He has relatives in the district and plans to launch a newspaper. He is staying at the Robinson Hall Hotel on Ridout Street. He has left there his valise containing the current volume of his extraordinary diary, which he started in 1819 in Tipperary County, Ireland.

In the Institute the congregation has progressed to the responsive reading of the psalm for the day, Psalm 68. The rector, Benjamin Cronyn, reads the first verse:

Let God arise and let his enemies be scattered;
let them also that hate him flee before him.

1845 US Congress sets presidential election day in the first week in November, after harvest, but while the roads are still passable.

The congregation, led by a distinguished visitor, the Honourable John Beverley Robinson, chief justice of Upper Canada, reads the response:

Like as the smoke vanisheth, so shalt thou drive them away and like as wax melteth at the fire, so let the ungodly perish at the presence of God.

Before the rector can continue with verse three, a hysterical cry from the street below is heard.
"Fire! Fire!"
There is immediate panic. People in wooden towns fear matches. The auditorium is on the second floor of the Institute. The stairs are narrow. A rush for safety can have tragic consequences. An unspoken message passes between the parson and the chief justice. The rector continues reading:

But let the righteous be glad and rejoice before God; let them also be merry and joyful.

With great equanimity the justice reads in a clear, loud voice:

O sing unto God, and sing praises unto his Name –

Other voices join in:

– magnify him that rideth upon the heavens, as it were upon an horse. ...

Quietly, but swiftly, the sidesmen lead the people down the steep stairs to safety while the parson and the chief justice continue their reading. Only when the last member of the congregation has reached the exit do the two men follow them. There's much to do. The chief justice is a guest at the hotel where the fire had started. His robes and other belongings are in his room. By this time the hotel is ablaze from front to back. At considerable risk to himself Judge Robinson rescues his belongings. The Scottish visitor, Marcus Gunn, is less fortunate. His valise containing his precious diary, with other manuscript materials, is lost.
The Reverend Benjamin Cronyn, always at his best in emergencies, is helping the occupants of nearby buildings to move their valuables to the street, where they are stacked up for later retrieval. The fire, fed by westerly

---

1845 John L. O'Sullivan coins the phrase "Manifest Destiny" to prophesy the fulfilment of the destiny of the United States "to overspread the continent allotted by Providence."

winds off the river, is spreading rapidly. The Robinson Hall Hotel is now gone and so are the adjacent structures on Ridout Street.

A squad of artillerymen under Captain John Herbert Caddy has placed itself under Cronyn's direction. By dint of great effort they manage to evacuate residents' belongings ahead of the fire, but the men are tiring. Suddenly there's a cry from the rear. Sparks from the burning buildings have touched off one of the stacks of furniture carefully piled in the middle of the street.

It has become a losing battle. Soon every building on the block bounded by Dundas, King, Talbot, and Ridout streets is ablaze, and structures south to the river are in imminent danger.

Before nightfall more than two hundred buildings are in ashes. The smoke and flames can be seen as far away as St Thomas and have attracted sightseers, scavengers, and looters from the surrounding countryside.

A further appeal to the garrison brings a number of men from the 2nd Royal Regiment of Foot to stand guard over the ruins with fixed bayonets to repel looters.

At the end of the day, Parson Cronyn, soot-stained and weary, retrieves the Preacher's Book of St Paul's from the Mechanics' Institute. Later, in the rectory, he records a laconic note under the current date:

"No collection ... Great Fire."

Almost before the ashes of London's business district had cooled, money was being collected to aid the sufferers. Like the nasty business of the looters, there were ugly aspects to this effort, too. Some fraud artists, representing themselves as victims of the disaster, began collecting funds in Toronto. They had the effrontery to call upon the Anglican Bishop of Toronto, the Right Reverend John Strachan, who at once wrote to Benjamin Cronyn suggesting that the latter call a public meeting of "the best-known and respectable of your inhabitants" to organize a proper relief fund.

The proposal was swiftly acted upon, and soon donations were pouring into the stricken community from cities and towns all over Canada, from the United States and Great Britain, for the story of the fire had received widespread publicity.

Estimates of the damage caused by London's "Great Fire" ranged as high as £300,000. No final accounting of the relief fund has been found, but by the summer of 1845 it had exceeded £100,000.

The village board of police, determined there should be no repetition of the tragedy, immediately passed a by-law prohibiting the erection of any more frame buildings within the village limits.

1845 First formal rules for baseball written by Alexander Joy Cartwright.

St Paul's Cathedral. The tower and nave were erected 1845–1846; the transept was added in 1897. Sketch by Silvia Clarke, from *London Heritage* – second edition (London: Phelps Publishing 1979).

The busy parson of St Paul's Church had much to occupy him that year. In addition to heading the campaign to raise relief money, he was deeply involved in a parallel effort to finance the building of the ambitious new St Paul's. The architect was William Thomas of Toronto, who may have been a pupil of Sir Charles Barry, architect of the British Houses of Parliament. The inside dimensions of the new church were commodious – fifty-nine feet in width by eighty-five feet in length. The walls of the tower were six feet thick at the base. Crowned by four slender pinnacles, it rose to a height of 114 feet, making it the dominant feature of the London skyline.

Despite the rector's acknowledged skill as a financier and money-raiser, the congregation faced a formidable debt of £4,100 ($16,400 US) when

1845 Fire in a theatre in Canton, China, kills 1,670 people.

the building was opened on Ash Wednesday, 25 February 1846, two years after the destruction of the first St Paul's. According to the editor of the London (Canada West) *Times,* Dr John Salter, 1,400 people crowded into the church, which had a seating capacity of one thousand, while several hundred more were unable to get in. Salter gave a knowledgeable account of the architecture, noting in passing that the style adopted "is that which prevailed throughout the greater part of the fourteenth century." The scholarly description descends into babbitry in the concluding paragraph:

The erection of such a church in this part of the province is a marked step and feature in that curious but interesting ... process by which a Country passes from the savage wildness of nature to that state of population, health and intelligence, in which the finest comforts of civilization are enjoyed in companionship with the blessings of religious ordinances and instruction.

The reference to the former primitive nature of the site was an obligatory feature of any public address, ever since Edward Allen Talbot wrote in his prospectus for the London *Sun,* back in 1830, that the site had formerly been only "the abode of the wolf and the haunt of the savage." Fourteen years after the opening of St Paul's the then-mayor of London, James Moffat, drew to the attention of the then-Prince of Wales (later Edward VII) that "at most it is only 40 years since, in the locality where you now stand, none but the red Indian dozed under the shade of the primeval forest."

A good cliché is a joy forever ... and forever.

The financial institutions that by the 1840s were doing business on "Banker's Row" on Ridout Street north of Dundas were certainly not trading in wampum. These were solid, conservative branches of Toronto and Montreal banks. Their managers and directors were reluctant to loan money to such insubstantial organizations as the Church of England and the board of police of the village of London. Both were refused loans on the grounds of "insufficient security."

Despite the dyspeptic cynics of Bankers' Row, the new year seemed to promise nothing but good news for the thriving – and growing – community. At the beginning of 1847 the population was more than 4,000, and steps were being taken to grant it the status of a town. Additional numbers were expected with the opening of navigation in the spring. Immigration from the United Kingdom was on the rise again.

It was well known that the newcomers would be mostly Irish and dirt poor. Throughout the winter of 1846–1847 Canadian newspapers reported

---

1845 Failure of the potato crop in Ireland causes the Great Famine.

at great length on the famine that had followed two years of crop failure. In fact, Canadian journals and their readers showed more compassion for Ireland's suffering paupers than did the English press.

Even so, until the tattered legions actually arrived in Canada, no one had any real conception of the true horror of the Irish situation. As it was, the enfeebled skeletons who limped, crawled, or were carried off the ships at Grosse Isle were pictures of health compared to the human wreckage they left behind:

At Castlebar people lay in the streets with green froth at their mouths from eating soft grass. Inquests brought in verdicts of "starvation," "Hunger and Cold," and "Died of famine". ... "As to holding more inquests," said the *Galway Vindicator* ... "it is mere nonsense. The number of deaths is beyond counting."

In the parish of Kilgless, Roscommon, seven skeleton bodies were found in a hedge, half eaten by dogs. The police shot seven dogs. In the mouth of one of them was a heart and part of a liver.

Canadian generosity and compassion were very soon stretched to the breaking point, for the immigrants were not only sick, but their sickness was contagious. They called it "ship's fever," we call it typhus.

Typhus is carried by body lice. The Irish paupers were generous hosts to the little horrors. Typhus is a disease of the blood vessels, the skin, and the brain. The symptoms are shivering, headache, congested face, blood-shot eyes, muscular twitchings, and a stupid stare, as if the sufferer were drunk.

The disease made its appearance in Canada on 14 May. By the end of the month there were more than a thousand cases, and the medical superintendent on Grosse Isle had trouble finding enough people able to dig graves. He wrote to the chief immigrant agent at Quebec:

I never saw people so indifferent to life; they would continue in the same berth with a dead person until the seamen or captain dragged out the corpse with boat-hooks. Good God! what evils will befall the cities wherever they alight. Hot weather will increase the evil. Now give the authorities at Quebec and Montreal fair warning from me. I have not time to write, or should feel it my duty to do so. Public safety requires it.

On 8 June the Canadian government ordered all municipalities to provide sheds to house healthy immigrants and hospitals for the sick. By that time the contagion had spread to Montreal, Kingston, and Toronto.

1846 United States declares war on Mexico.

At this time London had two public markets – the present Covent Garden Market and the "New Survey Market," in the block bounded by York, Bathurst, Wellington, and Waterloo streets. The board of police commandeered the New Survey Market House for the reception of the healthy Irish and had constructed two hospitals, each twenty by forty feet, and a shed of the same dimensions for cooking and washing, the whole at a total cost of £200 ($800 US). Houses in the vicinity were rented for the accommodation of the chief physician, dispenser, stewards, and nurses. The board of police named its president, Dr Hiram Davis Lee, as physician and employed Daniel Brown, a veteran of the Battle of Lundy's Lane (25 July 1814), as steward and a woman named Ann Peel as nurse.

For a few weeks all was well and the elaborate precautions seemed unnecessary. Then, towards the end of July, the epidemic struck with a ferocity not seen since the Asiatic cholera outbreak of 1832. All the village's doctors were pressed into service in an attempt to check the disease, but to little purpose. Potter's Field, west of Waterloo Street and north of Dufferin Avenue, gaped wide to receive the bodies of the known and the unknown. The burial register of St Paul's Church lost its desperate battle to remain current. There is now no way of knowing how many died between 15 July and 30 October 1847.

Throughout the epidemic Dr Lee and his staff fought like lions to contain the disease. Lee visited all his patients twice a day, pacing the packed-dirt floor between the rows of pallets laid on the earth, breathing the fetid breath of fever. It was inevitable that the plague would win the uneven contest. Daniel Brown died on Monday, 30 August; Ann Peel died on Wednesday, 1 September. With the fever abating finally, Lee struggled through the rains of September, but by the middle of October it was apparent to his friends and helpers that he was sick and confused, exhausted past caring. On Friday, 29 October, he visited the hospital one last time. He had been fighting to save the life of one particular patient, for no special reason. Perhaps in his fever-addled brain he felt that this was a battle he must win, or perish. He did not win. According to a contemporary, he looked at his dying patient and was seen "to turn aside with irresistible loathing."

He died later that day.

Nowhere in London is there a memorial to mark the name, career, and selfless sacrifice of the only chief executive of the city to die a martyr's death in office.

While Lee was fighting his last, lonely battle at the south end of the village, an old dream was being fulfilled at the north end.

1847 Charlotte Brontë, *Jane Eyre.*

On 29 March 1845, the act incorporating the London and Gore Railroad Company (1834) was revived under a new name – the Great Western Railroad Company. A year later the British government enacted a similar piece of legislation enabling British investors to participate in the colonial venture.

The infusion of English capital made it possible to proceed immediately with a survey of the proposed rail line, initially intended to link Hamilton and London, with later extensions planned to spots on the American border at Niagara Falls and Windsor.

The route chosen for the line through London was that later followed by the Canadian Pacific Railway. In 1847 the site proposed for the rail station was out in the country, by village standards. It was to be built on the west side of that part of the present Richmond Street then known as Sarnia Street, between Ann and Oxford streets.

The property in question was still forested, although it was adjacent to the northern boundary of the military reserve, roughly marked by a meandering watercourse known as Carling's Creek. The waters of this stream supported three local industries – Carling's Brewery on Waterloo Street, the Hamilton Brewery on Ann Street, and Water's Mill, west of Talbot Street where the creek empties into the north branch of the Thames River.

On Saturday, 23 October 1847, the site of the new station was the scene of the largest public gathering London had yet seen, as virtually the entire population of the village turned out to celebrate what George Brown, editor of the Toronto *Globe,* referred to as "the ceremony of breaking ground on this great national undertaking."

It was one of those crisp, sunny days October often confers on this part of North America, and the town was on holiday. All the stores closed at noon, and dignitaries from far and near began to assemble at the courthouse square. At one o'clock the procession set out, moving along Dundas Street to Richmond Street, and thence north.

The scene at the station site was described in colourful detail by the Toronto *Globe:*

On the ground, preparations had been made for the ceremony which was now to ensue; a wide space had been cleared in the forest around, and stands erected for the accommodation of the guests and spectators. The logs gathered from the clearance were piled around the scene of action, and ere the procession had reached the ground, these forest galleries were covered with people, and the ladies' stand was thronged with the beauty and fashion of the Metropolis of the Far West. The riflemen kept the ground clear in the centre,

---

1847 William Makepeace Thackeray, *Vanity Fair.*

and as the procession arrived the several bodies took up their stations around the inside of the large circle, forming as it were a spacious amphitheatre. The number present has been estimated at from 3500 to 5000 persons, and we feel certain that the smaller number is below the fact.

George J. Goodhue, now a member of the Legislative Council of the Province of Canada (a post roughly equivalent to that of a senator in our present terms), was chairman and opened the proceedings with the obligatory remarks comparing the "then and now." He then called upon the guest of honour, Colonel Thomas Talbot, to turn the first sod. According to the florid wording employed by the *Globe,* the aging founder of the Talbot Settlement (he was seventy-seven) "took the spade and inflicted the first wound on Mother Earth."

A man of few words, Colonel Talbot said them and sat down to thunderous applause and a salute from a battery of the Royal Artillery.

Lesser men followed and said a great deal more. Either because of the accumulated weight of the dignitaries or because of the burden of their rhetoric, the main stand collapsed towards the end of the proceedings, throwing them all to the ground. No bones were broken, there was a good deal of laughter and applause, Mr Goodhue said that that was all there was, the crowd gave "three times three" hearty cheers for the Queen, the procession re-formed for the march back to town – and that was the end of the public celebration.

At six o'clock that evening, 120 guests gathered in the dining room of the Western Hotel. This was Dennis O'Brien's original five-storey brick building on Dundas Street at Ridout. It was a large structure, one hundred feet by fifty-five feet, and contained sixty rooms; at this time it was operated by the firm of Paul & Bennett.

A copy of the menu for the evening, with a wine list on the reverse side, has been preserved. For the benefit of oenophiles, it may be noted that a Médoc could be had for 6s. 3d. ($1.25 US) a bottle. There was "champaigne" (Reinhart or Sillery) at $2 a bottle, in addition to madeira, port, sherry, brandy, ale, porter, and stout. The most expensive item was Hunts' Very Old Port, at $2.50 a bottle. When it is realized that a skilled artisan (like a newspaper compositor) could not hope to take home more than $8 or $9 US a week, it will be seen that the Western Hotel was no workingman's pub.

The "bill of fare" was a weight-watcher's nightmare. The diners had a choice of meats, roast or boiled – beef, pork, veal, lamb, mutton, turkey, chicken, duck, goose, ham, corned beef, tongue, and calf's head (ugh!).

1847 Emily Brontë, *Wuthering Heights.*

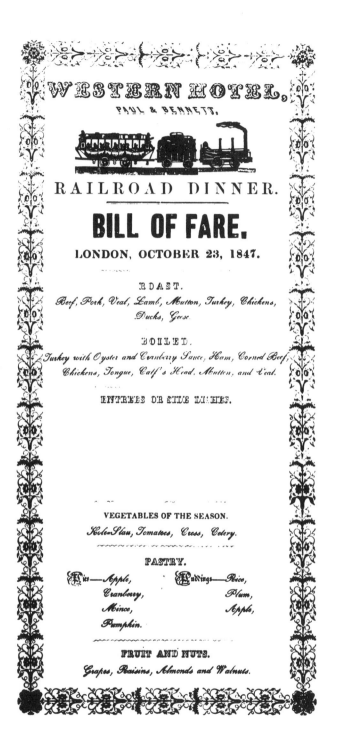

Bill of fare of the Great Railroad Dinner. UWO

Accompanying this Lucullan fare were the "vegetables of the season" – "kole-slaw," tomatoes, cress, and celery. It may be noted that this was a rather early appearance of the tomato on a restaurant menu. Originally considered to be poisonous, tomatoes did not become a popular edible in the United States until the 1860s.

Within the ensuing few hours no less than sixteen toasts were proposed and responded to. George Brown, on behalf of his paper, was keeping careful notes of all the toasts and responses (especially his own); but as the evening wore on, his notes got skimpier. All he could write about Lawrence Lawrason's response to the toast to "Agriculture and Commerce," was that it was given "happily." Since that was the twelfth toast, the adverb was probably well chosen.

Halfway down the lengthy list came the toast to the guest of honour. George Goodhue's introduction of "the Hon. Thomas Talbot" was rather fulsome, and the cheers with which it was greeted were slightly sycophantic or perhaps only maudlin. The Colonel's response was terse and humorous; his humour however, had its usual cutting edge:

I thank you gentlemen most gratefully for the honour you have done me this day. I have witnessed a scene which I never hoped to behold in this settlement – it is an event never to be forgotten. I believe I am the oldest inhabitant.
I slept on this spot 55 years ago, when my best friend was a porcupine. We were often excessively hungry in those days, but we all used to declare that we never were so hungry as the night we ate the porcupine. (Cheers and laughter.) What a change has occurred since then! Now I see different beings around me – no porcupine – no bristles; but in their place a company of half-civilized gentlemen.

This last sally was greeted with laughter and cheers.
They thought he was joking.

1847 All of California comes under United States control. Gold is discovered.

CHAPTER FOUR

TOWN

In my time, the follies of the town crept slowly among us, but now they travel faster than a stagecoach.
                                                                  Goldsmith, *She Stoops to Conquer.*

London was officially incorporated as a town on 28 July 1847. The first elections for municipal office took place in January 1848, the ward system being carried over from the previous village administration. Each of the four wards elected two council members; the mayor was elected by the entire electorate. A total of 384 votes was cast for the three candidates competing for the top office. This figure represented less than 9 per cent of the registered population of 4,668, as reported to the Legislature of the province.

The man chosen to lead London through the first of its exciting seven years as a town was a respected, God-fearing tanner named Simeon Morrill. Mr Morrill's features were obscured by an imposing white mattress of a beard that extended from neck to waist, obviating the need for a cravat, or indeed a shirt. He was "temperance and chapel," and hence to be trusted at a time when the excesses of the old Establishment were still vividly remembered. The old board of police had been largely Anglican. Of the nine men elected to office in 1848, only two were members of St Paul's Church.

Morrill's chief rival, who succeeded to the office in 1849, was quite another sort. He was Thomas C. Dixon, by trade a hatter, by avocation a trouble-maker. Dixon was a Tory extremist, violently opposed to the Rebellion Losses Bill, designed to compensate persons whose property had been destroyed in the 1837 uprising. The new governor-general of the Canadas, James Bruce, the eighth Earl of Elgin, favoured the bill, as well as a number of other Reform measures, thus earning himself a full charge of the London hatter's venom.

1849 General Zachary Taylor inaugurated 12th president, United States.

Dr John Salter (1802–1881), pioneer
surgeon, apothecary, dentist, and editor
of the London (Canada West) *Times*
from 1845 to 1849. Sketch by Stanley
Dale, from Seaborn, *The March of Medicine in Western Ontario*.

Of the nine members of the 1849 town council, four, including the
mayor, were Tories; the remainder, the majority, were Reformers. Trouble erupted at the first meeting. The issue was one that has continued to
split London municipal administrations ever since – education. A proposal
was presented to set a special tax of three farthings in the pound of assessed
value to pay for the erection of a central school on a site granted by the
government for school purposes. Apparently for no other reason than
that the motion had been made by his Reform opponents, Mayor Dixon
refused to put the question and therewith adjourned the meeting and left
the chair. Council carried on without him, put the motion, and passed it.

The meeting was covered by all four of the town's weekly newspapers
– the London *Times*, the *Western Globe*, the *Evangelical Pioneer*, and the
Canadian Free Press. The first was published by Joseph Cowley and edited
by Dr John Salter. It represented the local Establishment, and while politically Tory, consistently urged such liberal reforms as the abolition of
capital punishment and needed changes in the antiquated debtors' law.
The *Western Globe* was the London edition of George Brown's Toronto
Globe and was staunchly Reform. The *Evangelical Pioneer* was published
and edited by the Reverend James Inglis, a Baptist minister from Detroit.
While ostensibly a religious journal, the *Pioneer* incorporated much local
news in its columns, to the great annoyance of its secular competitors.

1849 Walter Hunt of New York invents the modern safety pin.

The *Canadian Free Press* was brand-new that January of 1849. Its publisher, editor, compositor, and sole reporter was a twenty-five-year-old Scots printer named William Sutherland. His little four-page newspaper, the first issue of which appeared on Tuesday, 2 January 1849, has grown into the largest metropolitan daily in the province west of Toronto, the London *Free Press*.

Sutherland was a fighting Reformer and promptly took off after the Tory mayor and his supporters. One of these was Alderman William Barker, an Englishman who came to London in 1835 as the agent of Major-General W.T. Renwick, who owned extensive properties in London and vicinity. In Old Country terms, Barker was the general's bailiff. He was a well-educated person, an amateur astronomer. If he kept environmental records as well, he must have made note of the extreme cold the district experienced in the winter of 1848–1849. For several days in January 1849 the thermometer hovered close to -40 Fahrenheit (-40 degrees Celsius).

Meanwhile the town continued to operate under what amounted to *two* municipal administrations – one representing the majority Reformers, the other, the minority Tories led by the mayor. Throughout January and February the pattern of the first meeting of the year was followed.

☐ The mayor convenes Council.

☐ The first order of business is the reading of the minutes of the previous meeting.

☐ The minutes are read, adoption is moved and seconded.

☐ The mayor refuses to put the motion.

☐ The majority of council members object to this act of absolutism.

☐ The mayor declares council adjourned *sine die*.

☐ The mayor leaves the chair and the chamber.

☐ The remaining members of council appoint a chairman and carry on with the agenda.

At the regular meeting of Monday, 12 March, after still another repetition of the Dixon ploy, the disgusted council passed a motion regularizing their own conduct:

Resolved in committee of the whole that the Mayor should not dissolve Council unless two-thirds of the Council are for it and if he is not satisfied they will appoint one of the Council to act as chairman.

At the next meeting, the mayor convened council, the clerk read the minutes, the mayor declined to accept them, the mayor adjourned the

---

1849 English archaeologist Sir Henry Layard excavates the site of Nineveh.

meeting, the mayor left the chair, the mayor left the chamber, and the council resumed its deliberations under a chairman of its own choosing.

Ho-hum!

As the year progressed, temperatures rose, both outside and within the council chambers. In March, word was received of fears being expressed in Quebec and Montreal about a new outbreak of Asiatic cholera in Great Britain, coincident with an expected new wave of immigration to North America. Locally, instructions were given to prepare the immigrant sheds on the New Market for the reception of the sick and healthy.

On April Fool's Day an arsonist burned the sheds to the ground.

On Wednesday, 25 April, Lord Elgin signed into law the Rebellion Losses Bill. His carriage was stoned by a mob as he left the Parliament Buildings in Montreal. Later that day the rioters set fire to the those buildings and embarked on a three-day mini-revolution.

The news reached London early in May. Council proposed a motion "expressing regret at the outrage at Montreal." Mayor Dixon refused to be associated with such a motion, dissolved council, and left the chamber. The remaining members named a chairman, then drew up and signed a "loyal address" to Lord Elgin.

William Sutherland let fly with a stinging editorial in the *Canadian Free Press* on the subject of "Tory hooliganism," ostensibly directed at the Montreal rioters but carrying unmistakable references to the local situation.

On Monday, 28 May, an arsonist set fire to the offices of the *Canadian Free Press*. Sutherland slept in the building but was able to make his escape unharmed.

On Monday, 29 May, the regular weekly edition of the *Canadian Free Press* appeared in an abbreviated form, consisting of a single sheet (two pages).

On Tuesday, 5 June, the paper announced that it had a new office and that the town council had offered a massive reward of £60 Provincial Currency ($240 US) for "information that will lead to the conviction of the person or persons who set fire to O'Brien's Buildings, Dundas street on the morning of the 28th ult."

No one ever claimed the reward.

Meanwhile the first ships to make the obligatory stop at the Quebec quarantine station had brought the first cases of Asiatic cholera of the new season. As usual, the precaution of quarantine failed and the deadly disease began its inexorable march westward with its immigrant hosts. Reaching the cities with their unsightly steaming middens, the cholera

---

1849 Mrs Amelia Jenks Bloomer (1818–1884) begins American women's dress reform.

William Sutherland (1824–1912), founder of the *Canadian Free Press* in 1849. Sutherland sold the paper to Josiah Blackburn in 1853, after which it became the *London Free Press*. Sketch by Maridon Miller.

bacteria throve mightily, the few hospitals filled up rapidly, and the grave-diggers prospered.

Early in the epidemic the board of health for the Canadas issued orders from its Montreal headquarters prohibiting burial of cholera victims until twelve hours after death, a measure taken to prevent live interment of patients in the third, deep-coma stage of the disease – a misfortune that occurred with hideous frequency.

At London the town council (unanimously for once) passed a by-law further restricting the burial of cholera victims to the hours of darkness. The dreary processions to the graveyards took on an even more macabre tone – flickering torches touching the worn logs of the corduroy roadbed with burnished highlights, the creaking halt of the ox-cart at the cemetery fence, a sheeted form (sans coffin) dumped over the fence, a grunted oath, a dull thud, the chunk of a spade in fresh-turned earth – the final anonymity:

> For no man knew his sepulchre
> And no man sought it e'er. ...

The first frosts of autumn killed off the cholera bacillus, and the relieved citizens returned to their social and political feuds. The political scene provided the most entertainment.

1849 Fedor Dostoevsky (1821–1881) sentenced to death.

The governor-general's office announced that Lord Elgin would visit London the first week in October.

The news galvanized the more or less static local political situation into feverish life. The Reform members of the town council decided to extend a cordial invitation to the father of cabinet government in Canada. Mayor Dixon and his three Tory compatriots refused to be associated with any such invitation, cordial or otherwise. He dissolved council and withdrew. Council appointed Murray Anderson as chairman and drew up the address over his signature.

Further word was received from Montreal. Lord Elgin would visit London on 3 October – henceforth to be known by London Reformers as "the glorious third of October."

On the eve of the great day, gangs of men set to work at the principal intersections, erecting "tastefully decorated" arches of greenery, under which the Earl and his entourage should pass.

A special meeting of town council was called to discuss some routine matters connected with the visit. The mayor was unusually amiable and cooperative. He remained in the chair throughout the meeting and raised no obstacle to the series of humdrum motions.

Obviously, something was up. Indeed, it was.

That evening, by candlelight, Dixon and his three Tory henchmen carefully prepared a "minority address" to Lord Elgin, its wording having absolutely nothing in common with the official address. Because of the conspiracy of silence observed by both the Tory *Times* and the Reform *Free Press* respecting the contents of this effusion, no hint of its nature or wording has survived the years beyond the obvious implication that it verged on sedition.

On the morning of the great day, Thomas C. Dixon was early abroad. Approaching the men putting the finishing touches on the last of the arches, he ordered them to stop the work. They refused.

The mayor then convened a meeting of his supporters at the Orange Hall. Instructions and axes were passed out to a score or more of town toughs. Within an hour the Tory commandos had levelled every arch in the town, as well as those on the Hamilton Road entrance into London.

With an expression of hypocritical outrage firmly fixed on his face, Mayor Dixon and his trio of fellow-conspirators rode out to meet the governor-general. Near the village of Dorchester, they reined up and made obeisance to the Earl, his wife, and the infant ninth-earl-to-be, fondly dubbed by his father, "the Canadian Bruce." The mask-like gravity of their faces belied by the inward jubilation in their eyes, Dixon and his

---

1849 British force Sikhs to surrender at Rawalpindi; Britain annexes the Punjab.

friends solemnly assured the Queen's representative that it would be unsafe for him to visit London.

They had misjudged their man. Lord Elgin received their news in silence and then curtly informed them that "if necessary, he should walk there, on foot" *(sic)*.

The governor's progress into the town took on some of the aspects of a Roman triumph. At every intersection more people fell into line behind the carriages, cheering, yelling, and generally bearing out William Sutherland's confident assertion that "three-quarters of the ... people of London are for the Earl and the Constitution."

Lord Elgin took his place on a balcony of the new brick-built Robinson Hall Hotel, across Ridout Street from the courthouse. The crowd was estimated to be several times the town's population of five thousand. The official address of welcome was given by Councillor Murray Anderson. It is reported that:

During the delay which was occasioned by preparing an answer to the address, a brutal attack was made upon a young man who was peaceably standing in front of the balcony, who was struck on the head by some ruffians. Immediately a rally was made by his friends and the scoundrels were beaten off. A pistol was then fired by some madman who had his skull fractured for his pains and was instantly borne off to gaol.

Following this violent interlude, partial order was restored and several more addresses read and responded to. The opposition wasn't finished, however.

During the Governor General's reply to one of the addresses, a number of Orangemen, partly intoxicated, commenced their usual annoyances by yelling, hissing and groaning. A body of Irishmen who had just taken up their positions in front of the Orangemen turned around simultaneously and with their shillelaghs made five or six of the grumblers kiss their mother earth in less than no time. The rest of the Orange party scampered off in wild confusion after which the immense crowd remained in undisturbed serenity.

The "undisturbed serenity" referred to in the account from the *Evangelical Pioneer* must have been a purely relative term, for the report is sprinkled with references to further rowdyism, most of them emanating from the vicinity of Mayor Dixon, who chose to take his position on the street, rather than on the official balcony.

1850 Jenny Lind appears in the United States under the auspices of P. T. Barnum.

All good things must come to an end, and finally the last of the long series of addresses and the brief courteous replies was over. Lord Elgin and his party went off to the home of Executive Councillor George Jervis Goodhue, and the crowd dispersed to London's twenty-five taverns and one temperance hotel.

The events connected with Lord Elgin's visit slowly rumbled into history, taking with them the reputation of the mad hatter. Thomas C. Dixon was turfed out of office in the municipal elections of 1850, when he was replaced by the patriarchal Simeon Morrill. Dixon's later career was more of the same. He lost a major parliamentary election to "Honest John" Wilson, the former duelist; appeared as a reluctant witness in a celebrated court case fought over the principle of freedom of the press; and left town a jump ahead of his creditors and moved to Hamilton. There he became a city alderman, was charged with embezzlement and bigamy, became a Mormon, and fled to Utah. He died in a fever hospital in Fort Worth, Texas, in the 1870s.

London's reaction to the fractious reign of Thomas Dixon was evident in the make-up of the council led by Mayor Morrill. The number of councillors was increased to twelve – three from each of the four wards – perhaps as a means of diluting political influence. The new councillors didn't play politics; business was their game. Among them was Lawrence Lawrason, a pioneer merchant and former partner of George J. Goodhue. John K. Labatt, the new brewer in town who had bought the old Balkwill brewery, joined his business rival Thomas Carling on council. Edward Adams was a leading wholesale-retail grocer, and Henry Corry Rowley Becher, an aristocratic English lawyer.

In other ways as well an era was coming to an end. The older settlers were dropping off. London's official first inhabitant. Peter MacGregor, died in his self-imposed exile in Westminster Township in 1846, at the comparatively early age of fifty-two. He is buried in the little cemetery at Scottsville, south of Lambeth on Highway 4.

Edward Matthews, who had been the contractor for the building of the Imperial barracks, shocked the town by putting a bullet through his head as he sat in his office at the corner of Dundas and Richmond streets on Saturday, 22 June 1850. Matthews's death ruined the plans for the annual celebration of the feast day of St John the Baptist (24 June) by his fellow-Masons; instead, the brethren turned out in numbers for his funeral. There are memorials in St Paul's Cathedral to the memory of Mrs Matthews and their children, but none for Edward Matthews himself, a suicide.

1850 American Express Company organized.

Thornwood, residence of Henry Corry Rowley Becher, pioneer London lawyer. As young men both King Edward VII and the Duke of Connaught visited here, and Winston Churchill planted a birch tree in the backyard in 1900. Sketch by Bill McGrath from *London Heritage* – second edition (London: Phelps Publishing 1979).

Less than a month later another leading Anglican Mason left the London scene. William King Cornish filled a positive constellation of posts in his Canadian career. A solicitor in England, he was prevented by provincial law from entering practice in Canada save after a probationary period. He thereupon turned to the study and subsequent practice of medicine, shortly becoming surgeon to the gaol and a district coroner. Later he returned to the study of law, became an attorney, surveyor, land agent, and, for a time, landlord and clerk of the village board of police. He was an inveterate prankster and practical joker. Probably the biggest joke he ever played on his fellow-citizens was siring a son, one Francis Evans Cornish, whose escapades, as we shall see, make his father's most inventive pranks seem tame. William King Cornish was known in his later days as

1851 Herman Melville, Moby Dick; Giuseppe Verdi, Rigoletto.

"Old Dr Cornish," yet he was only fifty when he died on 11 July 1850. Legend long credited him with setting fire to the Roman Catholic Church of St Lawrence in order to obtain possession of the land on which it stood. Unfortunately for the myth-makers the church fell victim to an arsonist more than a year after Cornish died.

The most illustrious of all the pioneers of southwestern Ontario, Colonel Thomas Talbot, died in London on Sunday, 6 February 1853, sixty years after he first saw the site of the city in the company of Lieutenant-Governor John Graves Simcoe. He was eighty-two.

The world in which Thomas Talbot died was vastly changed from the leisurely world into which he had been born. As he lay dying, not far from the forks of the Thames, the rails of the Great Western Railway Company were nearing the eastern outskirts of London. When the first train reached the city, later that same year, the journey from London to Hamilton had been reduced from a matter of days to a matter of hours.

When Talbot was born at Castle Malahide, near Dublin, Ireland, in 1771, the fastest speed attainable by a human being was astride a horse. Over a short distance a horse could run at perhaps thirty miles an hour. That had been the outside limit for many thousands of years.

In 1848 – the year London became a town – a locomotive on England's Great Western Railway managed to reach a speed of *seventy-eight miles per hour!*

The ordinary people of London, Canada West, refused to believe these reports. Seventy-eight miles an hour? Madness! A sober Londoner with pretensions to scientific knowledge told the *Free Press* that if a passenger thrust his arm out the window of a carriage travelling at such a speed, he would have the member ripped right off!

When the wood-burning locomotive and its two coaches rolled into London early in the evening of Thursday, 15 December 1853, the gaggle of Very Important Persons who comprised its passenger list was intact as to limbs, but tired and dirty. The trip from Hamilton had taken six hours. William Bowman, mechanical superintendent of the GWR, recorded his memories of the occasion a half-century later:

As I remember it, the weather was cold and raw, and the mud along the line was simply appalling.

We left Hamilton, where I was living at the time, early in the afternoon and it was near dusk when we arrived at London. The time was very slow, slow even for those days, owing to the condition of the roadbed; and it was my opinion at the time that it was a foolhardy notion to attempt the trip on such a

---

1852 State of Ohio limits working hours of women to 10 hours a day.

roadbed. The rocking of the coaches was frightful, and I thought at times we would go into the mud in the ditch.

We stopped at all the stations along the line, but it was difficult to leave the coaches, as there was no platforms as yet erected, and the mud was too deep to wade into. Woodstock was the largest place between Hamilton and London in those days, and it was small enough to be ridiculous.

We made the journey without incident, however, and upon our arrival in London we were met by a large crowd of people, who had awaited our coming. ...

The station at the time was a little frame building, which was shortly afterwards replaced by the present structure.

The artist who recorded the scene for the *Illustrated London* (England) *News* took a considerable amount of artistic license. The clean, sharp lines of the woodcut give no hint of the dull skies, rain, and mud that the passengers actually experienced, and the railway station shown is not the little shack that received them, but the later, permanent station.

The idealized picture conveys no suggestion as to the physical location of the event. It had nothing to do with the site where Thomas Talbot had wielded the ceremonial spade in 1847. This, the site chosen by the directors of the Great Western, was considered by the London merchant and financial community to be much too far away from the town centre. It was, after all, nearly a mile from the corner of Dundas and Richmond streets! The predecessors of today's Downtown London Business Association put pressure on the town council. The council put pressure on the Great Western. The company cited the additional cost a more central location would entail, and in effect said, "Put up or shut up." The town "put up" to the extent of investing £25,000 ($100,000 US) in the company – money, incidentally, which the municipality did not have and which the banks were unwilling to advance.

To compound this act of financial lunacy, the municipality proceeded to invest heavily in its very own railway line. The London and Port Stanley Railroad was incorporated by act of Parliament on Monday, 23 May 1853; capital stock, £150,000 ($600,000 US).

Among the incorporators of the new road was Freeman Talbot, younger brother of Edward Allen Talbot, the dreamer who, nearly a quarter-century earlier, had captured the vision of a nation whose cities would be linked by iron rails and iron horses.

Although the London and Port Stanley Railroad never, in its century of operation, achieved financial success, a second project with which Talbot

---

1852 Steamer *Atlantic* sinks in Lake Erie (20 August) with loss of 250 lives.

The Honourable Freeman Talbot (1811–1903) settled in London Township with his parents in 1818. He became a contractor, newspaper editor, and American senator. From F.T. Rosser, *London Township Pioneers* (Belleville: Mika Publishing, Inc.).

was associated made handsome profits for all its investors.

In 1849, Freeman Talbot was the chief architect of the Proof Line Road Company, a privately-owned toll road, the first such cooperative company in the history of the province. The Proof Line Road, which now forms part of Highway 4, ran north from London to Ryan's Corners (Elginfield), on the townline between London and Biddulph Townships.

By the time the Great Western's locomotive chuffed its way into London in 1853, the area already had the finest transportation network in the province. Thanks largely to the efforts of Hamilton Hartley Killaly, an Irish civil engineer, who represented London in the Legislature of the United Provinces of Canada East (Quebec) and Canada West (Ontario) from 1841 to 1844. Killaly became chairman of the Canadian Board of Works and, in typical pork-barreling style, spent nearly the whole of his first appropriation of £100,000 ($400,000 US) on improving the roads in his own riding and district.

With the completion of the Proof Line Road and the entry of the Great Western Railway, London had truly become the hub of one of the richest farming areas on the continent, a preeminent position never seriously to be challenged.

1852 The Duke of Wellington (b. 1769) dies: schooldays friend of Col. Thomas Talbot.

Long before the rails of the Great Western reached London, the town was already in the grip of as wild a real-estate boom as has ever afflicted any area in North America. Property along the right-of-way suddenly assumed fantastic values. As in London so in the surrounding countryside. Property not on the railway but in areas where it might reasonably be expected feeder lines would later be constructed also rose sharply in value. It was a rich field for the speculator. Packages of land changed hands with dizzying speed and frequency. Fortunes were made overnight – on paper. In very few cases was the full amount of the purchase price paid on the line. An instance is recorded of a lot of land changing hands several times in the course of a single day – and no actual cash involved. It was margin buying on a scale equalled only once since in this area – in the hectic days preceding the stock-market collapse of 1929.

The fever reached its most insane pitch in London. Real-estate promoters commissioned the survey of suburban building lots as far west as Komoka, north to Arva, east to Dorchester, and south to St Thomas. All these areas are still well outside the perimeters of the modern city of London.

As an example of the inflated values placed on London real estate in the years between 1851 and 1857, it will suffice to cite the case of the businessman who bought a building lot on the eastern fringe on the downtown shopping district during the boom. Unlike most of his fellow-speculators, he paid cash. For the ensuing fifty years he paid city taxes on the lot and the building he had erected on it. Finally, in 1905, he sold out for what was then considered a good price. It lacked a dollar of what he had paid for the land alone a half-century earlier.

As the land boom approached its giddy peak, events far removed from London thrust themselves forcibly on the attention of the townsfolk. The ancient political cauldron of the Middle East had boiled over again. Turkey declared war on Russia on 4 October 1853, launching attacks across the Black Sea on Russian positions in the Crimean Peninsula. Before the end of the year England and France were allied with Turkey, and troops of both nations were on their way to the battle zone. Faced with a major war, Britain recalled its troops from their Canadian garrisons.

Five or six years earlier the loss of London's garrison would have had a catastrophic effect on the town's economy. By 1854, the drying up of this source of income was scarcely noticed. Indeed the war resulted in a greatly increased demand for Canadian wheat. At the same time a reciprocity treaty with the United States, arranged by Lord Elgin, opened the southern frontier to a duty-free flow of natural products.

In the result the economic heart of London moved from the army

---

1854 Stephen Foster, "Jeannie With the Light Brown Hair."

barracks to Covent Garden Market, where a handsome new market building had been erected.

Meanwhile the town council, led by the mayor, Marcus Holmes, a carriage-builder, was pressing the Canadian government to pass the necessary legislation for the incorporation of London as a city. A population of 10,000 was required, and apparently London had passed that milestone in the year of the coming of the railway. By the summer of 1854, with prosperity breaking out all over, it was estimated that London had acquired at least a couple of thousand more inhabitants than the regulations called for.

Not all newcomers to the city were wealthy or healthy. Many were neither. They didn't stay at the town's numerous hotels, inns, and taverns. Some sixty-eight newcomers, including a group of six Norwegian immigrants, went straight from the railway cars to the city's pest house, and thence to Potter's Field, off the Hamilton Road. London's latest encounter with Asiatic cholera was short, sharp, and nasty. The town council decreed once again that all victims of the epidemic should be buried by night. Then as now, municipal authorities strove to preserve the fiction of a 100-per-cent-healthy citizenry. As an expression of the American Southland has it: "What the eye don't see, the heart don't grieve."

The poor immigrants whose remains were interred under cover of darkness were not the only exiles from the general paper prosperity. The inflationary spiral engineered by the rising values of land and wheat seriously inconvenienced middle-class Londoners and devastated the poor.

Over the years between 1848 and 1855, wages rose perhaps 20 per cent, while the cost of sheltering and feeding a family sky-rocketed by from 100 to 300 per cent.

As a consequence, those who could least withstand the economic turbulence suffered the most. So it was that a period of London's history superficially marked by financial progress and high expectations also saw the establishment of the municipality's first relief department, as some of the town's leading churches opened soup kitchens in an effort to meet some of the basic needs of the poor.

Meanwhile the flow of black refugees from the slave states continued. Harriet Beecher Stowe's phenomenally successful serialized novel *Uncle Tom's Cabin*, which appeared in book form in 1852, focused public attention on the plight of the Negro in the United States and on the humanitarian work of the Underground Railroad. As a highly visible, persecuted minority, the fugitive blacks won much sympathy from Londoners; more, in fact, than the indigent newcomers from Ireland.

1854 William Makepeace Thackeray, *The Rose and the Ring;* Henry David Thoreau, *Walden.*

5s, C'y.
Town Hall, London, C. W. _____ 184

Twelve months after Date, without acceptance, pay to _____

_____ or Bearer, FIVE SHILLINGS,

Currency, with Interest at Six per Cent. pe Annum.

TO W. W. STREET,
Treasurer of the Town of London.

Five Shillings.
One Dollar.
$1

Town Clerk. _____ Mayor.

Note of hand issued by the town of London in 1848 and used as currency. The notes, paying 6 per cent interest, were issued in five values: $1 (5 shillings Provincial Currency); $2 (10s.); $4 (£1); $5 (£1 5s.); and $10 (£2 10s.). UWO

The community that was about to achieve municipal maturity as Canada's newest city, was a far different place from the stump-strewn "New London" that had so amused the officers of the British garrison in the early 1840s.

Physically, it had expanded its boundaries to the north and east; boundaries that would remain static for a quarter-century. In April 1852, the town council advertised for tenders for a survey. The lowest bid received, for £125 ($500 US), came from Sandford Fleming of Toronto, later to become the father of Standard Time. It would be pleasant to be able to link the name of this great Canadian to the history of Canada's London, but in the result the contract was let to a local engineer, Samuel Peters, for £223 ($892 US). It was this survey that established the legal limits of the incorporated city of London, which came into being on 1 January 1855.

1854 Walter Hunt, who invented the safety-pin, now invents the paper collar.

CHAPTER FIVE

CITY

The City of London ... shall include all that part of the Province situate within the County of Middlesex, and lying within the following limits, that is to say: all the lands comprised within the old and new surveys of the Town of London, together with the lands adjoining thereto, lying between the said surveys and the River Thames producing the northern boundary of the new survey until it intersects the North Branch of the River Thames, and producing the eastern boundary line of the said new survey until it intersects the East Branch of the River Thames, and the eastern boundary line be known as Adelaide street. ...
Charter signed by P.J.O. Chauveau, Provincial Secretary, Quebec City, September 1854.

CITY OF LONDON COAT-OF-ARMS

The heraldic description, crest and motto and supporters are as follows: Per chevron gules and azure a chevron argent between in chief two garbs, or, and in base a beaver on a log of wood in sinister base and in dexter background a tree vert.

CREST: A locomotive and tender.
MOTTO: Labore et perseverantia.
SUPPORTERS: Dexter a deer and sinister a brown bear.
City of London Municipal Year Book 1981–1982.

A town is merely a large village. A city is another creature altogether, and no society has ever entirely succeeded in coping with the difference. Given a stable physical environment, a village may endure for thousands of years, as instance, ancient Jericho. Cities, on the other hand, are subject to acute stresses that eventually destroy them. The planet is littered with the bones of cities.

London's transition from village to city took only fifteen years, during which time the population soared from less than 2,000 to an estimated

---

1855 The Russians capitulate to the allied forces at Sevastopol, ending the Crimean War.

12,000. The sleepy little market town of 1840 became, in a decade and a half, the bustling transportation hub of what the people of Toronto thought of as "The West." (Many still do.) For the construction industry, the building trades, the railways, and the land agents it was bonanza time. Almost overnight, the corner of Dundas and Richmond streets became the heart of the community. Commercial and public buildings shot up like mushrooms around the intersection, changing the London skyline and forever obliterating the former dominance of the courthouse's mediaeval battlements. Now, only the tower of St Paul's Church (114 feet high) could look down upon the architectural Johnnies-come-lately.

Committed now to the god of Progress, Londoners knew this was only the beginning. There were some optimists who predicted a population for the city by the turn of the twentieth century of one million, and none was prepared to say them nay. To launch this ship of destiny the citizens were asked to elect twenty-eight men to the first city council – nine more than form the corporation of the 1980s. There were seven wards, and each ward elected four incumbents – two aldermen and two councillors. The councillors were junior to the aldermen who, by virtue of their higher office, were also magistrates and entitled to sit on the bench of the city police court, now for the first time served by a paid police force consisting of a chief and seven constables, one for each ward.

Since among the illustrious twenty-eight there were seven future mayors of London, two knights, and a senator, their names are worth noting here: **Ward One** – aldermen, Peter Schram and James Moffatt (mayor, 1860); councillors, John Blair and Barnabas Wheeler. **Ward Two** – aldermen, Murray Anderson (mayor, 1855) and Elijah Leonard (appointed Canadian senator, 1867); councillors, William McBride (mayor, 1859) and George M. Gunn. **Ward Three** – aldermen, James Daniell and Joseph Gibbons; councillors, Arthur Wallace and John Clegg. **Ward Four** – aldermen, R. Abernethy and J. W. Kermott; councillors, Frank Smith (mayor, 1867; knighted, 1894) and David Glass (mayor, 1858, 1865–1866). **Ward Five** – aldermen, Daniel Lester and George G. Magee; councillors, Thomas Carter and Robert Smith. **Ward Six** – aldermen, John Carling (knighted, 1893) and Thomas Peel; councillors, William Glen and P. Phipps. **Ward Seven** – aldermen, William Barker (mayor, 1856) and William Darby; councillors, Robinson Orr and John Wells.

From this galaxy of business and professional men, the council itself named the senior alderman of Ward Two, Murray Anderson, as first mayor of London City. Anderson was a pioneer Londoner, having arrived in 1835. He was a manufacturer of tinware and a dealer in furs, a rather

---

1855 David Livingstone, explorer-missionary, discovers Victoria Falls, in Africa.

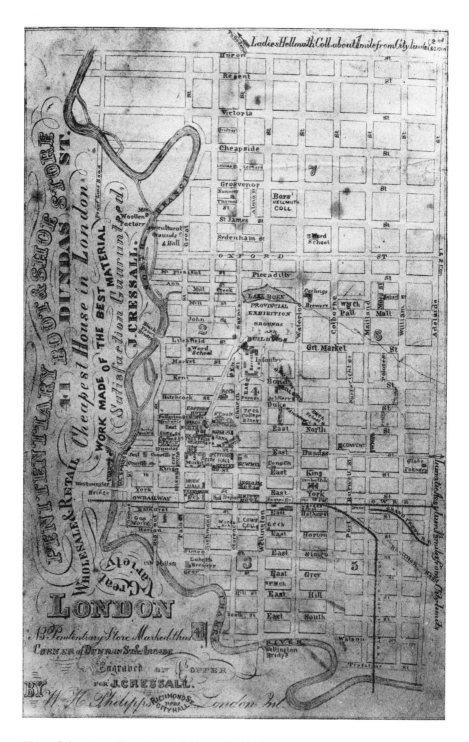

Map of the city of London as laid out in 1855. UWO

strange combination. In the fur markets he had an international reputation and often boasted of dining in New York with John Jacob Astor. Under his able guidance the city started off with great verve on its first year of corporate existence.

One of the first pieces of business accomplished by the new council was a decision to publish the official proclamation of incorporation in the city's three weekly newspapers – the London *Times,* the *Prototype,* and the *Canadian Free Press.*

The last-named had been bought in 1852, by a young Englishman, Josiah Blackburn, who had done some professional writing in England and in Canada. The name of the paper was changed, in 1855, to the London *Free Press.* Under that name and its Gothic masthead, the journal has continued in the ownership of the Blackburn family to the present time.

The occasion for the change in name was the appearance, on 5 May 1855, of a daily edition. The previous owner, William Sutherland, had launched a daily version of his little weekly in January 1852, but it had survived only forty issues. The community was not yet ready for it. Blackburn's timing was better. With one brief interruption, the daily has flourished ever since.

The new daily was a four-page sheet, six columns to the page. Pages one and four, as well as four of the six columns on page three, were given over entirely to advertisements, the life-blood of a daily newspaper. Here were listed the dentists, the physicians, the barristers, opticians, and daguerreotype artists. Here also were listed the commercial interests of the thriving city: the coppersmiths, the wholesale and retail grocers, the dry-goods merchants, the wet-goods merchants, the real-estate men, the booksellers, the plumbers, insurance men, hotel-keepers, and icemen. There was even a cigar factory in a place where, a mere hundred years earlier, Indians had grown and rolled their own coarse, vile-smelling rolls of tobacco leaf.

Page two carried the national and international news, the latter culled largely from English newspapers of a fortnight earlier. The principal item of European news dealt with Louis Napoleon's Universal Exposition, then in full flowering in Paris. A report received from New York by telegraph told of the bombardment of Sevastopol. Prominent among national news stories was a report from the sessions of the Canadian Parliament at Quebec City, detailing an abortive attempt to introduce a bill prohibiting traffic in intoxicating liquors.

1855 Henri Wadsworth Longfellow publishes his narrative poem, *The Song of Hiawatha.*

Page three contained about two columns of local news, headed by an editorial introducing the daily edition and inviting the cooperation of businessmen and the general public. The two chief news items told of the dedication of a chapel on Horton Street by the local congregation of Bible Christians (a branch of the Methodist movement) and the installation of J.B. ("Barney") Boyle as principal of the Union School.

Two letters from subscribers occupied considerable space. One, signed by E. Whitefield, is testimony of the extent to which the axe of the settler had denuded the once-tree-covered site. Mr Whitefield, an artist who produced a panoramic lithograph of the new city, strongly urged the planting of trees on London's bare and sandy streets – a recommendation that was finally adopted twenty years later.

The second letter, signed anonymously "Subscriber," complained bitterly of the behaviour of groups of juveniles who stood habitually at the intersections of Dundas Street with Richmond, Talbot, and Ridout streets, "seemingly for no other purpose than to obstruct the sidewalk and spew out upon each lady who may chance to be alone, the vilest language."

Apparently, even after fifty years of civilizing influence, the London area had not entirely ceased to be "the abode of the wolf and the haunt of the savage."

The continuing drama of the Crimean War, as reported in the local press, had a special interest for Londoners, due to the involvement of several British regiments, elements of which had occupied the barracks here. The 23rd Royal Welch Fusiliers held a particular place in the hearts of the citizens. This regiment and its goat mascot had been stationed in London on two separate occasions – the period 1843–1845 and the period 1850–1853. When it left the city the second time it was to go straight to the battlefields of the Crimea. There, on 20 September 1854, at the Battle of the Alma, nine young officers, many of whom had been guests of the Harris family at Eldon House, were killed attacking a Russian battery. A large memorial tablet in the narthex of St Paul's Cathedral is a tribute to the memory of these young men. The battle itself is commemorated in the name of a London street.

An event of considerable social significance took place in St Paul's on 11 August 1855. This was Emancipation Day, in remembrance of the passage, by the British Parliament, in 1833, of the Act that effectively abolished slavery throughout the British Empire. Seven hundred blacks attended a service of thanksgiving. Many were newcomers, refugees from the slave states of the United States; others were long-time residents, well established and, in the main, well liked.

1855 Stephen Foster, "Come, Where My Love Lies Dreaming."

The farmers of the area also had cause for thanksgiving, as the price of wheat continued to rise on the London market. By mid-January 1856, the best fall wheat was fetching the equivalent of $2.64 US a bushel.

This was the top of the inflationary spiral; from here on, everything was to go downhill.

Not being clairvoyant, the typesetters at the London *Free Press* chose this time to go on strike. In its issue of Tuesday, 12 February 1856, the paper announced that the London local of the International Typographical Union, then less than a year old, had pulled its members off the job:

The Journeymen Printers of this place have formed a combination for the purpose of compelling the employers to pay them higher wages. Yesterday morning they refused to go to work if the increased scale which they had prepared was not assented to, and as we, in common with some of our contemporaries, feel that the present rates are as high as it is possible for us to pay in order to leave a margin for profit, we resolved that the demand ... should not be complied with. It is quite evident that if A, B or C felt that his wages were not sufficiently high to enable him to live in comfort he was at liberty to remove his labour at any time to a better market. ... In the printing trade the mode of payment is made in two different ways; one is that of paying by the measure, at so much for a certain number of lines of type set up and the other mode is at so much per week. The price by the measure, or "per 1000 ems" set ... has been hitherto in this city 25 cents. At this rate a man can earn, with ordinary industry, $9.00 a week, or if he be an expert hand $11 to $12 and upwards. The rate of wages by the week has hitherto been $9. The combination of which we have spoken, seek to raise the wages to 28 cents per thousand letters, and to $10.00 by the week; and this demand is made quite irrespective of the capabilities of the man, so that the worst "botch" that ever slurred a sheet of paper with printers' ink is expected to be paid as much as his more practiced fellow-workman.

In defence of the paper's position, Blackburn pointed out that the local wage-rate of $9 per week was the same as that paid by newspapers in Toronto and Hamilton, by agreement of the Typographical Union. In Toronto, however, printers who chose payment by the measure received 30 cents per 1,000 ems, while in Hamilton the rate was 26 cents. While refusing to increase the weekly wage-rate, Blackburn offered to match the Hamilton rate of 26 cents per 1,000 ems. The offer was rejected and the printers walked out. The *Free Press* was optimistic as to the outcome:

1855 Florence Nightingale introduces hygenic standards into military hospitals during Crimean War.

To Merchants and Forwarders!

A NEW ROUTE OPENED

FOR THE CONVEYANCE OF FREIGHT

TO & FROM LONDON, CANADA WEST.

THE LONDON AND

PORT STANLEY RAILWAY

Will, on the 25th September, 1856, commence carrying

FREIGHT AND PASSENGERS

And no delay will take place in the immediate delivery of goods arriving at Port Stanley for London and intermediate stations.

A LINE OF STEAMERS

FROM MONTREAL,

TOUCHING AT OGDENSBURG & OSWEGO

FOR

AMERICAN FREIGHTS,

Will be placed upon the Port Stanley Route.   Arrangements are also making for connection, by Steamers, with

BUFFALO AND CLEVELAND.

The communication opened by the London and Port Stanley Railway will greatly increase the facilities for the transportation of Freights to and from the Seaboard, by the St. Lawrence, the Atlantic Cities, and all parts of the United States, direct with London, Canada West; at which City a great portion of the Northern and Western Trade is already concentrated.

W. BOWMAN,

Superintendent.

Office of the London and Port Stanley Railway Co., ⎱
London, Canada West, September, 1856.   ⎰

Advertisement for the municipally-owned London and Port Stanley Railway, 1856. UWO

The consequences may be that our sheet will not contain, for a few days, quite so much reading matter as usual, but we throw ourselves upon the generosity of the Public, and trust that the inconvenience will be but of a temporary nature.

To ensure that the interruption would be of short duration, the *Free Press* took a revolutionary step. In the same issue that carried the announcement of the strike, this advertisement appeared:

FEMALE
HANDS WANTED
Six Young Women

Of intelligence and respectability, have now an opportunity of learning the business of type setting.

Young persons of industrious habits could earn, after a month's practice, from Four to Six dollars a week.

Apply at this Office between the hours of Eleven and Twelve o'clock. Good wages to begin with.

Although this action must have shocked most of the journal's readership, it was quite in keeping with the objectives of the mid-century feminist movement, led by such women as Susan B. Anthony and Amelia Bloomer. The movement got formally under way at the Seneca Falls (New York) Convention in July 1848. In the "Declaration of Sentiments" the charges against the male domination of the species were made very clear:

The history of mankind is a history of repeated injuries and usurpations on the part of man toward woman. ...

He has never permitted her to exercise her inalienable right to the elective franchise.

He has compelled her to submit to laws in the formation of which she had no voice.

He has withheld from her rights which are given to the most ignorant and degraded men. ...

He has made her, if married, in the eye of the law, civilly dead.

He has taken from her all right in property, even to the wages she earns. ...

He has uzurped the prerogative of Jehovah himself, claiming it as his right to assign for her a sphere of action, when that belongs to her conscience and to her God.

1856 Verdi's *La Traviata* has its North American première in New York City at the Academy of Music.

Oddly, there was little in the way of editorial comment on, or public reaction to, the decision of the *Free Press*. It may be assumed that the male position was sufficiently entrenched in every facet of living to permit merely an amused tolerance. It will be noted that while the newspaper was prepared to employ women typesetters, no consideration was to be given to the principle of equal pay for equal work. It was still a half-century down the road before women got the right to vote in Canada and the United States; it took even longer for Canadian women to be acknowledged, in law, as "persons."

By the spring of 1856, with the printers out on strike, the bloom was definitely off the rose. The inflationary spiral was faltering and beginning to collapse in on itself. The riskier business ventures were going under. One of the victims was a city alderman. Dr J.W. Kermott, a homeopathic physician and patent-drug manufacturer, represented the fourth ward. He was one of the first persons to rent a store in the arcade of the hand-some new city hall on Richmond Street. He had invested heavily in land, with borrowed money, at the very peak of the boom. When his loans were called, he was unable to meet the demands. Faced with criminal charges of fraud and forgery, he skipped to the United States. From an unnamed location there, he wrote a letter to his former municipal colleagues. The *Free Press* printed it in its issue of 28 May, without any alteration, *verbatim et literatim:*

> To the Mayer   Unighted States, America
> Aldormen etc   & 7th May 1856
> of London

Gentlemen: I regret deeply the necessity of leaving you so unceremoniously but I felt it my imperrative duty after giving all I possessed in the world, but my Person. To take care of that I prefer freedom to confinement and so from the threats of my friends, the confinement of Prison was inevitable. I absquatulated, and here I am dreaming of the past and forming plans for the future, I believe that the time will come when I can pay up all arrears and I do assure you that nothing but a rich partner and a swindeling course of policy toward me and the business have involved me in the difficulty I now labour under, and what is worse those who were my friends are now sufferers. I defy the world to point out and prove one dishonest act in my whole life, and had my creditors not been quite so severe I could have done something to help them further out of trouble, that is, my presence is necessary to make the most of the Property. The City Physician purchased of me for use of the Hospital, one complete set of Surgeon's splints at 14£. They were charged to the

---

1856 British and French forces besiege Canton, China; take city the following year.

Committee. You will please allow me that amount on the note you hold, and as soon as Providence smiles I will send you the Ballance. You will please accept my resignation as a member of the Corporation. I do this as it may be necessry to fill my place. I shall confide my time and talents wherever Providence may cast my lot – as my time, aye, and my talents too are my creditors and I believe I have the Abbillity to make the raise to pay what may be lacking if there is any. Meantime I wish you all well. May you live long. Do not go too fast. You may learn something by experience, and your experience with me be an advantage both to yourselves and with the city. When you next hear from me I shall tell you what I am doing, perhaps digging gold, I shall however be at work. Your wellwisher.

By the fall of 1856 the strike was over and the city's printers were back on the job – and probably glad of it. The financial news had turned really bad. In September, the Royal British Bank in England failed, ruining

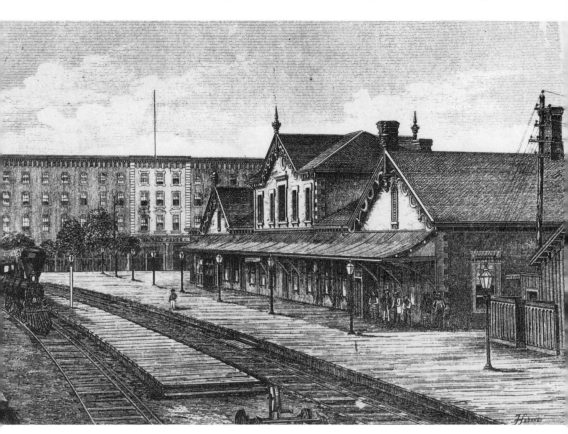

Great Western Railway Station, built in 1854. In the background is the Tecumseh House Hotel, built 1856–1860. From the *Canadian Illustrated News*. UWO

London, Canada West, 1855, from the usual vantage point on the Wortley Road
hill. From the *Illustrated London News*. UWO

thousands of small investors. By January 1857, unemployment was wide-spread in the United States. The New York *Tribune* estimated the jobless in that city at 100,000.

The whole western world was on the brink of a post-Crimean War depression. In this vast economic muddle, London, Canada West, was a very small factor indeed. Yet, when the depression struck here, it did so with singular ferocity. Few cities on the North American continent, and none in Canada, were hit as hard as London. The collapse of inflated wheat prices had a great deal to do with it, for wheat was still the economic backbone of the peninsula's existence.

The Thames flooded its banks in February, sweeping away many wooden bridges along its length. In March there was a ghastly accident at Hamilton on the Great Western Railway in which seventy-seven people were killed. This was the worst in the series of accidents that marked the early years of railroading in Canada, leading the newspapers of the period to make much editorial capital out of "Railway Murder."

The spring was late that year and the summer was cool and wet. A generation of careless husbandry was about to be paid for. Wheat rust and insect pests attacked crops that had been consistently robbing the soil of its nutrients for years, without replenishment. A heavy frost on the night of 15 June struck hard. A farmer near Komoka, west of the city, went out the next morning to view his ruined fields, then killed himself.

The big news of the summer was the election, on 9 July, of Dr Benjamin Cronyn, rector of St Paul's Anglican Church, as first bishop of the newly-created Diocese of Huron. Since this was the first time that a bishop of the Church of England in Canada had been elected by his peers, rather than appointed by the Crown, there was great general interest in the event. The local newspapers made capital out of the election. The *Free Press* in particular treated it like a political contest, drawing attention to the differing liturgical views held by Archdeacon Alexander Neil Bethune of Cobourg and Dr Cronyn. By simplifying the issue between "High Church" (Bethune) and "Low Church" (Cronyn), the editor of the *Free Press,* himself the son of a Congregationalist minister, was able to whip up a fine froth of partisanship on the part of the general citizenry.

In the result the synod voted for the man it knew best. As the accidentally appropriate words of the first lesson of Morning Prayer for the day had it: "Better is a neighbour that is near, than a brother afar off." (Proverbs 27:10). The clergy gave Dr Cronyn a rather narrow margin of support – twenty-two votes for Cronyn; twenty for Bethune. The laity were more generous in endorsing the man who had served congregations in the

---

1857 Indian Mutiny against British rule. Siege and relief of Lucknow.

The Reverend Benjamin Cronyn (1802–1871). This photograph, taken in Dublin in 1855, shows a close family resemblance between the cleric and his celebrated great-grandson, the actor Hume Cronyn. MRS JOHN HARLEY

London area for a quarter of a century; they gave Cronyn twenty-three votes to ten for Bethune.

The induced excitement of the ecclesiastical "contest" could not long obscure the deteriorating economic picture. By October the whole continent was in the grip of a major depression. In an editorial in the *Free Press* of 10 October, Josiah Blackburn summed up the situation in starkly simple terms:

The present monetary and commercial crisis is unquestionably the severest that has visited this continent for many years. Already many of the leading banking institutions of the chief cities of the United States ... have succumbed or suspended. ...

Just as twenty years earlier, the instability of the American banks wrought their worst hardship on Canadian farmers who had been paid for their wheat with bank notes that were now suddenly found to be worthless. That other form of paper transaction, notes of hand, became in many cases equally of no value. The *Free Press* noted that "many persons have resorted already to legal means in order to collect monies due them, but it may be stated as a general fact that out of 100 executions issued by the Sheriffs, at least 70 are returned 'no goods.'"

1857 American civil engineer E.G. Otis installs the first safety elevator.

By November, panic had London firmly in its grip. Businesses were declining and falling by the wayside in ever-increasing numbers, and the debtors' apartments in the London gaol were full to overflowing. The harsh provisions of the Debtors' Act, which decreed imprisonment for non-payment of a debt as small as $40, caused many a hard-pressed businessman to run for the international border when the shadow of the debtors' prison fell upon him. The *Free Press* attacked the abuse of the Debtors' Act:

We unhesitatingly affirm ... that by far the largest portion of the disaster that has fallen upon this place has arisen from the course complained of, and that those who practice it are the worst enemies of the city. In no other place in Canada has this mania prevailed, but to such an extent is it carried on here, that London has become a bye-word in the Province, as containing plenty of lodging room in the houses, but none in the jail.

As 1857 dragged into 1858 and 1858 collapsed into the arms of an equally-emaciated 1859, the tumor of poverty increased its hold on the vitals of this once flourishing city. The financial aristocracy continued to retrench; the middle class, the white-collar workers, rapidly approached the limit of their meagre reserves and looked forward only to more of the same. As for the unskilled labourer, his wife, or widow, there existed only an inadequate patchwork of reluctantly compassionate services. For the really desperate there were the soup kitchens operated by the larger church congregations, the cells of the city and county jails (the word now being spelled in the American fashion), and the grandly-named City Hospital, a log building on the barracks grounds rented from the military authorities for £5 a year. It had twenty-four beds, which were constantly in demand.

That winter London drank deeply of the dregs of its cup of bitterness. Poverty brought in its wake a rash of the queer, ugly perversions of the mind that batten on empty stomachs. Crime increased, with arson presenting a particularly difficult problem. Every week brought a fresh outbreak of incendiary fires. Some were traced to the fire companies, the members of which received a cash bounty for every fire they attended, but most of them were the work of pyromaniacs.

In the outskirts of the city, where pressures of population had forced the cemeteries operated by the various Christian sects to re-locate, in the dark of night, by the secret gloom of hooded lanterns, the "resurrectionists" plied their grisly trade, desecrating new-made graves for bodies to

---

1859 Karl Marx, *Critique of Political Economy*. J. S. Mill, *Essay on Liberty*.

View from the foot of Dundas Street looking east, in the 1860s. The courthouse and jail are at the left; in the right foreground is the sulphur springs spa patronized by Cornelius Vanderbilt in 1869. UWO

sell to the medical fraternity and their student apprentices for a few shillings each.

That winter the depression hit bottom. There was nowhere else to go but up. The cost to London had been enormous. It was said that 75 per cent of the businesses of London were bankrupt by December 1859. The city's population, which had been estimated at 16,000 in late 1855, was down to 11,000 four years later.

The lesson of that savage time was never forgotten. The financial conservatism that became London's best-known characteristic throughout the nation, was born of that bitter experience. The history of London in the ensuing century can be understood only in the light of that knowledge.

1859 Petroleum industry launched in the United States with the drilling of an oil well at Titusville, Pennsylvania.

CHAPTER SIX

ALARUMS AND DISCURSIONS

We, the Mayor, Aldermen and Commonalty of the City of London, Upper Canada, do, in the name of the inhabitants, most cordially welcome your Royal Highness. ... it is now only forty years since in the locality where you now stand, none but the red Indian wandered beneath the shade of the primeval forest. ...
From the official address to HRH the Prince of Wales (later Edward VII), 12 Sept. 1860.

There will be a large amount of speculation today at Sarnia, a quantity of land situated in what is known as the "oil regions" being about to be put up at public sale. ...
The London *Free Press*, 13 March 1861.

His Excellency [Sir W. F. Williams, commanding Her Majesty's forces in British North America] ... feels that, as some individuals are so constituted by nature they are without any sense of knowledge of right or wrong, of honour or justice, until it reaches their understanding through their pockets ... it is some satisfaction to his Excellency to inform the City Council ... that it is his intention to remove the military from London on the first opportunity. ...
From a letter by Colonel R. Rollo, military secretary, quoted in the London *Free Press*, 31 March 1861.

In electing James Moffat as mayor in January 1860 the electorate chose well. A native of Lanark, Scotland, and a London resident since 1845, Moffat had been a member of the municipal boards of both the town and the city. He was a prominent Mason and an ardent citizen-soldier, having been responsible for raising a company of Highland militia in 1856. A paid biographical notice published a quarter-century later described him as "a man of unbending honour and incorruptible honesty, generous in his feelings and dignified in his manhood, worthy as a citizen and true and faithful as a friend."

1860 Abraham Lincoln elected 16th president of the United States.

However exaggerated these attributed characteristics may have been, his appearance and manners made him a suitably distinguished chief magistrate to represent the city in its ecstatic welcome to Queen Victoria's heir, HRH Albert Edward, Prince of Wales.

It was London's first royal visit and made the year 1860 one ever to be remembered in the social history of the community. It came as a welcome antidote to the dreadful trauma of the depression years. Excitement was intense as the city prepared to receive its distinguished guest. The Tecumseh House Hotel – hailed at its construction in 1856–1857 as the largest such establishment west of Toronto – underwent an extensive and expensive refurbishing to make it worthy of its intended guest and his entourage.

The visit itself was a carbon copy of hundreds of similar events in the history of the royal family. The official greeting, read by Mayor Moffat, was, as may be seen from the brief quote at the head of this chapter, the standard haunt-of-the-wolf-and-abode-of-the-savage cliché first employed by Edward Allen Talbot thirty years earlier. Talbot should have copyrighted it.

The visit was brief and had no lasting impact on the history of London. However it left an apparently ineradicable mark on the city's mythology and folk history. The glittering ball held at the Tecumseh House lives on still in greatly time-enhanced images preserved in aging aspic. No lady survives who danced with the prince on the night of 12 September 1860, but that doesn't prevent the speculations that continue to surround any woman who gave birth within nine months of that event. Such matters are not susceptible of proof, but that in no way interferes with the amusement of gossip-loving Londoners.

One story connected with the royal visit has more basis in fact, although few of the details can now be confirmed. It depends on family tradition and a few scanty and discreet references in the papers of Marcus Gunn (1799–1878), diarist, newspaper editor, and land agent.

Gunn, a staunch anti-royalist and avowed republican, was also an inveterate writer of letters to the editors of various London newspapers. When the announcement of the prince's visit to London first appeared, Gunn launched a letter-writing campaign inveighing against the expense involved in entertaining the royal visitor, to whom he always referred as "the so-called Prince of Wales."

It appears that his publicly-expressed sentiments met with the approval of another visitor to the city, a member of the Fenian Brotherhood, the Irish terrorist secret society. The unnamed Fenian, in a state of aggressive

1860 Christopher L. Sholes, American inventor, devises primitive form of typewriter.

insobriety, called on Gunn to congratulate him on his stand. In the course of the conversation the Fenian made an unguarded reference to a "reception" the Brotherhood planned for the prince when he visited New York City.

Over the next few days Gunn brooded over his classic dilemma. Since he was an anti-royalist, a conspiracy directed against the heir to the British throne should have given him no cause for concern. On the other hand, Gunn was not a man of violence. Coincidentally, the young prince was the same age as the diarist's favourite son, Donald Marcus, at his death in Boston.

Gunn's letterbook for the period in question contains a laconic reference to a letter he sent to the Duke of Newcastle, Prince Albert Edward's principal equerry and adviser. Later, there is a notation concerning a letter Gunn received from the duke. It conveyed the duke's thanks. There is no indication of the contents of either letter.

The certain facts are these. There *was* a plot by the Fenians to assassinate the prince in New York City. Acting "on information received" American authorities were able to thwart the attempt on the life of the "so-called Prince of Wales."

There the matter rests.

Another plot connected with His Royal Highness's visit to London was more successful. While the cream of the city's society was cavorting in the ballroom at the Tecumseh House, a clever gang of burglars was robbing their homes. The loot was calculated to be at least $1,200, a large amount for the times.

Among the civic dignitaries who surrounded Mayor James Moffat as he read his stilted address to the Prince of Wales was the senior alderman for Ward Seven, Francis Evans Cornish. The alderman was destined to become an even more towering figure in local legend than the future king of England.

Cornish was the son of "Old Dr Cornish," the protean doctor-lawyer-surveyor-land-agent whose career was touched on briefly earlier in this history. Born in London Township, baptized in St Paul's Church, London, he was named queen's counsel in 1857, becoming, at age twenty-eight, one of the youngest men to be granted that honour in the history of the province.

This was the man who, in January 1861, was elected seventh mayor of the city of London. The elegant James Moffat had served his turn nicely; now, in the year the American states went to war against themselves, perhaps it was the time for a brawler. The electorate got one.

1861 Song, "John Brown's Body," words by an unknown author, published in Chicago.

Before he launched his career as the four-term "uncrowned king of London," Cornish was already well known to the gossip-mongers. For once, gossip was often outdone by the facts. What fiction, for instance, could improve on the veritable facts of the story of Frank Cornish and the city hall arcade?

Answer comes there none.

The arcade was a pedestrian walkway linking Richmond Street with the Market Square. It was not intended for vehicular traffic.

On a certain day, in a state of non-sobriety, the mayor drove his horse and carriage through the arcade. He was arrested by a constable. The following morning police-court spectators, including the press, were treated to a unique spectacle.

Mayor Cornish, in his official capacity as chief magistrate, called out his own name. He responded to it. He read himself the charge, delivered himself a lecture on the evils of drink, and fined himself four dollars, an amount he carefully removed from his right-hand trouser pocket and placed on the magistrate's desk.

Now it so happened that city magistrates received no salary, being entitled instead to collect all fines. Mayor Cornish accordingly transferred the four-dollar fine from the desk to his left-hand trouser pocket. Finally, after communing with himself, the chief magistrate decided to remit half of the fine on the grounds of the defendant's previous good conduct and subsequently transferred two dollars from the left-hand to the right-hand pocket.

The mayor's lenient treatment of himself was not extended to other drunks. During his term of office there was said to have been a marked decline in the number of charges of "drunk and disorderly." On the bench, the mayor was an unrelenting foe of public inebriety. He had a simple remedy for intemperance. Regardless of the social position of the offender, the penalty was the same. Clad in distinctive prison garb and toting a ball and chain, he was set to work grading, gravelling, raking, and otherwise improving the streets of the city. One such appearance in public was often sufficient to cure the most hardened toper. It was the principle of the old-fashioned pillory, somewhat modernized.

It were prolix (but highly diverting) to list all the juicy incidents that speckled the London career of Francis Evans Cornish. They included public assaults on the persons of the city's chief of police and an officer of the British Army, numerous charges of public drunkenness, one charge of bigamy, and a noisy suit for divorce.

The man suited times that, like himself, were flamboyant and dramatic.

1861 "Abide With Me," words by Henry Francis Lyte; music by William Henry Monk.

Cornish entered into office the same year as the sixteenth president of the United States, Abraham Lincoln, did. The London newspapers, like most of the Canadian press, tended to look on the new Republican head of state with disfavour; the *Free Press* considered him a dangerous demagogue.

When the seceding Southern states formed themselves into the Confederate States of America, they elected as their first and only president Jefferson Davis, a senator from Mississippi who had been secretary of war under President Franklin Pierce. There is a persistent local legend that says Davis had friends in London and that he drafted some of the clauses of the constitution of the Confederacy while a guest at the Tecumseh House Hotel. It is barely possible. Certainly the Confederacy had many supporters in this city, mainly among the members of the Establishment.

Nevertheless public opinion generally began to swing towards Lincoln and the North in February 1861, when a plot to assassinate the president was thwarted by the swift action of Allan Pinkerton, a private detective. This attitude hardened into active support when the Confederacy fired on Fort Sumter, South Carolina, on Friday, 12 April. Three days later Lincoln issued a call for 75,000 volunteers and one of the bloodiest civil wars in history had begun. Some of those who presented themselves at the recruiting offices were Canadians. Among them were some young Londoners. A few left their bodies on the battlefields.

The American Civil War had a deep and lasting effect on the history of Canada, and nowhere was it felt more strongly than in London. The issues were more clearly understood by the common people than they seem to have been by the politicians. The North stood for *paid* labour, the South for *slave* labour. The North represented the working man, the South, the Establishment. However many words the politicians wrapped around these issues, this was how London's artisan population – what an earlier generation had known as the "mechanics" – saw the matter.

The politicians – American, British and Canadian – of course tried to muddy the waters. William Henry Seward, Lincoln's secretary of state, tried to patch up the quarrel between the North and the South by proposing that the two join together to invade and annex Canada. Some of the Northern newspapers waxed enthusiastic about the suggestion, but Lincoln refused to adopt it, fearful of expanding the conflict by bringing in England, allied politically with its colonies and economically (cotton) with the Confederacy. Faced with these confusing developments, the politicians of British North America adopted the traditional national policy of speaking very softly and carrying a twig.

1860 Stephen Foster, "Old Black Joe."

Meanwhile there was plenty of local news to engage the attention of Londoners. The economic picture was changing rapidly. The farmers of southwestern Ontario had greeted the outbreak of the Civil War with some enthusiasm, expecting an increased demand for their wheat. They were disappointed. The newly-developed Kansas fields now provided the needed wheat. The armies of the North wanted beef. Canadian farmers responded. The changeover to beef production came just in time. The fragile soils of the peninsula were quickly wearing out under the merciless drain of a one-crop farm economy. Before the war was over scores of handsome new farm homes testified to the financial success of the region's beef barons.

The sand-and-clay soils of Southwestern Ontario, harrowed by the grinding teeth of the retreating glaciers ten millennia earlier, now revealed new hidden riches. The first commercial oil well in North America started production at Oil Springs, in Lambton County, in 1858. By 1861 the oil boom had replaced the real-estate boom. One account published in 1878 tells a graphic story of the feverish activity associated with the opening of the fields:

The success achieved by a few of the first operators fired the whole community with a desire to become millionaires and everybody got the "oil fever" and for a time the staple of conversation in the street, the store, hotel or office was oil and oil territory, flowing wells and royalty, until the whole community was oil mad; nearly every man became an oil speculator and nearly every acre of land in probable or improbable localities which could be leased, was leased for oil purposes, and lands worth intrinsically next to nothing were held at fabulous prices. ... Speculators rushed to the scene from all parts of the country and joint stock companies were formed by the dozen; test wells were sunk in every likely and unlikely locality and in every direction until the ubiquitous derrick disfigured the whole landscape. Staid and sober business men, yielding to the allurements of the day, became sanguine and visionary speculators in oil lands and spouting wells and immense fortunes were made in a day and lost in a night. London was the centre of this speculation and was the market where the oil lands in several counties were bought and sold.

While some Londoners were making money in oil, others were making whoopee at the City Hospital. The nature of this institution was quite different from that of today's hospital. In the 1860s it was a refuge and treatment centre for the very poor. In the frequent outbreaks of epidemic disease of those days, it served as a pest house. Dr Robert Hobbs was for a time the official physician. His duties were to "attend to and render

1861 Great Britain recognizes the Confederate States of America.

Medical aid to all sick persons at the City Hospital and to all poor persons within the limits of the city ... to provide and furnish all Medicines, Medicinal and External applications for the restoration of health (Bandages excepted) ... to vaccinate all poor persons who may attend for that purpose, the fee to be charged not in any case to exceed fifty cents."

The city's relief committee, headed by Councilman David Hughes, was responsible for the operation of the hospital. Mr and Mrs John Helstone were steward and matron. For some time rumours had been circulating about the rather hedonistic behaviour of the staff. Finally, in early 1861, as the result of a complaint laid by Dr Hobbs, an investigation was carried out. The report "charged a few of the aldermen with being too intimate with the matron and other female attendants at the hospital." Councilman Hughes admitted "that the Matron would throw her arms around his neck and kiss him as would the other servant girls in the establishment and he would kiss them in return."

It is difficult to tell from the report whether favours other than kisses were exchanged. It is clear, however, that Councilman Hughes was most assiduous in his duties, being seen at the hospital "four of five times a week."

In the result the Helstones were dismissed and the husband-and-wife team of Thomas and Helen Warren appointed in their stead. The new steward and matron had barely time to get settled in when the peripatetic City Hospital had to move its operations again. On Monday, 18 November, the city council received word that the Crown authorities would again require the use of the hospital and the other buildings on the barracks grounds for military purposes. Before the end of the year the city had taken on the appearance of an armed camp, with an estimated 2,000 British troops overflowing the facilities of the military reserve. A number of downtown buildings were rented for officers' quarters and administration offices. The premises formerly occupied by Hope, Birrell and Company, general merchants, at the southeast corner of Carling and Ridout streets, became a military prison.

The unexpected return of the Imperials was due to what came to be called the *Trent* affair. A British ship bearing that name was stopped on the high seas and boarded by a Union vessel, the *San Jacinto,* and two Confederate diplomats bound for England were forcibly removed. When the news reached Britain, the government reacted angrily. An army of 10,000 troops boarded transports bound for Canada. The prime minister, Lord Palmerston, sent an ultimatum to Washington: apologize and return the Confederate commissioners, or prepare for war.

1861 Charles Dickens, *Great Expectations.*

Palmerston's precipitate action was taken during the temporary absence from London of the Queen. The royal consort, Prince Albert, although gravely ill, insisted on taking a hand in the affair. The belligerency of the British demand was toned down. The troops already on their way to Canada were ordered distributed among the existing garrisons rather than being sent to the frontiers prepared for a state of war.

By the time London's quota of nearly a fifth of the expeditionary force had reached the city, the worst of the crisis had passed. The North was not in a position to fight a war on two fronts. The mutual threats were reduced to the normal mutterings and mumblings of diplomatic communication. It had been a near thing, and Londoners continued to have bad dreams about the possibility of a Yankee invasion.

While the crisis was still very much current, nervous Londoners were treated to a charming diversion. On Friday, 15 November, General Tom Thumb (Charles Sherwood Stratton) visited the city under the auspices of Phineas Taylor Barnum. The midget was then in his twenty-fourth year, nudging three feet in height, and was at the peak of his fame. To the delight of cheering crowds, he rode in his miniature carriage from Strong's Hotel on the north side of Dundas Street, between Richmond and Clarence streets, to the city hall where he was received by Mayor Cornish and other members of the city council.

Happy memories of this pleasant event were still being savoured when the sad news was received of the death on Saturday, 14 December, of Queen Victoria's beloved Prince Albert. The news cast a gloom over the Christmas celebrations of citizens and soldiers alike, as the flags at the garrison and the city hall stood at half-mast.

Frank Cornish was returned to office in 1862. A new generation of municipal politicians was emerging as death and boredom removed some of the older men. The new council members were businessmen, professional men, and artisans; few belonged to the old London Establishment. One who shared some of the characteristics of the old clique was Simpson H. Graydon, a native of Ireland and, like Bishop Cronyn, a graduate of Trinity College, Dublin. Graydon first visited the area in 1840 as a member of a group of young adventurers who came to Canada "for the hunting." Still looking for thrills, the young men drifted on to the Australian gold fields. Graydon, when he finally decided to settle down, chose London for his home and entered into the study, and subsequently the practice, of law.

Meanwhile, relations between the citizens and the British garrison were not as friendly as they had been formerly. There were many more soldiers

---

1861 Italy proclaimed a kingdom; Victor Emmanuel II is king.

The Crystal Palace, built for the Provincial Exhibition of 1861 on the military reserve south of Lake Horn. From *Canadian Illustrated News*. UWO

than there had been back in the forties. They had overflowed the military reserve into the downtown areas of the city. Soon there was friction.

In the eight years since the redcoats had marched off to the Crimean War, civilians had virtually taken over the barracks property. To the north, Lake Horn had become a community playground. South of it, on the northeast corner of Central Avenue and Wellington Street, a large octagonal building known as the Crystal Palace was built to house the annual

1861 Louis Pasteur proves that micro-organisms cause fermentation and disease.

Provincial Exhibition of September 1861. As has already been noted, the
city was using one of the two hospitals on the reserve. Many of the other
buildings had been taken over by poor squatters. Part of the parade square,
which the Imperials had used as a cricket pitch, had been pressed into
use by London sportsmen for the more plebian game of baseball, which
had been steadily increasing in popularity.

As invasion fears receded, local tensions increased. Succeeding barracks
commanders faced a difficult double task of pacifying the civilian population while at the same time finding peacetime occupations for the troops.
They were, after all, fighting men who chafed at inaction. There was a
fine old war going on just a few hundred miles away. Furthermore the
Union's pay-scale was better than the Queen's. The recruiting officers at
Windsor and Port Huron asked few questions. The rate of desertions
increased dramatically.

Frank Cornish was re-elected mayor in 1863, but this time around victory
didn't come quite so easily. His perennial opponent David Glass, a former
mayor (1858), was steadily building a powerful challenge to the incum-
bent. Cornish's ace-in-the-hole was his use of the British troops. The story
is that he bribed a considerable number of soldiers to take up temporary
residence in tents pitched on Tipperary Flats, in the city's north end, for
a time sufficient to entitle them to a vote in the municipal elections. Factually
true or not, this story has become a part of the Cornish legend.

The next incident in the Cornish saga is solidly factual. It happened
during a ball at the Tecumseh House Hotel sponsored by the garrison in
honour of the marriage of the Prince of Wales to the Princess Alexandra
of Denmark, which took place that very day (10 March 1863) in St George's
Chapel, Windsor.

A Major Bowles, of the 63rd Regiment, second-in-command of the
garrison, was the official host of the event. Rumours had been circulating,
linking Bowles' name with that of Mrs Cornish. Cornish set out to confront
the major.

The confrontation took place in the hotel in the early morning hours
of 11 March. It was short, sharp, and farcical. A brief bout of fisticuffs
ended with the victorious mayor landing a magisterial boot on the major's
posterior. Despite the attempts of two other officers to prevent further
assaults on the honour of the regiment, Cornish succeeded in ripping off
the major's decorations and hurling them in his face.

At the city police-court hearing that followed, Cornish was found guilty
of unprovoked assault and fined six dollars. In his defence the mayor said
only that he had been denied admission to the ballroom and had been

---

1861 First horse-drawn trams appear in London, England.

aggravated by the major's abrupt manner. This restraint on the part of Cornish stimulated the gossip concerning the alleged relations between the major and Mrs Cornish.

The major, for his part, created a bad impression when he explained with some *hauteur* that he had been stopped at the entrance to the ballroom "by a civilian whom I at first took for a cabman, but afterwards recognized as the mayor of the City of London."

Such an unfortunate remark insulted not only the mayor but the council over which he presided. In consequence, when the Army demanded an official apology from the council for the behaviour of the mayor, the suggestion received a chilly and almost unanimous refusal. The mayor, they said, had acted as a private citizen.

The Army, in the person of Sir William Fenwick Williams, Bart., KCB, commander of the forces in British North America, then dictated a blistering letter threatening to withdraw all the troops from London. This was drastic punishment indeed, promising serious consequences to the safety and economy of the city. It was the economic effect that troubled the *Free Press:*

On the removal of the troops, house rents will fall thirty or forty per cent; trade, which has been active, will diminish; the minor produce from the country, which had risen largely in price, will fall; and thus not only will the citizens of London, but the farmers in the neighbourhood, be called upon to suffer.

The matter had gone too far for either side to retreat. The council refused to alter its original stand and General Williams would accept nothing but a complete and abject apology. Driven to action by the widespread publicity given the affair, he gave the order to reduce the garrison at London. There could be no thought of removing the troops altogether. Tension at the border remained great. There had been riots in Detroit and Windsor, and a bad racial incident at Oil Springs, when a number of American well-drillers attacked a black settlement.

Meanwhile the armies of the South under their brilliant general Robert Edward Lee had taken the offensive, driving north into Pennsylvania. There, at the town of Gettysburg, what was probably the most decisive battle of the war raged for three days. That battle must have struck splinters of fear into the hearts of Londoners, for on the first three days of July 1863 the sun was obscured by the smoke of the guns of Gettysburg, which is less than 350 air miles away.

1862 Naval cadet, Nicolai Rimsky-Korsakov visits Niagara Falls on world tour.

That same month brought chilling news from New York City. Until the end of 1862 Northern armies consisted, in the main, of volunteers. Their numbers were not sufficient. The Conscription Act was passed into law. The draft was highly unpopular in the cities. On Monday, 13 July, a mob trashed the draft office in New York. As their numbers grew they turned to looting, burning, and raping. The riot went on for four days, causing enormous property damage and costing 1,000 lives.

The thirst for news was intense. London, with a population of less than 15,000, had three daily newspapers. A young printer named John Cameron didn't think that was enough. On Tuesday, 27 October 1863, he published the first issue of the London *Advertiser,* an evening daily. The *Free Press* was a morning paper. The *Advertiser* was an immediate success and remained the principal competitor of the *Free Press* for the next seventy-three years.

On Wednesday, 2 December, both newspapers covered an event of far-reaching significance in the history of education in the city. On that day Huron College, a theological institution, was opened officially. While the event was of specific interest only to members of the Church of England, the college's first principal was destined to exert a tremendous influence on the development of secondary and post-secondary education in the province.

The Reverend Dr Isaac Hellmuth was born near Warsaw, Poland. The son of a rabbi, he converted to Christianity and studied theology in England. He was brought to the Diocese of Huron by Bishop Cronyn for the express purpose of establishing a theological college based on low-church principles (as opposed to the high-church teachings of Toronto's Trinity College).

Such doctrinal and liturgical matters are of importance mainly to those who have a vested interest in partisan churchmanship. However, it was the man chosen by Cronyn as his instrument whose work transcended these rather petty considerations. Dr Hellmuth, as dean of Huron and later as the second bishop of the Diocese, introduced the kind of academic secondary schools known as collegiate institutes and was instrumental in founding and funding the University of Western Ontario in 1878. His stature as the greatest educator in the history of the peninsula cannot seriously be challenged.

With the aid of his coterie of bully-boys and his British Army pals, Francis Evans Cornish was elected to his fourth and final term as mayor in January 1864.

It was to be a vintage year.

1863 On New Year's Day, President Lincoln issues the Emancipation Proclamation.

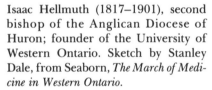

Isaac Hellmuth (1817–1901), second bishop of the Anglican Diocese of Huron; founder of the University of Western Ontario. Sketch by Stanley Dale, from Seaborn, *The March of Medicine in Western Ontario.*

Graves Simcoe Lee, son of Dr Hiram Davis Lee. A player with the Gentlemen Amateurs, Lee became a professional actor, specializing in Shakespearean roles. Sketch by Stanley Dale, from Seaborn, *The March of Medicine in Western Ontario.*

The Canada Trust Company under its birthing name – the Huron and Erie Mortgage Corporation – got its start in life. So did the James Cowan Hardware Company.

It was the year of the tercentenary of the birth of William Shakespeare. The Perth County town of Stratford, after a very slow start, staged a modest little celebration. London had a much bigger, three-day "monster" festival capped by a performance in the city hall auditorium of *The Merchant of Venice.* In keeping with Elizabethan stage tradition, all the female roles were played by young, clean-shaven men. (Portia was Edmund Meredith, a leading lawyer.) Graves Simcoe Lee, a son of the pioneer innkeeper, Hiram Davis Lee, returned to the city to take part in the festival. A former member of the Gentlemen Amateurs, he had gone on to become what was called "a luminary" of the American professional theatre.

Another cultural event of consequence was the laying of the cornerstone of Dr Hellmuth's London Collegiate Institute (not to be confused with the later secondary school bearing the same name). Citizens came to know it better as "Hellmuth College."

The year was marked by some less pleasant events, of which the worst was an outbreak of incendiarism. It would appear that arson is the oldest signature activity of the urban guerrilla. London's tiny police force, consisting of a chief and seven constables, was unable to cope with the firebug. The city council appointed forty citizens to serve as special constables and offered a reward of $200 for the apprehension of the arsonist. (It should be noted, parenthetically, that decimal currency had been adopted by Canada in 1858.) The money was never claimed.

The police force had no "fraud squad" in 1864, and so when William Oakley, a municipal collector of taxes, was found to have a notable shortage in his accounts, the matter was settled by the parties themselves. All of Oakley's real estate, goods, and chattels were seized, and his two sureties paid the city's claim. No one yet knew that the city treasurer, John Brown, had already embarked on his unparalleled thirty-year-career of embezzlement of the city's funds.

London Collegiate Institute, opened 1865. Later renamed Hellmuth Boys' College, and still later, Dufferin College. Demolished 1895. From the *Illustrated London News*. UWO

These local affairs were minor irritants compared with the major anxiety Londoners were subjected to in that critical year. In 1864 the American Civil War impinged directly on the lives of the people of London. Driven to desperation by the growing certainty of its defeat by the Union, the Confederacy tried a mad scheme involving the use of Canadian territory as the base for an attack on the cities of the North. The so-called Northwest Conspiracy was led by Jacob Thompson, a member of Jefferson Davis's cabinet. From his headquarters in Toronto Thompson presided over a network of Confederate spies, guerrilla fighters, refugee Southern soldiers (said to number 2,000 in Canada West), Canadian sympathizers, and dissident Northern Democrats. Chiefest among this last-named group was Senator Clement Laird Vallandigham, of Ohio. Banished by Lincoln for his treasonous activities as leader of the anti-war Copperhead movement, and as a kingpin of the secret society, the Knights of the Golden Circle, Vallandigham spent at least part of 1864 in London.

In London, conveniently situated with respect to the cities of Toronto, Detroit, and Buffalo, Vallandigham met and parlayed with Thompson's agents, among whom were an unidentified young woman from Maryland and a dashing young officer from Kentucky. The officer, Captain Thomas Henry Hines, was a physical double of the actor and Confederate sympathizer John Wilkes Booth. Hines was the military commander of the Northwest Conspiracy.

Hines's plan, in broad outline, was reported to his secretary of war in June 1864:

Two regiments [of guerrilla fighters] now in the process of formation in Chicago will be placed under my command to move upon Camp Douglas and free the prisoners.

Simultaneously with this movement, the Democrats in every county of Illinois and portions of Indiana and Ohio will rally to arms. A force of 3,000 Democrats under a competent leader will march upon Rock Island [Illinois] for the release of the 7,000 prisoners at that place.

The remainder will concentrate upon Chicago and Springfield. State governments of Indiana, Ohio and Illinois will be seized and their executives disposed of. By this means we hope to have, within ten days after the movement has begun, a force of 50,000 men.

In the crunch, thanks to excellent intelligence work in Ottawa, Washington, and London, England, the conspiracy fizzled out, with nothing to show beyond an abortive naval excursion on Lake Erie, fire-bomb attacks

---

1864 Lincoln re-elected as president; Andrew Johnson elected vice-president.

on twelve buildings in New York City, and a border raid on the community of St Albans, Vermont. It was a pitifully meagre return for an investment of several million dollars.

None of this, of course, was known to the Londoners of Canada West in the summer of 1864. They only knew the worry of it all. The streets of the city swarmed with Confederate and Union spies, counter-spies, double agents, and moles, along with a sprinkling of Allan Pinkerton's men, Canadian secret agents, and a clutch of eager newspaper reporters. The situation in London was similar to that experienced in Toronto by the head of the Confederate mission. Jacob Thompson complained of "the bane and curse of carrying out anything in this country due to the surveillance under which we act. Detectives, or those ready to give information, stand on every street corner. Two or three cannot interchange ideas without a reporter."

Londoners did have some idea of what was going on. So did the Northern press, which grew more and more belligerent in its demands for the final elimination of British power in North America. In these circumstances London's Imperials began to look more like saviours and less like nuisances. The late unpleasantness with Mayor Cornish was glossed over. But then the 63rd Regiment was replaced by the 47th. The men of the 47th were a tough, hard-bitten crew. They cared nothing at all for the feelings of the "colonials." Little frictions became big tensions, resulting finally in the "Battle of the Gore."

The "Gore," as noted before, was a triangular piece of land bounded by Central Avenue and Richmond and Clarence streets. The Clarence Street allowance was within the boundary of the military reserve, which was marked in part by the big stump fence. During the eight-year absence of the troops from the city, local people had breached the fence and used the street allowance as a short-cut to downtown London. The 47th replaced the fence. Citizens tore it down. The soldiers replaced it again and, with loaded guns, prepared to confront and repel the invaders. Undaunted, the citizens again began dismantling the fence. On command, the Imperials fired a volley over the heads of the activists, who paid no attention whatever to it. Three or four subsequent volleys likewise had no effect. A blank charge fired from one of the barracks cannons succeeded only in setting one of the stumps on fire. While the troops laboured to extinguish the blaze, the London loyalists triumphantly drove farm wagons down the reactivated street allowance, which experienced no further blockage.

In September and October, the Charlottetown and Quebec conferences

---

1864 George Mortimer Pullman began the construction of his railroad sleeping cars.

launched the British North American provinces on the road to national unity. London's member of parliament, John Carling, played a special role behind the scenes in smoothing the way for cooperation between the two great political enemies, George Brown and John Alexander Macdonald.

The first day of the municipal elections of January 1865 followed the pattern of the four previous years. The candidates were, as usual, Frank Cornish and David Glass.

There were many signs that the London electorate was becoming a little bored by the Cornish antics. Glass shrewdly took advantage of the mood.

The first day's vote went to Cornish.

That evening David Glass met with some members of the 1864 council. He claimed that the voting had been marked by so much violence that a fair contest had been impossible. He asked that balloting be continued for a second day in order that all who wished might vote, and that the militia be called out to guarantee the security of the polling stations.

The next morning Frank Cornish's supporters found a ring of armed militiamen surrounding every polling place in the city. The news spread rapidly. Assured of a fair opportunity to voice their choice, the Glass men turned out in great numbers. When the count was complete, London had a new mayor.

One of the first problems Mayor Glass faced was the bill for the militiamen – $282.60. There was much opposition to the discharge of the debt. Those councillors who were faithful to Cornish claimed there had been no necessity for the show of military strength and, furthermore, there was some question whether the council's action had been decided by a legal quorum of that august body.

The account was finally paid, under protest.

April brought an end to the savage war across the border. General Lee surrendered at Appomattox courthouse on Sunday, 9 April. Five days later Abraham Lincoln was assassinated by the actor John Wilkes Booth. On the following evening, Saturday, 15 April, the Confederate officer Captain Thomas Hines fled from a mob in Detroit, Michigan, who mistook him for Booth. At the point of a pistol he commandeered the Detroit-Windsor ferry and joined friends in London and, eventually, Toronto.

In common with other communities throughout North America, London mourned the death of the man whom less than five years earlier the London *Free Press* had dismissed as a ranting demagogue. Josiah Blackburn, in company with a number of other Canadian newspaper editors, visited the White House toward the end of the war and came away with a totally

1865 New fads: mascara and pork-pie hat.

different impression. The power of the president's personality affected the Canadians deeply.

The North Street Methodist Church, on the southwest corner of Queens Avenue and Clarence Street, which on its completion in 1854 was said to be "the finest church west of Great St James Street, Montreal," was chosen as the site of a memorial service. The huge church was packed to hear a funeral address delivered by W.G. Moncrieff, a former Presbyterian minister, newspaper editor, historian, school-teacher, and acknowledged dean of London letters.

The death of the martyred president was not viewed with compassion by everyone. At Lucan, north of London, a village already notorious because of an imported Irish feud, the community's flag had been lowered to half-staff in tribute to Lincoln. A Southern refugee named White fired a shot at the flag.

The end of the war did not mean the end of danger to Canada. Northern newspapers were still trumpeting their demands for the annexation of Canada. By their posturings they actually hastened the advent of the Confederation of the British North American colonies. As George Étienne Cartier declared, "When we are united, the enemy will know that if he attacks any province he will have to deal with the combined forces of the Empire."

An anxiety closer to home was the epidemic of burglaries that broke out in 1865. The police force was unable to cope with it. Eventually the situation became so bad a citizens' vigilance committee was formed to patrol the streets at night. A reward of $200 was offered for the capture of the burglars. Like the earlier reward for nabbing the mysterious arsonist of 1864, this one, too, was never claimed.

In the folklore of the United States the citizens' committee of vigilance is usually represented as a spontaneous expression of the community's need to establish law and order where no official legal machinery exists. In these cases the community takes the law into its own hands, with often tragic results.

This was not the intent of the ancient English *posse comitatus* (power of the county). The "posse," as it is more generally known, does not exist *outside* the law. It is called into being by representatives *of* the law, to assist them in carrying out their legal functions.

The London area has had examples of both kinds of committee – the vigilance committee and the posse. The notorious vigilance committee of Biddulph Township, which was responsible for the mass-murder of five members of the Donnelly family in 1880, was organized outside the law.

1865 Jefferson Davis, President of the Confederate States, charged with treason.

It later arranged for some of its members to be appointed as justices of the peace and constables, to give its murderous work the colour of legality.

On the other hand, the citizen committees of London in the 1860s were true examples of the *posse comitatus*. They were called into being by legally-constituted authority (the city council) to assist the official police force in carrying out its legal tasks of protecting life and property.

Before 1865 was out, there was even more serious work for the city's volunteer peace-keepers. This time the threat came from outside the city; indeed from outside the provincial border. The Fenian Brotherhood had enlisted thousands of disbanded and jobless veterans of the American Civil War in a mad adventure – to invade and conquer Canada in order to use it as a base to drive the English out of Ireland.

By early fall, thanks to superb intelligence gathered by Canadian and British operatives (including one working within the Fenians' executive circle), it was known that one of the principal centres of Fenian activity was Chicago, and that a major attack was to be launched from there on the Canadian border at Sarnia. Sarnia was chosen because of its excellent rail connections with such Canadian nerve-centres as Stratford, London, and Toronto. Sufficient credence was given these reports that on Wednesday, 15 November, Lieutenant-Colonel James Shanly was ordered to hold the London militia in readiness to defend the frontier.

(It was Shanly who, earlier in the year, had defended the city against its late mayor, Frank Cornish.)

Time passed. There was no invasion. A reaction set in. Mocking editorials and news stories belittling the "Finnigans" began to appear. However John A. Macdonald had access to secret information that led him to consider the Fenian threat a very real one. Accordingly, in March 1866 a call went out for 10,000 volunteers for the Canadian militia. More than 14,000 presented themselves for duty.

Nothing happened. As the weeks dragged by, London's factory-owners and businessmen became restive at the continued inconvenience and expense caused by the volunteer call-up. On 30 May the *Free Press* editorialized:

The prolongation of the Fenian sensation is a sad bill of expense to Canada, and the people are anxious to see a period put to the Volunteers' term of service. ...

Two days later the balloon went up. The *Free Press* was on the streets by five o'clock on the morning of Friday, 1 June, with disturbing news:

1865 Lewis Carroll, *Alice's Adventures in Wonderland.*

The fourth office of the London *Free Press,* 1862. This building on Carling Street (then called North Street) now houses the Marienbad Restaurant. From Tremaine's *Map of Middlesex County* (1862). UWO

We had hoped we had got to the bottom of these Fenian scares, but it seems we were mistaken. ... the redoubtable Sweeney is assembling his Fenian loafers at Buffalo for a raid on Canada. ...

Within an hour anxiety had replaced irritation. An "extra" issued free at 7:30 am reported that a large force of Fenians had landed at Fort Erie on the Niagara frontier.

1865 New York City replaces its volunteer firemen with a paid fire department.

At 1:30 pm the city council held a special meeting to consider the question of the formation of a home guard for the protection of the city.

By late afternoon both the *Free Press* and the *Advertiser* had published extras reporting much in the way of sensation but little hard news. All that was certain was that the Fenians were in Canada in undisclosed numbers.

Some idea of the size of the invading force was spelled out in a story from Port Stanley, on Lake Erie:

All day yesterday, a fleet of between thirty and forty schooners were cruising off Plum Point and Port Stanley. It is expected they carry supplies for the Fenians. During the afternoon, about five, they all tacked off in the direction of Port Colborne.

By nightfall the *Free Press* had its own war correspondent in the field. He was Malcolm G. Bremner. Another Londoner represented the Toronto *Globe* – Donald Cameron, who later became sheriff of Middlesex County.

A telegram from the front, routed via Paris, Canada West, was received some time before midnight:

News has just been received that the Fenians are entrenched about four miles from Fort Erie, and our troops are closing in at Chippewa, Port Colborne and Dunnville.

There was little sleep for anyone in London that night. The telegraph offices and the newspapers were fully staffed, but no trustworthy information was received. The first reliable news was not available until late afternoon, Saturday, 2 June, and it was bad:

A skirmish took place about eight this morning between 600 Fenians, under Col. O'Neill, and about an equal number of our Volunteers. Troops firing was heard for about three-quarters of an hour in the neighbourhood of Frenchman's Corners. Three of our dead lie in the road. No other dead reported. It is said our men were repulsed, and retreated in good order. ...
The march has been exceedingly fatiguing, and Corporal Wm. Corrington, of the 4th, is now lying at the point of death from sunstroke. ... A number of Fenian rifles have been captured. A hard battle is expected tomorrow.

M. G. BREMNER,
Free Press Correspondent.

1866 Alfred Nobel invents dynamite.

The decisive battle – "skirmish" would be a better word – was fought near the village of Ridgeway the following day, Saturday. It resulted in the rout of the Fenians and their retreat back across the border.

News of the victory did not reach London until late on Sunday. It was the strangest Sunday London had ever known. The city had become a war zone. Rumour had a field day. The *Free Press* reported:

The most excited state of feeling prevailed in London all day Sunday. Crowds gathered at every corner in the most intense state of excitement after news. ...

At 12:30 Sunday morning the bugle sounded an alarm in London, and the fire bells rang, causing an intense excitement. People turned out of the churches in crowds in a state of the utmost alarm. The occasion was a report that the Fenians had landed at Sarnia and Windsor. It turned out to be false, however.

Many years afterwards William Hayman, a soldier in the British 53rd Regiment, recalled the tensions of that day:

Many a Sunday I have gone to St Paul's Church with my rifle on my shoulder and forty rounds of ball ammunition in my cartridge pouch, expecting to have to fight my way back home from the church to the barracks ... Col. Harence was our commanding officer then, and a fine fellow he was too. Many a night I have seen him on the streets until morning, ready at a moment's warning to turn his men out.

By Monday morning, 4 June, the "war" on the Niagara frontier was over. That evening 4,000 Londoners gathered at the Great Western Railway depot to greet the returning volunteers. Later, at a banquet honouring them, Mayor David Glass proposed a toast: "To the health of our guests, Her Majesty's troops, and the noble volunteers who have gone to the front in the hour of danger."

That's where most popular accounts of the Fenian raids end. It wasn't over for London and Southwestern Ontario. The threat of invasion via the St Clair River border was very real. On at least three separate occasions British troops and Canadian militiamen were ordered to Sarnia to repel threatened attacks by Chicago-based Fenians. The threats proved false alarms. However, the fears remained and finally proved the glue to bind together the eastern provinces of British North America in a defensive union.

1866 Aeronautical Society of Great Britain founded.

The Music Hall at the northwest corner of Richmond and York streets, as it appeared in 1866, the year of its construction by E.W. Hyman. UWO

As the curtain came down on the seriocomic drama of the Irish adventure, London buried its saint on Wednesday, 3 October 1866.

He was Ensign The Honourable Henry Edward Dormer, late of the 60th King's Royal Rifles. He was the youngest son of Joseph Thaddeus Dormer, eleventh Lord Dormer, and his wife Elizabeth Anne Tichborne. Both families had long histories of deep attachment to the Roman Catholic faith; in the case of the Tichbornes the record extended back to the twelfth century. The Dormer family motto expresses well the fervour of that connection: "Ciò che Dio vuole io voglio" (What God wills, I will).

From his arrival in London in February 1866 until his death some seven short months later, the young Englishman was an exemplar of the life in

1866 "When You and I Were Young, Maggie," copyrighted by J.A. Butterfield.

Christ. Attaching himself to a preaching mission being conducted at St Peter's Church by the Dominican Order, he made of himself an honour-guard for the priests taking the Eucharist to the poor and ill. There were many sick in London at this time, due to twin outbreaks of Asiatic cholera and typhoid fever.

It was while attending an old lady suffering from the latter disease that Dormer contracted the fever himself. It swiftly proved fatal. He left a personal estate of $13.95 and a reputation for piety and charity that has endured. His closest London friend, Father Stephen Byrne, a Dominican friar, wrote to Dormer's parents:

In all sincerity of my soul I believe, my dear Lord and Lady, that you have brought into this world and reared to manhood a great saint.

Posterity has not seen fit to challenge the good friar's judgement. It was at Dormer's grave at St Peter's Cemetery in 1912 that the bishop of the Roman Catholic Diocese of London, the Most Reverend Michael Francis Fallon, launched a campaign (which continues to the present) "to glorify God's faithful servant with the crown of sainthood."

As the short career of Henry Edward Dormer shows, charity in 1866 was still largely an individual matter. The only official recognition given to the needs of the poor came from the relief committee of the city council, which dealt out its funds with a niggardly hand. The indigent sick went to the city hospital, a peripatetic institution now located in a rented house on York Street near Thames Street.

The need for a more permanent structure led the council to petition the provincial legislature for a grant. That was in 1863. The request was denied. London was on its own. To the city's everlasting credit, its own came through. On Monday 9 January 1865 the trustees of the London Savings Bank wrapped up its affairs and directed that its surplus of some $15,000 be donated to the city of London and the County of Middlesex on condition that the interest on this sum be applied to the maintenance of a general hospital for the use of both city and county. In typically deliberate London fashion it was another eleven years before the London General Hospital (now known as Victoria Hospital) could claim its inheritance.

Slowly, the humanitarian instincts of Londoners were finding organized outlets. Charity was still being expressed by "Lady Bountifuls" distributing goods to "the deserving poor." However, the Lady Bountifuls, like the recipients of their graciousness, were becoming more numerous and the

1866 Robert Whitehead, English engineer, invents underwater torpedo.

The Labatt Brewery on the left and the family residence on the right. UWO

line between the deserving and the undeserving poor was becoming less well defined. Intemperance as a cause of economic and social distress cut across all social levels.

Since God was still alive and well in London in the 1860s, His flourishing temples were the natural originators both of charity and the means of its distribution. And just as in our own times, women were the leaders. The concerns of the Roman Catholic Church were expressed in its orders of nuns, chiefly the Sisters of St Joseph. The Protestant women, headed by Mrs Isaac Hellmuth, organized a committee to establish a House of Refuge in April 1865.

Men's organizations were less charitable. A proposal brought before the Middlesex county council in 1867 to open a House of Refuge was rejected

1866 *The Black Crook* (play), by Charles M. Barras, opens in New York City.

HRH Prince Arthur, as he appeared in 1869, when he officiated at the opening of Hellmuth Ladies' College. Prince Arthur (1850–1942) was the third son of Queen Victoria. AUTHOR'S COLLECTION

out of hand. The gentleman councillors expressed an opinion that is still held by many opponents of aid to the disadvantaged: to provide such a facility would only encourage them in their dependence.

Nationally, great things were brewing. The third Confederation Conference was meeting in London, England, to hammer out the details of the British North America Act. The new Dominion of Canada came into being on Monday, 1 July 1867. The celebrations were low-key. There were many speeches. Of the new union George Cartier said:

In our confederation there will be Catholics and Protestants, English, French, Irish and Scotch, and each by its efforts and success will add to the prosperity of the Dominion. ... We are of different races, not to quarrel, but to work together for the common welfare.

Brave words, those!

London's mayor that year was an Irish Roman Catholic, Frank Smith. Smith had come to London in 1849 to open a grocery store. It prospered so mightily that he eventually moved to Toronto. He was knighted by Queen Victoria in 1894.

1867 The Emperor Maximilian is executed in Mexico.

Frank Smith's council made no plans for a suitable municipal recognition of the new national holiday. The *Free Press* was critical of the oversight:

This day ... will long be remembered as the day on which a new Dominion will be added to the nations of the world, and it is meet that all should celebrate the day in a befitting manner ... It is to be regretted, however, that no fitting celebration will be made here, but "what's done can't be undone," or vice versa, and consequently it's of very little use to harp upon this matter.

There was no holiday for the students at W.G. Moncrieff's private school. Their teacher was determined that they should remember the day. Fascinated, they watched the Scottish scholar stumping up and down the room on his wooden leg as he repeated, over and over:

"Now, remember this day. I want you all to remember it – the first Dominion Day in Canada. Will you remember it?"

They did. Not a single boy or girl in that room seems ever to have forgotten W.G. Moncrieff and Canada's first Dominion Day.

It was much more difficult to remember to write "London, Ontario" instead of "London, Canada West."

1867 The United States buys Alaska from Russia for $7,200,000 (equal to 2 cents an acre).

CHAPTER SEVEN

A QUIET TIME

Therefore all seasons shall be sweet to thee,
Whether the summer clothe the general earth
With greenness, or the redbreast sit and sing
Betwixt the tufts of snow on the bare branch
Of mossy apple tree, while the night thatch
Smokes in the sun-thaw; whether the eave-drops fall
Heard only in the trances of the blast,
Or if the secret ministry of frost
Shall hang them up in silent icicles,
Quietly shining to the quiet moon.
Samuel Taylor Coleridge, "Frost at Midnight."

The governor-general of the new Dominion was Sir Charles Stanley Monck, fourth Viscount, born, by the good judgement of his parents, in Tipperary County, Ireland, and educated at Trinity College, Dublin. The Moncks had been in Canada all through the difficult years of the American Civil War and had won the good opinion of the Canadas, East and West.

On the other hand, the lieutenant-governor of the new Province of Ontario was virtually unknown to the people, although he had commanded the troops defending the province against the Fenians. He was Major-General Sir Henry William Stisted. His was a temporary appointment. He was gone by 1868.

These two gentlemen represented the Queen. In a London cemetery, in a newly-made grave, lay the remains of a woman who, if her story were true, had a powerful, prior claim to the throne Victoria occupied.

Today, a modest tombstone in Mount Pleasant Cemetery marks the last resting place of the lady who had herself thus immodestly immortalized:

1867 Karl Marx, *Das Kapital*, vol. 1.

In
Memory of
LAVINIA HERMIONE
GERTRUDE AMANDA
GUELPH
Daughter of George 4th
and wife of
CHARLES WETHERBEE
Died
Jan. 25, 1867
Aged 46 Yrs.

London's "Princess" has attracted the attention of historians as well as collectors of the curious and the trivial for more than a century. Despite all, the truth of the matter remains elusive. If her age, as given on the memorial and in the local newspaper obituaries, is correct, then her story was a fabrication. In 1821 her supposed father, George IV, was ill and impotent and her purported mother, Maria Fitzherbert, was sixty-five.

Mrs Wetherbee's death and burial drew little interest from the general public. The big sensation of Confederation year and the twelvemonth following was the case of Slippery Jack.

"Jack" was nameless at first, and his escapades drew little attention. It was apparently to remedy this oversight that he developed the technique that guaranteed him a place in the folklore of London.

The police were baffled.

What they confronted was a series of "break and enters," but with a bizarre difference. Nothing was stolen. Week after week homes were entered illegally, furniture piled in the middle of a room or turned upside down. The intruder made no effort to disguise his presence. He made a lot of noise. It was as if he wanted to be found out.

Soon the unknown tired of furniture-arranging. He turned to more direct methods of announcing his presence, such as wakening the householder by shaking him or shouting in his ear.

This method also palled in time, and he took to tickling feet. They were male feet at first, but he soon found it was much more fun using this method to arouse young women. (The verb "arouse" is here used in its nineteenth-century meaning, as in "to wake up.")

A brilliant young writer on the staff of the *Free Press* coined the nickname by which the night visitor was forever afterwards known – Slippery Jack. The journalist was Robert J. Devlin, known to his readers by the

---

1867 Horatio Alger, *Ragged Dick, or Street Life in New York.*

"Slippery Jack," the mysterious intruder who baffled London police for a year. Sketch by Maridon Miller.

nom de plume Korn Kobb, Junior. In later life he became a prominent Ottawa merchant.

By the turn of the new year Slippery Jack was a London institution, and the city police force was a laughing-stock. Once again a vigilance committee of citizens was formed. The committee had no luck either. Twice Slippery Jack was actually seen, and once an irate householder got hold of the long black duster that Jack habitually wore, but couldn't hold on to the midnight marauder himself.

The series of break-ins came to an abrupt end in September 1868. After several weeks a letter appeared in the London *Advertiser* signed "Slippery Jack." The writer announced that he had made – and won – a wager that he could enter at least one London home a week for a period of one year and escape capture. Out of his winnings he was prepared to pay for any damage caused during the prank.

Long, long afterwards it was revealed that Slippery Jack was a young officer of the Imperial garrison, who later succeeded to a Scottish peerage. He had been assisted by a London cabinet-maker. Both were members of a club of young mischief-makers called the Hellfriars Club.

An era was coming to an end. Slippery Jack, the Hellfriars Club, the annual Bachelors' Ball–all these light-hearted entertainments were enriched by, if not indeed dependent upon, the presence of the British garrison. Now the troops were to be withdrawn. The new Dominion was to be responsible for its own defence.

Economically, it made little difference. The city was no longer dependent on the military payroll. It was London's society that suffered most from the loss. The officers, many of them members of the British aristocracy, had provided a social standard against which many of the local élite showed up rather dismally. Korn Kobb, Junior, portrayed this contrast rather wickedly in a multi-stanza poem, "The Bachelors' Ball," from which these stanzas are excerpted:

> Some London bachelors met one day,
> In a very agreeable sort of way,
>   And, putting their heads together,
> Decided forthwith on giving a ball
> To their very dear friends and acquaintances all,
> On a scale so grand, so exceedingly tall,
> As would make other balls for the future sing small,
>   And astonish the natives rather. ...

1868 Skeleton of Cro-Magnon Man found in France.

Now, of all the parties held in the west,
This one was most essentially blest
  With what's known as good society
First on the list most conspicuously shine
A number of gents in the military line –
Colonels and Majors and Captains Divine,
  And subalterns in great variety.

And home-brewed nobs so very genteel,
Who had drawn a prize in Fortune's wheel,
  If I might be allowed the quotation;
Of these there certainly was no lack,
If I had the time I could mention the pack
Who could easily trace their lineage back
  At least through a whole generation. ...

It was, to be sure, a delicious treat,
To see our gorgeous city elite
  (That's French for aristocracy),
As they walked the quadrille with courtly grace,
Or plied the gallop with quickened pace,
For not the closest observer could grace,
Neither in figure nor yet in face,
  Slightest taint of democracy.

Compared with such sophisticated high-jinks, a country fair was pretty poor competition, but it was the best "the locals" could offer. In 1868 London obtained its own permanent annual agricultural exhibition with the establishment of the Western Fair Association. The former provincial exhibitions, with their yearly change of venue, gradually settled into a home in Toronto, in time becoming the Canadian National Exhibition. In the same way the Queen's Plate, the oldest continuously-run horse race in North America, which had previously been held in a number of communities, including London, became permanently anchored in Toronto. London's Newmarket race track, off the Hamilton Road, became lost to memory.

Such changes as these, which gradually, almost imperceptibly, centralized the province's social and economic powers in Toronto, led to a corresponding creeping parochialism in the smaller cities and towns. The process continues to this day; Torontonians find it difficult to conceive of life

---

1868 Fyodor Dostoyevsky, *The Idiot.*

west of Mississauga or east of Oshawa, while nearly everyone hates Toronto, a.k.a. Hogtown.

The process still had some way to go in 1869. London was still on the major social circuit, thanks in part to the Church of England Establishment. Huron College and Hellmuth Boys' College ranked among the most important educational institutions in the province. Now their founder added another school to the list – Hellmuth Ladies' College. The new school was the answer to a question put to Dr Hellmuth by a British educator, Mrs Mary Mills. "Why." asked Mrs Mills, "should so many girls of good social position have to go to Convent Schools? Why cannot the Church of England start a school for them?"

"It can," Hellmuth replied, "if you will come and take charge."

Mrs Mills accepted the challenge.

The new college was inaugurated on Thursday, 23 September 1869, by HRH Prince Arthur, aged nineteen, third son of Queen Victoria and Prince Albert. The prince, a lieutenant in the Royal Engineers, was stationed in Montreal at the time. It was his first visit to London. More than forty years later, when he was the first Duke of Connaught and tenth governor-general of Canada, he again came to London, to open a tuberculosis sanitorium.

The mayor who welcomed Prince Arthur to London was not the mayor who assumed the office in January of that year. John Christie, who had served as an alderman for several years, occupied the office of mayor for one month, and then, according to a contemporary account, "he got tired of the office and resigned." The council appointed as his successor Simpson H. Graydon, the local lawyer and former Irish sportsman.

As well as entertaining British royalty London hosted, that same year, a representative of the American aristocracy. Cornelius Vanderbilt, the transportation czar, was enticed to London by the claims made for a sulphur-water spa that had been opened at the forks of the Thames. The London Sulphur Baths quickly gained an international reputation for the allegedly rejuvenating powers of the heated water. Vanderbilt believed the rather extravagant claims made for the facility. He decided to take the cure before his December-May marriage to an eighteen-year-old American socialite. Never one to waste time, he arranged to marry the girl at London's Tecumseh House Hotel immediately after "taking the waters." The marriage was performed by the Reverend William Briggs, founder of the Methodist publishing house that became the Ryerson Press (now absorbed by McGraw-Hill). History does not record the success of the London treatment in restoring the "Commodore's" virility, but he survived another eight years, dying in 1877 at the age of eighty-three.

1869 Hudson's Bay Company transfers its territory to the Dominion of Canada.

The Tecumseh House Hotel, completed in time for the visit of the Prince of Wales (later Edward VII) in 1860. From H.R. Page's *Middlesex County Atlas* (1878). UWO

Just up the Dundas Street hill from the spa, in front of the old court-house, a few months previously, a life had been cut short at the hands of the common hangman in the presence of a large concourse of people, drawn from the city and the surrounding countryside. It was to be the last public execcution in the county. More than 8,000 sightseers came to see Thomas Jones of Delaware "topped off." He had capped a long criminal career by murdering his niece Mary Jones.

1869 Louisa Mary Alcott, *Little Women.*

Tradition has it that the timbers used in erecting the gallows for Jones were the same pieces of wood employed in the execution of the six tragic victims of the Rebellion of 1837 and its aftermath. The clergyman who had attended those young men himself died on Saturday, 2 September 1871. Bishop Benjamin Cronyn was immediately succeeded by the coadjutor bishop of Huron, Dr Isaac Hellmuth.

A hanging that affected Londoners deeply was carried out within the jail yard on Thursday, 20 June 1872. Mrs Phoebe Campbell was the first, and only, woman to be executed in Middlesex County. She had murdered her husband. A solemn community mourned the occasion as the sexton tolled the great bell in the tower of St Paul's Cathedral.

The Campbell case, traumatic as it was to Victorian sensitivities, was overshadowed by a criminal case with dangerous international ramifications.

On the Queen's Birthday, Friday, 24 May 1872, a man known as James Simpson, a newcomer to the city, attended a cricket match on the former barracks grounds, now vacated by the military. After the game he was shadowed by two men who followed him to his rooming house on Wellington Street, near the Hellmuth Boys' College. During the next few days Simpson's "tails" made a careful study of his habits.

In the late afternoon of Tuesday, 4 June, a hansom cab driven by Robert T. Bates drove up alongside James Simpson as he strolled on the grounds of the college. His two passengers leaped out of the cab, accosted Simpson, applied chloroform to his face, and dumped him into the cab, which then raced off to the Great Western Railway station. The sole witness of the incident was a nine-year-old-girl, Mary Alice Overholt.

At the station Simpson's captors bundled him aboard a westbound train. At Windsor their prisoner was identified for the authorities as a Major Avery, for whom they had a legitimate warrant for arrest on a charge of murder. The man's condition (still under the influence of drugs) was explained to the train crew as a case of insanity.

Once safely across the border in Detroit, the chief kidnapper, an American detective named Hester or Hunter, arrested Simpson legally under his real name. He was Dr James Rufus Bratton of South Carolina. A former surgeon in the Confederate Army, he has wanted by the authorities in his native state as a suspect in the murder of a black man during a raid by the Ku Klux Klan. The charge was never proceeded with. Dr Bratton was later awarded damages for wrongful arrest and imprisonment.

Within a few hours of Bratton's abduction, a fellow-South Carolinan,

1870 Red River Rebellion collapses. Manitoba becomes a province of Canada.

Looking south from the roof of Hellmuth Boys' College, about 1870. In the foreground is the intersection of St James and Wellington streets, near where Dr James
Rufus Bratton was kidnapped in 1872. In the background are Lake Horn, the
Crystal Palace on the fairgrounds, several of the buildings of the military barracks,
the tower of St Paul's Cathedral, and the chimney of Hyman's Tannery. UWO

Gabriel Manigault, informed London authorities of the incident. An investigation was promptly launched by Charles Hutchinson, clerk of the peace
for Middlesex County. To everyone's astonishment the trail led swiftly
and directly to Hutchinson's own department. On Tuesday, 11 June,
Gabriel Manigault swore out information in city police court against Isaac
Bell Cornwall, deputy clerk of the peace, that on the fourth day of June,
Cornwall "without lawful authority, did forcibly kidnap one Rufus Bratton

1872 Jules Verne, *Around the World in 80 Days.*

within Canada, to wit, at the said city of London, with intent to cause the said Rufus Bratton to be unlawfully sent or transported out of Canada against his will."

Several witnesses, including Mary Alice Overholt, Bratton's landlady Mrs Sarah Hill, the cabbie, Robert Bates, Gabriel Manigault, and Isaac Cornwall himself were examined by Police Magistrate Lawrence Lawrason, after which Cornwall was committed for trial at the next following court of assizes.

The seriousness of the case was at once recognized by the Canadian government. It was, in fact, the first truly important challenge to the sovereignty of the new Dominion. The prime minister, Sir John Alexander Macdonald, was asked in the House of Commons what reaction the government intended. Sir John had taken all appropriate steps. Canada did not yet have jurisdiction over its foreign affairs. The British ambassador in Washington and the Colonial Office in London, England, had been informed. The next move was up to them.

Feelings ran high throughout the country. Canada had been grossly insulted. Reaction in the press ranged from the restrained to the hysterical. George Brown's Toronto *Globe* put it as well as any:

It is the duty of the government to act promptly and decidedly in this matter, and demand that the stranger taken with violence from under the protection of the British flag, be returned unharmed, and rendered secure from further molestation. If he has been guilty of an extraditable offence there is a proper and lawful way of obtaining his arrest and removal. ... Official outrages of the above nature must not be tolerated if we desire to maintain the national honour unsullied.

The British government was less restrained. The message conveyed to the administration of President Ulysses Simpson Grant (né Hiram Ulysses Grant) was curt. It demanded that Dr Bratton be returned forthwith to British jurisdiction.

If the fire-breathing Republican expansionist William Henry Seward had still been secretary of state, the challenge could well have led to war. It was Seward who had arranged the purchase of Alaska and the Virgin Islands, pushed for the annexation of Hawaii, and had urged Lincoln to invade and conquer Canada. However, Seward was out of office, the problems of the Reconstruction period in the South were daunting, the United States and Great Britain had recently signed a fence-mending treaty, the

---

1872 Ballot Act in Britain makes voting secret for the first time.

nation was heartily sick of war – and it was a presidential election year.

The politically-dangerous international incident was settled in an amazingly short time. Washington "discovered" that the doctor was in the custody of a United States marshal in North Carolina. Assurance was at once given Ottawa that "our Government will send him back to Canada without delay, and indemnify him for the arrest."

The whole affair was laid to rest on Wednesday, 17 July. Isaac Bell Cornwall was found guilty of kidnapping and sentenced to three years' imprisonment. From first to last the incident occupied only one day more than six weeks.

After his triumphant return to Canada, Dr Bratton, under his proper name, practised medicine in London for some years. He eventually went back to South Carolina, where he died in September 1897 at the age of seventy-six.

With the amicable solution of the Bratton case, London and its citizens settled into the peaceful ambience of what a Canadian writer has called "The Age of Innocence." It is doubtful whether "innocence" is the *mot juste* for a period that was marked rather by a quiet sophistication in manners, art, and dress.

In fashion, women's dress achieved a quiet elegance, free of the extreme exuberance of the late Victorian age still to come, and free of the often frivolous experiments of the 1860s. Gone were the ridiculous hoopskirts and the inelegant bloomers of the early Railway Age; still to come were the ballooning skirts and sleeves and the caboose-like bustles of the 1880s.

It is in the art of the period that the reason for this charming *entr'acte* in the affairs of the western world may be most clearly discerned. The soft summer skies of the great European painters tell the story. The weather of the 1870s was probably as bland as any within the range of the last one thousand years. The summers were gentle, the winters kind, the wine vintages exceptional.

During this time London put away its frontier-town image forever. A slow metamorphosis began to alter the physical appearance of the city. It started with the military reserve, which was now the property of the municipality. The barracks buildings were sold and removed from the site. A far-sighted city council resisted the blandishments of nineteenth-century real-estate developers and reserved 15.5 acres (6.2 hectares) of the site for a public park. In August 1874, the governor-general, Frederick Temple Blackwood, Lord Dufferin, named the park after his Queen. In return, the London council changed the name of the street that formed the southern boundary of the park from Bond Street to Dufferin Avenue. The

1872 The *Mary Celeste* found abandoned in Atlantic Ocean; all aboard ship are missing.

Covent Garden Market in the late 1860s. UWO

governor-general was an Irish peer, which suited London's predominantly Irish establishment very well indeed.

Victoria Park, situated in the very heart of the city's core area, has played a big role in shaping London's character. It is a miniature version of New York City's Central Park. In a special issue of the London *Advertiser* published in October 1888, an account of the park's early years provides some amusing sidelights:

1872 Claude Monet, *Impression: Sunrise.*

Frederick Temple Blackwood (1826–1902), first Marquess of Dufferin, governor-general of Canada 1872–1878. UWO

When the park was laid out London was not as large as it is now, nor had its residents such metropolitan ideas. They were at that time very fond of allowing their cows, horses, pigs and geese to roam at large, destroying what they pleased. Therefore the Council in its wisdom had a high picket fence put up around the park. In time this fence decayed and became an eyesore. For years the *Advertiser* called for its removal and advised the putting down of straight walks from corner to corner, to stop people cutting pathways through the grass. However, the *Advertiser's* views were too far ahead of those of the Council to prevail at once, but in the end the suggestion had to be acted upon. ... The removal of the fences ... had the effect of raising the value of property in the neighbourhood very considerably. When the trees on it get a little larger, there will probably not be another spot like it in the Province.

It was the trees that made the difference, finally.

For forty-five years Londoners had worked hard to eliminate all the trees on the site. They did their work well. By 1871, as all the surviving photographs indicate, the city had an oddly naked appearance. The lack of greenery showed off the major public buildings to great advantage, but the overall impression was one of raw newness and impermanence.

1872 Yellowstone area becomes first national park in the United States.

The London Tecumsehs v. the Syracuse Stars. International baseball came to London in the 1870s. The field is Tecumseh (now Labatt) Park. UWO

A campaign launched by public-spirited citizens led to a decision by the city council of 1871 to buy 15,000 trees, at 25 cents each, to plant along the city streets and in Victoria Park. The success of this pioneer venture in landscaping surpassed all expectations. It has led to a widespread misunderstanding of the origin of the city's nickname, the Forest City. It was so called not because of its tree-lined streets, but because for many years it inhabited a cleared space in the encompassing forest. A more descriptive, if less elegant, cognomen was "London-in-the-Bush."

As the carefully-tended saplings grew, so did other civilized amenities. The city could boast of an important cadre of artists, two of whom — William Lees Judson and Paul Peel — later achieved international distinction. The theatre, both amateur and professional, persisted as always to scale the peaks and explore the valleys of success and failure. There was a small but active musical community centred largely on the churches and the two Hellmuth colleges. St John Hyttenrauch, formerly of the Danish

1872 Lewis Carroll, *Through the Looking-Glass.*

Royal Symphony, and George Sippi, an Irish descendant of an old Italian family, were both connected with the musical life of St Paul's Cathedral.

Londoners "of the better sort," as the newspapers of the day referred to the upper-middle class, played whist indoors and cricket out. Baseball was still considered a more plebian sport, but it was catching on rapidly with all classes as local teams like the London Tecumsehs gained a measure of national and even international renown.

"The better sort" travelled to their offices and businesses in their own carriages and behind their own horses. The upkeep of stables, vehicles, and steeds represented a substantial yearly outlay. Those who could not afford such an establishment either employed the city's fleet of hansom cabs or, at need, rented a horse and carriage from one of the city's many livery stables.

In the mid-1870s still another choice became available when the London Street Railway Company began the operation of its three horse-drawn trams on a one-mile route along Dundas Street from Richmond to Adelaide streets. The leading figure in the new company and its president for its first twenty years was Verschoyle Cronyn, son of the late bishop of Huron.

Meanwhile the second bishop of Huron, Isaac Hellmuth, had launched still another of his grand projects. This time it was to be a new cathedral to replace St Paul's. It was to be called the Cathedral of the Holy Trinity and was to be built on a large lot at the southeast corner of Richmond and Piccadilly streets. The first building to be erected on the site, intended to be the chapter house of the new cathedral, was opened with due ceremony on Sunday, 2 November 1873. For the next fourteen years this fine stone building served as the cathedral (technically, the pro-cathedral) of the diocese. It was levelled to the ground in 1982 to make way for a parking lot to serve a neighbouring whited sepulchre, a former shoe factory converted into a shopping centre.

The premier Anglican family, the Cronyns, continued to play an active role in the city's affairs. Verschoyle Cronyn's younger brother Benjamin was elected mayor in 1874 and re-elected the following year. In his two years in office the London Life Insurance Company was incorporated, the city's general hospital was finally opened, the extraordinarily-influential Women's Christian Association was founded, and Blackfriars Bridge was erected. All four still serve their community faithfully and well.

The bridge, which crosses the north branch of the Thames River at the northern end of Ridout Street, is a living tribute to nineteenth-century structural technology and artistry. It is a single-span truss bridge, which

---

1873 Andrew Hallidie invents cable car for use on the hills of San Francisco.

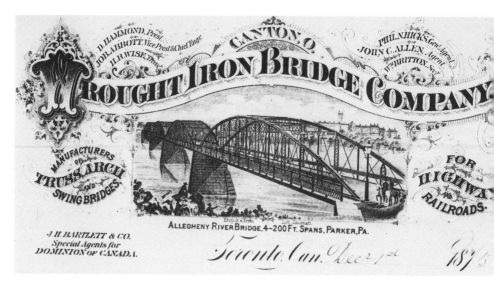

The Wrought Iron Bridge Company of Canton, Ohio, produced prefabricated iron bridges. London's Blackfriars Bridge, over the north branch of the Thames River, is a surviving example. UWO

was actually assembled from a do-it-yourself kit! The Wrought Iron Bridge Company of Canton, Ohio, carried on a mail-order business, sending out, to prospective customers, catalogues detailing the various kinds of bridges available. The pieces for Blackfriars Bridge were shipped to London by railway, accompanied by a skilled foreman to supervise the construction. Fragile in appearance, with simple, effective lines, it is a memorial to the superb artistic judgement of the 1870s.

The great international showcase of the decade was the Philadelphia Centennial Exposition, celebrating the one hundredth anniversary of the Declaration of Independence of the United States of America. Among the scientific displays, which were the main feature of the exhibition, were demonstrations of the electric arc light and the telephone. Both involved men with strong southwestern Ontario connections – Thomas Alva Edison (the electric light) and Alexander Graham Bell (the telephone). One visitor to the Exposition, Dom Pedro II, the last emperor of Brazil, was especially impressed by Bell's telephone and subsequently travelled to Canada to visit Bell at his Brantford home. He apparently also visited London at that time. Whether this visit had anything to do with the subsequently

1877 Queen Victoria proclaimed Empress of India.

high Latin American registration in women's colleges in London and St Thomas is a matter for speculation.

Of more real and lasting importance to Londoners than the peregrinations of Brazilian royalty was the introduction of free mail delivery. The mail service was one more indication of the degree to which London had become a fully modern city, ready to take its place among Canada's metropolitan centres.

This feeling was reinforced in 1877 with the opening of the London Collegiate Institute, a secondary school based on the academic principles that Bishop Hellmuth had introduced. In that same year another remarkable man, Dr Richard Maurice Bucke, took over the administration of the London Insane Asylum, practically next door to the farm on which he had grown up, east of the city. This institution, the largest in Ontario dealing with mental illness, had been established in 1870.

Under Bucke's direction new forms of treatment were introduced at the Asylum. All unnecessary and cruel restraints were done away with, and sports and entertainment programs were introduced. It is pleasant

McClary Manufacturing Company's stoves carried the name of London around the world. UWO

to be able to report that the new, enlightened approach received the support of London's social Establishment. The concerts and sports days soon attracted the attention and attendance of the élite.

However, as far as the artisan class was concerned, the Asylum was for lunatics and its patients became the butt of innumerable cruel jokes. A much more important institution for the working class was the Young Men's Christian Association. The YMCA, established in London in 1856, had campaigned stoutly for a shorter working day and a five-and-a-half-day week. Some members had also been prominent in promoting a summer holiday for all, which in time became our present Civic Holiday. On the first Monday in August the streets were deserted while hundreds took advantage of special railway excursion rates to Toronto and Detroit. These excursions were generally organized by the volunteer fire departments, often on a reciprocal arrangement.

In this informal manner Londoners added two terms to the common language pool of Canada and the United States – Civic Holiday and the expression, "visiting firemen."

Among the "visiting firemen" of those days was the American poet Walt Whitman. Whitman first met Dr Bucke, who was to become his fast friend, physician, and literary executor, in that busy year, 1877.

While Whitman and Bucke were getting acquainted, that other doctor of men's minds, Isaac Hellmuth, was preparing to launch the greatest of all his achievements in education, the founding of the University of Western Ontario. The university was incorporated by act of parliament in March, 1878, as "the Western University of London, Ontario." Both the founding title and its present name serve to mask the pioneer nature of the institution and the area it served. A *Free Press* editorial in December 1876 commented on the need to "institute a seat of learning to which the young men of the West would naturally incline."

Many of the "young men of the West" were at this time migrating to the great plains, then referred to as the "Far West." Among the number, although no longer a young man, was the city's former mayor, Francis Evans Cornish. In 1874 he became the first mayor of the city of Winnipeg. He died four years later.

The decade of the 1870s saw many of the city's leading pioneers leave the scene. George Jervis Goodhue, the first president of the village board of police (1840), died in 1870; Simeon Morrill, the first mayor of the town (1848), died in 1871; and Marcus Holmes, the last mayor of the town (1854), followed in 1872.

These men had seen London grow from a collection of log and frame buildings clustered around the courthouse to a busy city of nearly 20,000.

1878 Electric street lighting introduced in London, England.

Richmond Street, looking south from the Queens Avenue inntersection, about 1875. The three buildings in the right foreground – the Commercial Bank, the London Post Office, and the Albion Block – are now gone. The next row of buildings, from Carling to Dundas streets, still stand. From the *Canadian Illustrated News*. UWO

Everything had changed, including the courthouse. For twenty years the structure had been condemned by successive grand juries as being inadequate to the needs of the expanding community. At last, in 1878, the building was altered and remodeled to answer the complaints.

The alterations were carried out with due respect for the 1829 plans, but when they were completed the courthouse had been doubled in size, a new tower dominated the front of the building, and any resemblance to Colonel Thomas Talbot's ancestral home, Malahide Castle, had been obliterated.

It will be recalled that the courthouse had initially been planned to face the River Thames, the cause of its being. The 1878 front elevation, with its tower facing Ridout Street, declared what had been true for a long time: the future of the city lay to the east, not the west.

The city had symbolically turned its back on the river.

The river would soon have its revenge.

1879 Leon Trotsky (Lev Davidovich Bronstein) born 7 November.

CHAPTER EIGHT

A BAD TIME

Who slew all these, whose has laid them so low?
From the thousands around us in sorrow and woe
The cry is ascending, from whence came the blow?
  Who slew all these; who slew them?

Who slew all these? Was it ravaging war
That hurl'd forth the dead from his thundering car,
Gory and ghastly in death, as they are?
  Who slew all these; who slew them?

Who slew all these? Did the pestilence sweep
O'er the great Forest City to lull to sleep —
In but one short hour to awake and weep?
  Who slew all these; who slew them?
Archibald McKillop, London, Ont., 26 May 1881.
(quoted in *The Victoria Day Disaster* by Kenneth D. McTaggart, 1978.

In the summer of 1879 the village of London East served notice on the
corporation of St Paul's Church. Burials in St Paul's Cemetery on Dundas
Street East within the village limits were to be prohibited and the cemetery
to be "closed forthwith."

The church immediately set about finding a new site. The search was
a success. A beautiful riverside location was secured west of the city, and
Woodland Cemetery came into being.

Once the fifty-six-acre (22.4-hectare) plot had been cleared and land-
scaped, the task began of moving the bodies and the memorials. Londoners then witnessed one of the most bizarre events in the community's
history. The work took several weeks. Some of the bodies were being

---

1879 A British churchman, W.L. Blackley, proposes a scheme for old-age pensions.

moved for a second or, in a few cases, a third time: from the original graveyard opposite the courthouse to the churchyard of St Paul's; from St Paul's to the Dundas Street site; and finally to Woodland Cemetery.

Most of the coffins were transferred by wagon, but at one stage a fleet of local hansom cabs was pressed into service. The resulting uproar from the cab-using public filled the editorial columns of the city's newspapers for weeks. The cab business fell off sharply. A generation accustomed to the dread effects of such epidemic diseases as Asiatic cholera, typhus, and smallpox feared contagion from long-dead victims of those scourges.

With the advantage of hindsight, we may see this macabre procession of sightless cab passengers as a sinister harbinger of the series of big and little disasters that plagued the city and its neighbourhood in the 1880s. We might, if we so wished, look further abroad for signs of the coming woe. It was in 1880 that James Garfield, the Republican senator from Ohio, was elected twentieth president of the United States. He was assassinated the following year after serving for only 199 days. It was in 1880 also that the American painter George Inness exhibited his morbidly popular painting "The Coming Storm," full of ominous clouds.

The south side of Queen's Avenue, near Clarence Street, in the 1880s. UWO

The local horrors of the 1880s were ushered in on Wednesday, 4 February 1880, by the massacre of five members of the Donnelly family, farmers in Biddulph Township north of London, by a so-called "vigilance committee" of their neighbours.

Although these shocking murders were committed outside the city, it is impossible to pass over the event without recording something of its effects on the people of London. As the principal market town of the county and the terminal of a busy stagecoach line from the north, London knew both the victims and the perpetrators of the crime.

Sensation piled on sensation as the newspaper press of the continent converged on the little village of Lucan. The outline emerged, quite soon, of a long-standing feud with social, political, and religious ramifications, which had originated in Tipperary County, Ireland. The London police force, under its new and able chief, W.T.T. Williams, was called in to conduct the investigation. Two eye-witnesses identified six men who were arrested, charged, and tried at the London assizes. A "hung jury" resulted in a second trial, at which all six were acquitted at the direction of the presiding justice. The case left a legacy of bitterness that is still, more than a century later, capable of causing acrimonious debate.

A final, sensational disclosure involving the Lucan parish priest was overshadowed (to the relief of many) by the greatest tragedy in London's history – the sinking of the pleasure steamer *Victoria* in the Thames River on Tuesday, 24 May 1881.

The day dawned bright and clear, "perfect weather for the holiday," Ken McTaggart writes:

One jubilant holidayer startled most of his neighbourhood by touching off a small signal cannon on his front lawn. The reverberating boom echoed across the area announcing the beginning of celebrations. Little boys scrambled for their supplies of firecrackers. One popular sized package selling for five cents on the previous Saturday, cost seven cents on Tuesday. Hundreds of Londoners stayed at home for the holiday, many others went on picnics or excursions. Old buses and even stages had to be brought out in order to move the crowds. Many of the people headed for the river and the new popular picnic area called "Springbank." They would either take the boat cruise or row boats down the river, or walk. The more affluent rode horse and carriage. Many people took time to visit the graves of relatives or friends at Woodland Cemetery. ... Farm people came to London for the day and a trip on the river.

1881   Fire in Vienna, Austria, burns the Ring Theatre, leaving more than 600 people dead.

The Grigg House, at the northwest corner of Richmond and York streets. Built in 1879, it is now the Clifton Arms Hotel. UWO

Those who chose the river could select one of the three river steamers operated by the Thames River Navigation Company. These vessels – the *Forest City, Princess Louise,* and the *Victoria* – made several trips each daily from the dock at the forks in front of the Sulphur Springs Health Spa to the pavilion in Springbank Park at a cost of 15 cents per round trip.

At 5:25 pm the SS *Victoria* pulled away from her Springbank dock with an impatient load of 600 to 800 holiday-makers anxious to get home for the evening meal. This was roughly three times the safe capacity of the forty-three-ton vessel (gross weight). The draught of the hull was only sixteen inches because of the many shallow places in the river. She was seventy feet long, with a beam of twenty-two feet. There were two decks. By modern standards the vessel was probably dangerously top-heavy.

The last voyage of the *Victoria* ended just west of the railway bridge over the Coves, where she capsized, throwing her human cargo into the

1881 A violent storm and tidal wave in China and Indochina kill some 300,000 people.

water. Many victims were crushed to death when the decks and machinery fell onto them.

Many eye-witness accounts of the death of the *Victoria* have been recorded. One of the most graphic is that of Lambert Payne, a reporter on the staff of the London *Free Press*. Payne, who had been the first reporter on the scene of the Donnelly murders, was also one of the first to reach the wreck on the river. Years later he recalled in vivid detail his part in the events of London's blackest day:

I was having an after supper smoke in my lodging on Maple Street and half an hour later I heard a man shouting on the street. I went to the door and saw that it was Mr James Stewart, a stove merchant on Richmond street, who lived a few doors farther eastward on Maple street. He was shouting: I'm saved! I'm saved!" I tried to find out from him what had happened; but he was too frantic to even notice me. I caught, however, the words "all drowned," and that gave me a clue.

In the office we had often talked about the possibility of a tragedy some day on the river. In particular, Jack Dewar shared my suspicion that the *Victoria* was unsafe. So when Mr Stewart had said "all drowned," I did not hesitate. I grabbed my hat and ran. At the foot of Dundas street I got definite word that the *Victoria* had sunk just below the Cove bridge. I was in good training, and was soon on the spot. As I neared the wreck I met Mr Eckhart, principal of the London East School. He had been on the steamer, and said at least a hundred had been drowned.

It was now dark, and two large bonfires were blazing on the bank. These fires cast a weird light over the scene – a scene which will never be blotted from my mind while memory lasts. It was unreal. It took on the character of a nightmare. Scores of men were breaking up the two decks of the steamer, which lay like a blanket over the surface of the water. The drownings had all taken place within 30 or 40 feet of the shore – most of them within 15. The sister vessel, the *Princess Louise,* was drawn up alongside, and to her deck the dead were being carried. I pulled myself together and began getting names.

At midnight the *Princess Louise* left the scene of the disaster with her cargo of dead, and 20 minutes later was at her dock. I made the count on the way up to the city, and there were 152 bodies. These were laid out on the lawn at the old Sulphur Springs bathhouse. ...

At four in the morning, without having thought of either food or sleep, I returned to the river. I joined in the search for bodies, and before 10 o'clock my pike pole had brought up more than a score. Two of them, I remember, were children of my associate at *The Advertiser* Charlie Matthews. I got back to

---

1881 Czar Alexander II of Russia is assassinated by a member of a terrorist organization.

the office at 12 and wrote a couple of columns for the evening edition. Then I practically collapsed from sheer exhaustion. Mr Blackburn ordered me home for sleep. But the outrage on nature had been too great. I couldn't sleep. I simply lay staring at the ceiling. Every nerve in my being jangled. To make matters worse, my feet began to swell from their prolonged wetting. It seemed to me I lay tossing for hours; yet oblivion finally came. For the ensuing two days I had to go about in slippers.

A completely accurate tally of the number of fatalities has never been made. Initial estimates ranged as high as 230, but this was an obvious exaggeration. A total of 182 interments were made in London-and-district cemeteries and this is probably as close as one can now come to the truth. Of these burials, a majority – about 125 – were of women and children under the age of sixteen. Many of the eighty-five female victims drowned as a result of being pulled under the water by their heavy clothing.

As usual, the disaster brought out the good, the bad, and the ugly. The city prefers to remember the good deeds done, of which there were many; but memory chooses to overlook some other reactions. There was the farmer who ordered the first survivors to reach the shore to get off his land. Looters worked through the night, stealing watches, wallets, and jewelry from the bodies in spite of police efforts to stop the ghoulish trade. Drivers of hearses, hacks, and wagons turned profiteer, charging two or three times the regular price to return the bodies of victims to their homes. In this connection, a macabre story is told about one team who found nobody at home at the victim's residence. They propped the corpse up on a chair on the porch, with a brief note attached.

The funerals went on for a week. There was a shortage of children's coffins. Priests and ministers were worked off their feet. Nearly every home in London was affected by the loss of a family member, a relative, a friend, or a near-neighbour.

There was an inquest. The blame was neatly and proportionately divided among – first, the passengers themselves for crowding the boat beyond its capacity; second, the owners and crew for allowing the craft to be overloaded; and third, the shipping inspector for certifying as seaworthy a refitted, previously-condemned hull, without ever having seen the completed job. The captain and the owner were charged, tried, and acquitted.

As in the case of the Donnelly murders, the *Victoria* disaster captured the attention of the newspaper press of the continent. The city swarmed with reporters from the major dailies and the American and British news

1881 Helen Ridley Young and Ira David Sankey, "I Am Coming" (hymn).

services. Queen Victoria sent condolences. The chap-book writers, minor poets, and balladeers ground out yards of lugubrious verse and prose. A sample of the better verse heads this chapter.

In time, the tide of sensationalism ebbed, and London was allowed slowly to drift back into its normal state of conservative indecision. But not for long.

The year 1882 produced two events of more than passing interest. In May, the first meeting in Canada of the Salvation Army was held on the market square. A monument today marks the approximate spot. Then came the shocking news of the suicide of the city's popular treasurer John Brown.

Brown, a native of Ireland, had arrived in London in 1832, at the age of twenty-five. He soon became involved in Masonic matters. For nearly a half-century he devoted much time, energy, and money to the Order's affairs. About the same time he was appointed treasurer of the town and continued in that office for the city of London until his death.

Several times during Brown's thirty-year tenure in office rumours had surfaced concerning irregularities in the city's bookkeeping, but in each instance the matter was cleared up. Finally, however, an official audit in 1882 revealed a startling shortage in the city's coffers of nearly $70,000 – a very large amount for the times. It appeared that for almost the entire three decades of his city service Brown had been dipping his hand into the treasury. No legal action was taken following the discovery. Like a true Irish gentleman, Brown shot himself, and that was that.

It was a big funeral. Brown had been gregarious and generous. Many had profited from his generosity with the citizens' own money. There was little bitterness about his defalcations; the treasurer had not benefited to any great extent personally from his steady drain on the city's exchequer. In fact, viewed as an exercise in community compassion, that funeral was one of London's better moments.

The year 1883 was marked by some very odd meteorological phenomena. April saw an outburst of aerial anomalies. On Sunday, 15 April a number of irregularly-shaped bodies (flying saucers?) were seen crossing the face of the sun at Marseilles, France. The same thing occurred at the same place on Monday, 23 April. Peculiar atmospheric effects were noted in Trinidad and the western United States.

Locally the spring weather was erratic, but that was normal for the area. Summer brought the usual number of thunderstorms. Be it noted here, London is the thunderstorm capital of Canada, with an average of thirty-four days of such weather per annum.

1882 Knights of Columbus, a fraternal organization of Catholic men founded.

Jack Addie and Joe Ludgate, who began the work of the Salvation Army in Canada on London's market square in 1882. From *"What God Hath Wrought": A History of the Salvation Army in Canada* (Toronto: Salvation Army, 1952).

Even in view of this record, the storm of Wednesday, 11 July 1883, was phenomenal. The rain came down in torrents for eight hours straight, ending with a shattering cloudburst effect.

The electrical display that highlighted the storm was awesome. Toward its close, a bolt of lightning struck the Imperial Oil Company refinery in London East, completely destroying the plant. It was a stubborn blaze. It was after one o'clock when the London firemen finally got the fire under control.

William Thompson, a reporter for the London *Advertiser* covered the fire. The storm suddenly stopped, the stars came out, the air was rain-washed and sweet. Thompson walked back to his office, relishing the night. It was nearly two o'clock when he reached the corner of Dundas and Richmond streets. He was in no hurry. The *Advertiser* was an afternoon paper. He had plenty of time to write his copy. He decided to see if the downpour had had any effect on the flow of the river. William Thompson was very conscious of the Thames. Two years before he had been one of the lucky ones to escape drowning in the capsizing of the *Victoria*. (Other members of the paper's staff had not been so fortunate; out of nine staffers and family members on that fatal cruise, five had died.)

1883 The first skyscraper, a ten-storey building, erected in Chicago.

LONDON EAST POST OFFICE

AND

TELEGRAPH OFFICE

TELEGRAMS SENT TO ALL PARTS OF THE WORLD.

Lilley's Corners, London East.

The Savings Bank and Money Order Office open daily from 7 a.m. to 7 p.m.

Money Orders issued and paid on and from any Money Order office in the Dominion, England, Ireland, Scotland, and the United States.

Savings Bank Deposits received from one dollar up. Four per cent. allowed.

Pass Books and every information given free, on applying.

All business done at our office strictly confidential.

CHARLES LILLEY,
POSTMASTER.

The village of London East was incorporated 1 January 1875. It was amalgamated with the city of London in 1885. UWO

As he approached the river, Thompson heard a peculiar sound to the north – a low-pitched roar. As the sound grew louder he broke into a run.

At the Dundas Street bridge he halted and looked across the water at the village of London West. The air was clear and the roofs of houses stood out in sharp detail against the sky. Few lights showed. Most of the suburb's one thousand residents were asleep.

The noise to the north became deafening. Then Thompson saw what had happened. The tortured bed of the north branch of the river had proved unable to contain the great mass of water poured into it. As he watched, the river jumped its banks north of Oxford Street and crashed down in a solid wall of water on the sleeping village.

Within minutes Thompson saw London West converted into a whirling gully of wildly-tossing water, broken houses, drowning animals, and screaming human beings. Wrenching his eyes from the scene, the reporter turned and ran back up Dundas Street, yelling the news through the deserted, gas-lit streets:

"Flood! London West is flooded! Help!"

Inside of a half-hour, the streets bordering on the river, and the banks of the river themselves, were black with people, launching boats, helping survivors, hauling up bodies, and getting in one another's way.

The first light of morning revealed a slime-coated, tangled mass of wreckage in what had been the path of the runaway river from the Oxford Street bridge to the main branch of the Thames. Smaller buildings, of which there were a great number, for this was a modest, workingman's suburb, had been reduced to matchwood. Larger structures were twisted, gouged, and scarred as though they had been the toys of a demented giant.

William Thompson and the *Advertiser* had got the newspaper "scoop." However, it was Lambert Payne and the *Free Press* that got the "colour story." Payne, covering his third disaster in four years, was appalled by what he saw. At one place a mother, standing at an upper window, had passed down her baby to willing hands below, only to see it snatched out of the rescuers' hands by a runaway barn and ground to death against the sidewall of its parents' home. There, against the wall near the window, was the crimson imprint of the child's body.

Lambert Payne turned away, sick at heart.

The scene was chaotic. Wreckage and bodies were strewn over a large area. One thing was certain. The residents of London West had been fortunate. In spite of the fact that the flash flood had struck at an hour

---

1883 Clement Attlee and Benito Mussolini born.

when most people were in bed, the death toll had been remarkably low. The best estimate was seventeen or eighteen.

It took some time for the lesson of the July flood to register with the people of London and the Thames River basin – something over sixty years, in fact. Floods on the Thames have occurred at every season of the year – spring, summer, fall, and winter. Since the first really damaging flood in 1852, the cause has been constant. The removal of the forest cover throughout its 163-mile (262-kilometre) length has left the stream susceptible to uncontrolled run-off. That was precisely what happened in 1883 when the denuded soil of the watershed had nothing on it to hold back the immense amount of water suddenly dumped upon it.

In August 1883, the volcano Krakatoa, in Java, blew up, sending shock waves around the world, and thousands of tons of dust into the stratosphere to change the world's weather patterns for several months and to leave a legacy of green suns, blue moons, and spectacular sunsets.

The year also marked the eclipse of one of the brightest careers in Canadian education. The Right Reverend Dr Isaac Hellmuth submitted his resignation as bishop of the Diocese of Huron in the summer of 1883. He cited as the principal cause of his surprise decision the grave illness of his wife. (She died on Wednesday, 21 May 1884.) This was not, however, the only reason. The two colleges named for him were in financial difficulties. The Hellmuth Boys' College (later named Dufferin College) had ceased operation in 1882. The mother-church of the diocese, St Paul's, was heavily in debt. The clergy and laity of the diocese were sharply divided on the matter of their bishop's grand plans for his new cathedral and the new university. In addition there were many who resented his autocratic administration.

The reluctance of Dr Egerton Ryerson, director of the Ontario school system, to acknowledge his debt to Hellmuth is unfortunately typical of his contemporaries' reactions to Hellmuth and Hellmuth's ideas. It is true that the bishop drove others as he drove himself; it is true that in the pursuit of his own goals he could be stubborn to the point of intransigeance; it is true that he often rode roughshod over the feelings of others and could not bring himself, even in Christian charity, to suffer fools gladly; but the great tragedy of this brilliant man's life lies in something much more basic and intellectually shocking than these human faults of character.

Isaac Hellmuth was a *converso*, to use the Spanish term – a converted Jew. Furthermore he had that intellectual arrogance that so often characterizes the scholar of the Diaspora. It is barely possible that his provincial

1884 Gold discovered in the Transvaal.

Gracious days at Hellmuth Ladies' College, 1885. Lower left, a general view of
the grounds; upper, the chapel; lower right, a view over the tennis court. UWO

Canadian fellow-citizens could have accepted a properly humble *converso*, but never one of such obviously superior intelligence.

The very silence of his contemporaries and his later biographers in respect of these facts is in itself eloquent evidence of the ambivalent character of the community's reaction to the son of a Warsaw rabbi. Today, eighty-six years after his death, there is still a tendency among Londoners in speaking of Hellmuth to emphasize rather the fact that he was a former Jew than that he was the founder of the University of Western Ontario.

In fact he was, and still is, regarded as something of a freak – a sport, a graftling on the family tree of the Church of England in Canada. It is for this reason, disturbing as it may be to the good consciences of the "Anglo-Saxon" founders of London, that the failure of Hellmuth's Canadian career must be attributed. His lonely and unequal battle ended, as it had to, in his defeat. The man who had a foot in each of two camps had a home in neither. Of him it could be said, as of the master he followed so faithfully, "Foxes have holes, and birds of the air have nests; but the Son of man hath not where to lay his head."

Of quite a different nature was the ebullient young man whom Londoners elected as their mayor in 1884. Charles Smith Hyman, aged thirty, was head of the tannery founded by his late father Ellis Walton Hyman. The younger Hyman had launched his political career two years earlier as an alderman. He presided over the city council in the year designated by the province as the centennial of its first settlement by the United Empire Loyalists.

The success of the UEL celebrations in Ontario and New Brunswick sparked an enthusiastic interest in local and regional history. This in turn led to the establishment of historical societies, libraries, and archives in both provinces.

A distinctive London institution also made its first appearance in that landmark year. The Baconian Club is still pursuing its aberrant course in its one-hundred-and-fourth year. The club is variously described as a literary society devoted to the proposition that Sir Francis Bacon wrote the plays and sonnets attributed to William Shakespeare; as an association of professional eccentrics; and as a debating society conducted somewhat along the lines of a "roast." It is all of these things and none of them. It is, quite simply, the Baconian Club.

There is no such ambiguity about the club to which the mayor belonged – the London Club. After an abortive beginning in 1875, the club was incorporated by an act of Parliament in 1880, and by 1884 it was settling nicely into its present quarters on Queens Avenue, in the heart of the city.

1884 Grover Cleveland elected 22nd president of the United States.

Town and country: a busy day at the Covent Garden Market. The market house is in the right background. UWO

Both this club and its sister-organization, the London Hunt and Country Club, were socially exclusive and until recent years denied membership to Jews.

The long financial recession that gripped Canada for the last quarter of the nineteenth century claimed two London banks as victims. Fawcett's

1885 D(avid) H(erbert) Lawrence, Ezra Pound, and Sinclair Lewis born in this year.

"They never fired a shot in anger": London veterans of the Riel Rebellion of 1885.
UWO

Bank collapsed in 1884, and the Bank of London three years later. The Fawcett disaster involved a shortage of $47,000 and a number of lost or destroyed bank records, and resulted in severe hardship for many depositors. It was a very unfortunate period for the private banks. Ten of them went belly-up between 1879 and 1887.

Many of these banks had invested heavily in land and timber in northern Ontario and Manitoba. Political developments were coming to a head, with the second insurrection of the Métis under their leader Louis Riel.

On Thursday, 26 March 1885, the Métis fought an engagement with a force of the North West Mounted Police at Duck Lake, Saskatchewan. The Mounties were defeated, suffering a loss of nine men. One of the dead was Skeffington Connor Elliott, son of the Middlesex County judge, William Elliott.

1886 Robert Louis Stevenson, *Dr Jekyll and Mr Hyde*.

Within a few days orders were received for the mobilization and dispatch of the 7th Fusiliers, City of London Regiment, to the scene of the rebellion. The "call to arms" was sounded by a bugler mounted on one of the popular "penny-farthing" bicycles, tootling on his instrument while guiding his unwieldy vehicle over London's gravel, dirt and, cobbled streets. It was a courageous feat, but received little notice from the members of the regiment. One by one they woke up, remembered the date, snorted, and went back to sleep. It was the morning of Wednesday, 1 April – April Fool's Day.

Eventually assembled, the regiment, under the command of Lieutenant-Colonel W. De Ray Williams, travelled west on the nearly completed main line of the Canadian Pacific Railway. They returned in July without having fired a shot in anger. The heroes received a great civic welcome. One Fusilier, an employee of Hyman's Tannery, was greeted by a banner stretched across Richmond Street that read:

"ARE YOU THERE, MORIARITY?"

Moriarity was.

Like the other members of the regiment Moriarity received a big dinner and a cigar later that day. One of the city's cigars, encased in a glass tube, survived into the fifth decade of the twentieth century, one of the less-treasured objects in the museum of the London and Middlesex Historical Society.

In fact, the manufacture of cigars had become a booming local industry. By the late 1880s there were at least ten firms producing many different brands, some with exotic names. An allied trade was manufacturer of cigar boxes. One of the most successful of these was the Beck Brothers Cigar Box Manufactory, which moved to London from Toronto in 1884. One of the two Beck brothers was Adam (later Sir Adam), who became one of the city's most famous adopted son, and the founder of Ontario's publicly-owned hydroelectric power system.

London had already been introduced to the joys of electricity. In a public demonstration of Ball's Electric Light Machine in July 1882, 7,000 citizens came to see the lights turned on in Victoria Park. Thereafter, progress was swift. Within four years many of the principal streets were lit by electricity.

Despite the long-dragged-out, continent-wide recession, London was beginning to earn its reputation as a solid, conservative money centre. Opulent family homes began to grace such thoroughfares – properly called avenues – as Queens and Dufferin in central London, and Grand Avenue in the south.

1887 Queen Victoria celebrates her Golden Jubilee.

Some of these mansions, like Charles Smith Hyman's home "Idlewyld," boasted ballrooms of elegant dimensions – and cramped, cell-like rooms for the domestic staff. An American writer, Joanna Barnes, in her recent novel *Silverwood* (New York: 1985), provides an evocative picture of the domestic arrangements in a large home in New York City:

One day, though it was forbidden, I had surreptitiously made my way to the fourth floor of the Madison Avenue house, where the servants' quarters were. What I found there were not rooms at all but tiny cubicles, most of them windowless, separated from each other by thin, wooden partitions which denied all but an illusion of privacy. In each a single gas jet provided all the light and heat there was. The rooms were identically outfitted with a cot and a chamber pot, a washstand, pitcher and basin, a narrow chest of drawers and four clothes pegs. These were the dreariest, meanest surroundings I had ever seen, and I found it nearly impossible to believe that our mother, who was the soul of kindness and forever reminding us that charity began at home, could possibly be aware of the conditions in which our help lived.

Even the smaller, middle-class homes usually had two staircases leading to the upper floors, the "front stairs" carpeted, with shallow risers; the "back stairs" uncarpeted and steep, leading to the "help's quarters" under the eaves.

In the late years of the nineteenth century, the public conscience was becoming aware of the gulf between the classes. Slowly, charity became an organized rather than a hit-or-miss affair. The leadership in the charitable movement was taken by the Establishment, especially by its female members. Over the decades generations of social reformers have learned that the way to achieve their laudable goals is through the lady consorts of the movers and shakers.

As the century neared its close there was a proliferation of philanthropic enterprises in London. Most of them originated with the churches, especially those associated with the Roman Catholic Diocese of London. The Sisters of St Joseph were the pioneers. They had already established a House of Providence and the Mount Hope Refuge, and in 1886 they opened their own hospital. Not to be outdone, the Women's Christian Association started a women's refuge, a home for aged women, and the Protestant Home for Orphans, Aged, and Friendless.

It must be pointed out that these institutions bore little resemblance to those with which we are today familiar. The late Victorians continued to tend towards the view that the poor and distressed were the authors of

---

1888 Blizzard paralyzes New York City; 400 people die.

their own misfortune. There is an unmistakably censorious tone to many of the regulations guiding the administration of these places. This is especially true of the institutions operated by the municipalities. The rules laid down for the poor house of the County of Norfolk in 1871 are typical:

Rule IV   Every inmate, unless sick, shall rise at 7½ o'clock, and retire at 8 o'clock, in winter; and rise at 5½ o'clock and retire at 9 o'clock in summer. And all that are able to work must be kept employed.
Rule V   No inmate is allowed to leave the premises without a pass from the Inspector. If any one wishes to visit friends, or go away on business he, or she, must apply to the Inspector, at his usual visits, for a written pass, which pass must be presented to the Keeper before he or she will be allowed to leave the premises. ...
Rule VIII Any one infringing any of the above rules will be placed in solitary confinement, with bread and water diet, for such period as the Inspector shall direct, subject to the approval of the Medical Superintendent.

Many of the occupants of these poor houses were local people who, for one reason or another, had fallen on evil times. The harsh rules represented a pretty general public attitude toward the distress of other people. The feeling about needy newcomers was even harsher.

The Guthrie Home for English orphans was established in the 1880s in an old building on the Governor's Road south of London that dated back to the 1820s. In 1887 John T. Middlemore, founder of the Orphan Children's Emigration Charity, brought out a party of fifty girls and one hundred boys from Birmingham to this facility. On that occasion a local newspaper had this to say about the philanthropic effort:

This work Mr Middlemore has made a study. During the 15 years of his career in ridding England of an unprofitable class of persons, he has bestowed upon Canada at least 2,000 members of that class, a few of whom are said to have made useful residents.

Before we condemn the Londoners of a century ago for their lack of compassion, it would be advisable for us to consider the difficulties experienced by the social agencies of 1988 in locating group-homes in residential areas.

1889 The Johnstown, Pennsylvania, flood destroys four towns and takes 2,300 lives.

CHAPTER NINE

HORSE-AND-BUGGY DAYS

The horse and buggy made the reporting of fall fairs an enviable assignment because on such occasions it was possible to take along the Little Lady, and while the reporter ... was engaged in copying the prize list, the L.L. could always be depended on to make a few notes about the women's fancy work, the cookery, and the preserves, so dear to the housewives' hearts.

And then there was always the drive homeward – mostly by moonlight, as it seems in retrospect. And how surely those livery stables nags could make their way, unguided and untended, until the lights of London appeared over the hill and it became necessary once more to come from out the clouds and pick up the reins to restrain a now impatient horse from foundering on the last long mile that led to stable and to feed box. Steady Bess, old girl; whoa Dan!
George W. Yates, Ottawa, in the London *Free Press*, 21 June, 1939.

The fact is, as the extract above illustrates, London *liked* the nineteenth century and was reluctant to give it up. It required two world wars finally to convince the die-hards that Queen Victoria really was dead and that the "good times" were no more.

Of course the good times were never that good, in spite of the rosy memories of George Yates and thousands of others. The best that could be said of them was that those times were slower and less noisy than our present environment.

These memories are summer memories. In the spring the roads that Dobbin traveled that halcyon evening would have been deep in mud; in winter they would have been choked with snow. What prevailed in the rural areas also held true in the city. London's streets were a hodgepodge of materials. Some streets were dirt on one side of the street, gravel on the other. Some of them were brick, covered with asphalt; others, in the downtown area, were paved with cedar blocks. All types froze in the winter,

1890 Feminine fashions emphasized the hour-glass figure, leg-of-mutton sleeves.

heaved in the spring, and potholed in summer – just like the ones we travel today.

The statistical relationship between rural and urban areas was changing rapidly. The farm population of Middlesex County began a slow decline, while that of London began to rise. From a figure of 19,941 in 1880, London's population rose to 30,705 in 1890. A good part of the increase came from the annexation of suburbs. London East "amalgamated" with London in 1885. Soon afterwards the factory suburb's smelly petroleum industry was banished to Lambton County, where it had originated. In 1890 the city took over the unincorporated areas of what is commonly called London South. London West was added in 1897.

The atmosphere of the age served to enhance London's social insularity. Its citizens were intelligently aware that there was a world outside London and felt sympathetic towards its shortcomings. This attitude often infuriated or amused the city's critics. When a London newspaper once commented, smugly, that London was "better laid out" than its traditional rival Hamilton, an editor in the latter city wrote acidly that when Hamilton had been as long dead as London, it too would be "well laid out."

McClary Manufacturing Company in its new incarnation as General Steel Wares. Later still, until its demolition in 1988, it was known as CamCo Inc. UWO

Canadian Packing Company building under construction at Pottersburg, East London. The cornerstone was laid by Sir John Carling on 8 February 1893. The building burned in the early 1900s. It was rebuilt and later came to be known as Coleman's. UWO

London modestly acknowledged its reputation as one of the wealthier Canadian cities. At the same time, its citizens were well aware of the social and economic gulf fixed between its richest residents and its poorest. They were proud of the first group and tolerant of the second.

London was, and is, a tolerant community. This is not to say that Londoners are incapable of racism. They have resented Jewish business success and erected subtle social barriers against blackness; but while these

1891 Dr James A. Naismith, a native of Almonte, Ontario, invents the game of basketball.

attitudes have been persistent, they have never been terribly popular. The people of London have always felt somewhat embarrassed by the *existence* of differences between individuals.

The city had a few minority groups. The largest at this time was the Italian newcomers. They had begun to arrive, in numbers, in the 1880s. They were not penniless immigrants. They came prepared with capital to establish businesses and to become full-fledged citizens of the new land. Many settled in the downtown area west of Richmond Street, a district later referred to by many as the "Latin Quarter." Almost inevitably, music was a common interest. Such family names as Venuta, Olivastri, Lombardo, and Cortese became well known throughout the continent.

There had been Jewish families in London from almost the beginning of settlement, but they seem not to have established any formal religious institutions until the 1860s. Many of the founders of the oil companies were men with Jewish backgrounds. This was especially true of the Imperial Oil Company.

Of what we have come to call the "visible minorities" the blacks were, of course, the first. It was not until the 1870s that Asiatic immigrants became a feature of Canadian life. One local record states that "Wahelee Angnee was the first Chinese laundryman in London." He began business here in 1878. The census of 1881 reports 4,383 registered Chinese in the country, most of whom had been brought to Canada to undertake the back-breaking work of building the Canadian Pacific Railway through the Rocky Mountains.

As London society grew more complex, the nature of the charitable impulses of its citizens changed. Charity became more specialized, and specialized agencies arose to meet those needs. By 1896 there were no less than fifty recognized charities in the city. In that year the groups came together to form the Charity Organization Society, London's first community welfare council. Its main objective was to prevent duplication of effort. Organizations of a similar type have pursued this same worthy goal ever since, with mixed success.

The "Widow of Windsor" celebrated her diamond jubilee in 1897. It was even grander than the golden jubilee extravaganza of ten years earlier. Most Londoners had known no other queen but Victoria. The very name of the community spoke of its strong attachment to the capital of the Empire and to its Empress. During the jubilee year a visitor from the older London found great amusement in the duplicated street names – Pall Mall, Oxford, Piccadilly, Grosvenor, Cheapside, and Regent. He was Harry Furniss, noted *Punch* cartoonist and illustrator of the novels of

---

1893 Anton Dvořák, *Fifth Symphony* ("From the New World").

Charles Dickens, William Makepeace Thackeray, and Lewis Carroll. Through him, London, Canada, made the scene in London, England, by way of a satirical cartoon.

The city made the international scene again in January 1898, but this time it wasn't amusing. On municipal election night, Monday, 3 January, a crowd gathered in the second-floor auditorium of the city hall on Richmond Street. They were celebrating the mayoral victory of Dr John D. Wilson. Suddenly, without warning, a section of the floor gave way, pitching 250 people on to the ground floor. Seconds later, a 500-pound safe slid into the hole, crushing many of the victims. A total of twenty-three people died; 150 were injured.

Less noted nationally, a single death in April 1898 provided a local

Special Edition.

The Free

ONE CENT.   LONDON, ONTARIO, CANADA, SATURDAY,

THE CITY HALL CATASTROPHE

PART OF THE FLOOR GIVES WAY

And Upwards of Three Hundred Citizens Went Down With the Debris.

Twenty of Them Dead, While Two Hundred Others Are Injured, Some of Them Fatally—Scenes of Horror and Excitement—Successful Municipal Candidates Were Addressing the Electors, When the Terrible Crash Came—The Cause of the Disaster—The Work of Bringing Out the Dead and Injured — Many Prominent Citizens Among the Victims—Names of the Dead and Injured.

From the Daily Free Press of Tuesday.
An appalling accident happened in London last evening. The first list of dead totalled 18, but this number will be augmented, in all probability. The

dows from outside. And thus the hall was cleared.

IN THE PIT OF HUMANITY.
The cloud of dust was not dispelled so as to make vision across the hall possible for several minutes.

they were almost powerless to keep back the crowd and make way for those going to and coming from the City Hall. The place was besieged until a late hour this morning by men

City hall disaster of 1898. The collapse of part of the floor of the building plunged twenty-three people into eternity. UWO

sensation. It was a murder case. Since it was a truly theatrical murder, it is necessary to set the stage for the telling.

The Mechanics' Institute building, 229–231 Dundas Street, erected in 1877, had been vacated in 1895 when the London Public Library opened its new building at the southwest corner of Wellington Street and Queens Avenue. The municipal library took over the function and the collections of the Institute.

The Dundas Street building then became the home of the Music Hall (later Bennett's Theatre, and later still, the Majestic Theatre). The box

1898 Spain declares war on the United States.

Inside page of a theatre program for a performance of 24 May 1894 in the Grand Opera House. The Grand occupied the western portion of the Masonic Temple on Richmond Street. None of the firms advertising on this page survive. UWO office was on the ground floor, the theatre auditorium on the second level.

On the night of Friday, 1 April, the touring Wesley Stock Company, under its manager James Tuttle, was performing a play called *The Candidate,* which was billed as "a satire on Canadian politics." The male lead was played by an American actor, William D. Emerson, whose wife was also a member of the cast.

That evening, just before curtain time, there had been a dispute between Tuttle and Emerson on a matter of overdue wages. There was a confrontation on stage, in the course of which Emerson shot Tuttle in the face at point-blank range with a .32-calibre revolver, a stage property that unaccountably was loaded with live ammunition.

In the ensuing confusion someone told the crew to raise the curtain. As the bleeding corpse lay stage-centre, a member of the cast stepped forward to the footlights and cried out, "Is there a doctor in the house?"

This hoary stage line drew howls of laughter from the three hundred members of the audience as they recalled the date. Someone put a name to it:

"April fool!"

Eventually the audience was apprised of the true state of affairs, but unfortunately

– there *was* no doctor in the house.

After a long delay a doctor was found, some two blocks distant. Dr Frederick P. Drake drove his finger into the facial wound of the obviously deceased manager and solemnly announced to the house, now eagerly assembled on the stage:

"This man is dead."

This, the second theatrical cliché of the evening, was followed by a third when a member of the London police force stepped up to William Emerson, and declaimed:

"You, sir, are under arrest."

The second act of this real-life drama lived up to the promise of the first. From the beginning of the case the London public was on the side of the actor. When the grand jury brought in a true bill on a charge of first-degree murder, there was widespread indignation. The late manager, James Tuttle, weighing in at 250 pounds, had been unpopular with everyone. He had struck the first blow in the altercation with the slender actor. Emerson was a member of the United States Naval Reserve and was expecting to be called up for service in the Spanish-American War. That, in itself, made good newspaper copy. The female lead in the drama of the trial was Emerson's wan and weeping little blonde wife Laura, who at

---

1898 *Way Down East,* a play by Lottie Blair Parker.

Masonic Temple and Grand Opera House, built in 1881 at the northwest corner of Richmond and King streets. Fire gutted the theatre portion in 1900. The entire struture was demolished in 1968. UWO

every critical moment was to be seen "clasping her flaxen-haired little daughter to her breast."

In these circumstances the prosecution didn't have a chance, despite the unexplained loaded revolver in the hands of the defendant. The jury stayed out just long enough to appear to have considered the matter, then brought in the expected verdict:

"Not guilty."

1898 Pierre and Marie Curie discover radium and polonium.

The crowd inside and outside the courtroom was ecstatic. When Emerson, his wife, and daughter emerged, some men loosed the horses from the shafts of the carriage that was waiting for their hero, and themselves pulled the vehicle to Emerson's boarding house, preceded by an improvised band.

The story is worth retelling. It epitomizes the romantic sentimentalism of the period. A less lovely aspect of this attachment to the romantic ideal was the outburst of patriotic fervour for the cause of Britain in the South African War. Less lovely because the war cost Britain a great deal of credibility in world circles. The spectre of a powerful empire pitting half a million troops (including 7,300 Canadians) against a mere 88,000 independence-loving Boers was not a pretty one. Toward the end of the conflict, which began in 1899 and lasted until 1901, England's use of a scorched-earth policy and the establishment of concentration camps in which 20,000 men, women, and children died, offended Britain's friends and enraged her enemies.

Nevertheless Londoners and English-speaking Canadians generally supported Britain. Citizens played tinny-sounding recordings of "Soldiers of the Queen," on their hand-cranked Edison phonographs and prayed for the success of the Empire's arms.

For a time in 1899 residents of the Forest City had plenty of excitement on their own turf.

Four years earlier, in 1895, the London Street Railway sold its horses and converted its trams to another kind of horsepower – electricity. This was an enormous leap forward. Service on the lines was increased. So were the labour problems. In earlier times almost anyone could handle a horse-drawn vehicle. Now it required an engineer to operate the electric cars. The "motorman" came into his own. He joined a union, Branch 97 of the Amalgamated Association of Street Railway Employees of America. On Thursday, 27 October 1898, the AASREA called its members out on strike. It lasted less than a week. The employees won an extra one third of a cent an hour on their former wage of fifteen cents an hour.

The labour peace lasted only a few months. On Monday, 22 May 1899, seventy-nine motormen and conductors walked off the job, without notice.

This second strike proved to be the most vicious in the city's history. It dragged on for more than three months and was accompanied by the worst civic violence London had ever seen. The strikers and their supporters attacked the street cars, which were now being operated by replacement workers, known to the unionists as "scabs."

So much damage was done to the rolling stock that the police were

---

1898 Edward Noyes Westcott, *David Harum.*

A piece of music composed locally to celebrate the introduction of hydroelectric power from Niagara Falls. UWO

called out. Londoners were then treated to the astonishing spectacle of the trams and their strike-breaking crews being guarded by constables carrying loaded revolvers.

The violence reached a peak on Saturday, 8 July. Many businesses were now operating only a half-day on Saturdays. This meant that many employees were at liberty to join the crowd that was beginning to assemble in the downtown area. By 2:30 in the afternoon several thousand rioters had taken over control of the city's core. The authorities hoped against hope that the rioters would run out of steam as the supper hour approached. Hunger apparently only made the mob meaner.

At midnight, Dr John D. Wilson, in his second year as mayor, called out the militia units to restore order. He then read the Riot Act to the noisy, unruly mob. It was the first and only time in the history of London that this legal instrument has been employed.

The replacement workers, a.k.a. "scabs," did a good job throughout the strike in spite of the harrowing conditions. It was a highlight in the lives of many, an exciting interlude in the boredom of their daily lives. Joseph Albert Miller, a tailor's apprentice, never forgot the experience and delighted, ever after, in showing off his knowledge of London's streets, the locations of which he had to memorize as a replacement conductor.

Kensington Bridge (built 1884), looking east on the Dundas Street hill toward the courthouse and jail. The photograph was taken after the London Street Railway was electrified in 1897. The conductor at the rear of the car appears to be replacing the trolley on the overhead wire that provided the power. UWO

The union lost the strike, most of the strikers were fired, the damage was repaired, and life went back to nearly normal.

A prettier tale, one that has long been held dear to the hearts of romantic Londoners, unfolded its fairy-tale climax in the Gay Nineties.

Cy Warman, an American journalist and poet, fell in love with a girl from Kansas, Myrtle Marie Jones, who was attending the Roman Catholic Academy of the Sacred Heart in London. After seeing her home one evening, Cy sat down on a bench in Victoria Park and composed a poem to her, which he looked on as a proposal of marriage.

So did she. She accepted.

In 1893, Raymon Moore set the poem to music. The song was called "Sweet Marie." It made Cy Warman's fame and fortune.

In 1899, the Warmans returned to London, built the house at 100 Cheapside Street that still stands, and lived there happily ever after – at least until he died.

An important date was coming up and the "battle of the century" began on Monday, 1 January 1900. Thousands – perhaps millions – of people celebrated that New Year's Day as the beginning of the twentieth century. A fewer number of brave souls declared that the first day of the new century would not come until Tuesday, 1 January 1901. Although much outnumbered, the second group was right. The reader may work it out for himself, or herself. The next occasion for debate will come in twelve years' time, on Saturday, 1 January AD 2000.

The first year of the new century started out on a sad note. Queen Victoria died on the Isle of Wight on Tuesday, 22 January 1901, to be succeeded by London's favourite prince, as King Edward VII. As a foot-note to history, it may be noted that a remarkable number of boy babies born that year were christened Albert Edward in honour of the new king, just as another crop of children forty-one years earlier had been given the same two names in honour of the same royal personage when he was the Prince of Wales.

The new king's son, Prince George (later George V), visited London that year with his wife, Princess Mary (of Teck). The city's greeting was a warm one, but somewhat marred by an unaccountable oversight on the part of the committee in charge. There was no official welcome at the railway station.

September 1901 marked the opening of the palatial new Grand Opera House on Richmond Street, between Fullarton and Maple streets. The new theatre succeeded the former Grand Opera House, which had occu-pied premises in the Masonic Temple building on Richmond Street, south

---

1901 George Bernard Shaw, *Caesar and Cleopatra.*

Theatre program for *La Grande Duchesse,* an entertainment for the Queen's Birthday in 1894. The Holmans were a family of professional actors; but many of the performers – like William C. Coo, alderman and owner of a shorthand school – were local amateurs. UWO

of Dundas. The building had been destroyed by fire on Friday, 23 February 1900.

The new theatre was the queen of a massive chain of some ninety houses controlled by Ambrose Joseph Small, of Toronto, one of the best known and most cordially hated theatrical figures in Canada. The importance of the new theatre lay in its large seating capacity (1,850), its modern equipment, and the extraordinary dimensions of its playing area, which may be judged from the following description from *Julius Cahn's Official Theatrical Guide for 1905-1906*:

LONDON – Pop., 50,000. Grand Opera House. A. J. Small, proprietor. J. E. Turton, bus. mgr. Communications regarding time at this theatre should be addressed to A. J. Small, Grand Opera House, Toronto, Canada. S.C., 1,850. Prices vary. Illum, electricity. Volt, 110; amperes, 125; Edison system. Width prosc. opening, 42 ft. Height, 34 ft. Depth footlights to back wall, 45 ft. Dist. curtain line to footlights, 3 ft. Dist. bet. fly girders, 55 ft. Height to rigging loft, 70 ft. Dist. bet. side walls, 80 ft. Depth under stage, 12 ft. Usual number of traps, in usual places. Height to fly gallery, 24 ft. 2 bridges, third and fourth entrance. Scene room. Theatre on ground floor. A. Schabacker, stage carpenter. Jas. Cresswell, orches. leader. 9 in orchestra. London Bill-Posting Co. Printing required, 10 stands, 50 3-sheets 200 1-sheets, 200½-sheets. Dates read, Grand Opera House. City Transfer Co. Express offices, Dominion and Canadian. T. H. Purdom, lawyer.

A less dramatic but no less important event occurred on Tuesday, 22 October 1901, when a group of distinguished Londoners met to form the London and Middlesex Historical Society. Its honourary president was Sir John Carling, former minister of agriculture for Canada (1885–1892); the president was Dr Cl. (for Clarence) T. Campbell, who became mayor of London in 1905. Dr Campbell was responsible for many useful papers on the city's history, much of which he had experienced personally.

London's volunteer soldiers returned to the city from the battlefields of South Africa as that part of the world settled down to an uneasy peace. An organization of patriotic London ladies began a campaign for funds to erect a memorial to London's heroes.

While dead heroes were being mourned, new ones were making their entrances. On Thursday, 19 June 1902, Guy Albert Lombardo was born. His mother, the former Angelina Paladino, had been the first child of Italian parentage to be born in London. Her own small claim to fame is forgotten in the blaze of glory surrounding her band-leader son.

1902 Arthur C. Benson and Edward Elgar, "The Land of Hope and Glory."

Sir John Carling (1828–1911). Carling represented London as a Conservative in many provincial and federal administrations from 1857 to 1895, and was knighted by Queen Victoria in 1893. UWO

In his show-business heyday Guy Lombardo became almost as famous for driving fast boats as for his "sweetest music this side of heaven." Guy was born into a generation that worshipped speed. At his birth the internal combustion engine was about to come into its own. There were a few automobiles in the area, and by the time Guy was two years old the London Automobile Club was able to muster a caravan of five autos carrying a total of nineteen persons for a road trip to Aylmer and St Thomas by way of Belmont. It was a test of endurance for both humans and machines.

It was a time of transition in the field of transportation. Since at least the 1850s the steam engine had reigned supreme. Now it was being challenged by the gasoline-powered engine, and by old Benjamin Franklin's discovery – electricity. The first self-propelled passenger vehicles were steam-driven and had appeared on the public highways in England as early as the 1830s. The first vehicle powered by electricity generated by storage batteries appeared in France in 1881. Carl Benz produced his first gasoline-powered tricycle in 1885.

All three methods of propulsion entered the twentieth century, with steam in the lead. Some 40 per cent of the automobiles on the roads of the United States were steamers, many of them built by the Stanley Brothers – Francis Edgar and Freelan O. A close second were the electric cars – at 38 per cent; only 22 per cent were powered by the internal-combustion

1904 Rolls-Royce Company founded in England.

gasoline engine. The electric cars were the quietest, steam cars were the fastest – a Stanley Steamer set a record of 127.66 miles (205.4 kilometres) per hour in 1906 – but in the end, thanks largely to the brilliant manufacturing methods introduced by Henry Ford, gasoline buggies became the cheapest and easiest to maintain.

London adjusted itself faster to the quiet power of the electric current than it did to the efficient but noisy gasoline engine. In large part this was due to the activities of the man who for three years served the city in the dual capacity of mayor and London's representative in the Ontario Legislature. Adam Beck's greatest achievement was the establishment of the Hydro-Electric Power Commission of Ontario in 1906.

Memories of the city hall disaster of 1899 were awakened in 1907 when another downtown structure proved unequal to the stresses placed upon it. During alterations to the premises of I.W.J. Reid and Company, known as the Crystal Hall, on Dundas Street, some injudicious changes to an endwall caused the building to collapse, carrying an adjoining property down with it. Seven people were killed, a number injured.

A little over a year later, another building on Dundas Street collapsed, claiming three more lives. During a bad fire at Westman's hardware store, the upper stories of the building fell, crushing to death Fire Chief Lawrence Clark and two of his men.

These three tragedies within a decade had taken thirty-three lives. The city accordingly passed a building inspection by-law. There were a few Londoners who remembered a similar municipal reaction fifty-three years earlier. After the Great Fire of 1845 the town had enacted legislation prohibiting the erection of wooden houses in the core area. It now appeared that even solid brick structures were not always safe.

One downtown building put up during this period certainly conveyed the impression of solidity and permanence. The Canadian Bank of Commerce branch at the northeast corner of Dundas and Richmond streets, built, according to the date-stone, in 1905, stood as a monument to the Canadian mood at the turn of the century. Its huge pillars, inset in the south façade, seemed to say, "We are here to stay." Little children, hoisted up by adult arms to sit in the embrasures between the pillars to watch a parade, could well believe in the certainty of life as it was and ever would be, world without end. British was the Empire on which the sun would never set. And, of course, the "Maple Leaf, our emblem dear" would likewise be forever.

The storm that would shatter these cherished ideals was just over the horizon, but its ominous shape was unseen by all but a few Londoners.

1905 Ignace Jan Paderewski, the Polish pianist, gives a concert at the Grand Opera House, London, Ontario.

It was known, indeed, that King Edward VII, "The Peacemaker," was having some trouble with his nephew, Kaiser Wilhelm II, but it was, after all, a family matter and would soon be straightened out.

As the city's good-natured contribution towards smoothing over the quarrel, London's first self-propelled fire engine was named "Kaiser Bill."

London was now getting used to noisy automobiles. Their number was increasing. The first fatality occurred on Tuesday, 23 August 1910, when Anson Wallace was run down by a McLaughlin Runabout manufactured at Oshawa. The McLaughlin cars were a typical Canadian product; the carriage-work was done in Canada, the Buick engine was imported from the United States.

The great transportation disaster of the era was, of course, the sinking of RMS *Titanic* in April, 1912. The loss of the great ship and 1,517 of its passengers and crew shocked the London business community in particular. Many of them were frequent transatlantic travelers, like John Bamlet Smallman and Thomas F. Kingsmill. Mr Kingsmill made an average of two ocean-crossings a year on buying trips for his store.

A month later, the aeroplane came to London.

On Thursday, 23 May 1912, Beckwith Havens, a member of the staff of the Glenn Curtiss aeroplane factory, arrived in London accompanied by several packing cases, containing his plane – "some assembly required." An "aviation camp" had been set up on Carling Heights. There everything was put in order for a publicized flight on the Queen's Birthday.

A severe electrical storm on the holiday prevented Havens from keeping his scheduled date. By the following afternoon the weather had cleared and the plane was able to take off. Havens's course took him from the camp in the northeast part of the city northwestward to the north branch of the Thames, and thence in a great semicircle over the business section and back to the camp. The entire flight took place at what would now be considered the dangerous altitude of 600 feet and occupied some twenty minutes. An awe-stricken newspaper reporter described the flight in these words:

After the aviator had taken his seat in the machine and the engine was started, several of the spectators held the big bird until the momentum was reached. Then with a rush along the field the machine lifted from the ground within 100 yards from the starting point and gradually climbed to an altitude of nearly 600 feet. In the downtown section of the city, Mr Havens manoeuvred over the National Bowling Alley building, swaying at times, but keeping well on his course. He looked like a gigantic bird, traveling along at a terrific speed, a

---

1912 Glenn Curtiss invents a "flying boat," or seaplane.

cloud of white smoke trailing behind him. The landing operation at the aviation camp was simplified. Making an abrupt circle over the C.P.R. tracks, Havens turned his machine toward the meadow from which he had made his ascent, drooped his planes and took a long, graceful glide to earth. When about 20 feet from the ground he silenced his engines and brought the machine lightly to the field. ...

A 60-horsepower engine, developing a speed of over 70 miles per hour, faster than almost any ordinary railroad train, was the power behind the air voyage.

That was a big year for London. In May the governor-general visited the city, and in July, Dora Labatt went for a ride in an aeroplane, the first London woman to do so.

The governor-general was His Royal Highness The Duke of Connaught. Elderly Londoners must have found it difficult to recognize, in the distinguished seventy-two-year-old soldier, the gay young officer who had officiated at the opening of Hellmuth Ladies' College back in 1869.

Few governors-general have had a closer association with Canada than the first Duke of Connaught and Strathearn. During his first posting to this country he was a member of the Red River expedition that was sent west in 1870 to deal with the first Riel Rebellion. Port Arthur, now submerged along with Fort William in the modern city of Thunder Bay, was named for him. In the European war that was a little over two years away at the time of his visit to London, the Duke organized the Canadian Patriotic Fund to help the dependants of servicemen, and his daughter assisted in raising a regiment named for her, the Princess Patricia's Canadian Light Infantry. The "Princess Pats" served with distinction in both world wars. The Duke himself lived to see Great Britain go to war for the second time against the German state. He died on Friday, 16 January 1942.

Among the crowds that greeted the Duke in the spring of 1912 were many newcomers from the British Isles. The Liberal prime minister, Sir Wilfrid Laurier, and his minister of the interior Sir Clifford Sifton were responsible for attracting more than three million immigrants from the United Kingdom, the United States, and Europe in the years between 1897 and 1914. Like the earliest arrivals to the London area back in the 1830s, these new people brought little with them except a desire "to get ahead."

The effects in London were marked. Hundreds of "workmen's cottages" sprang up, with a concentration along the Hamilton Road in East London.

1913 A destructive storm on the Great Lakes sinks 30 ships.

Strange new languages were being heard on the city's streets. One of these languages was German. Suddenly, beginning in 1913, this was not a popular sound. Rumours began to circulate around one man, Otto Becker, an employee of the Public Utilities Commission. It was said he was a member of the German Reserve Army. It was said he was a spy.

And then it was August 1914. A hot month.

Since the assassination of Archduke Ferdinand of Austria at Sarajevo on Sunday, 28 June, things had been heating up in Europe. It was all too complicated for the average person to understand. However, it all came down to the fact that Great Britain had served an ultimatum on Germany. The Kaiser had until 11 pm on Tuesday, 4 August 1914, to withdraw his troops from the territory of the neutral state of Belgium.

Crowds began gathering in front of the newspaper offices in the early evening hours of that day. From time to time copy boys emerged to put up fresh bulletins on the boards in front of the offices, printed by hand with grease pencils on newsprint. The crowds were quiet until the last bulletin of the night was put up:

"GREAT BRITAIN DECLARES WAR: GOD SAVE THE KING!"

The following day the *Free Press* reported on the city's reactions to the news:

Scenes of the wildest enthusiasm, with every display of patriotic regard for the motherland in the present European situation followed the official announcement of the declaration of war by Great Britain on Germany last night. ...

Within a few minutes after the announcement was made on the *Free Press* bulletin and in extra edition a hundred patriots gathered in front of the *Free Press* and calling upon a group of bandsmen organized a procession and demonstration that grew as it proceeded through the business section.

At midnight the throng was even greater. ... Wild cheers went up when the declaration of war was announced and gathering at Richmond and Carling streets the crowd lustily sang "God Save the King," "Britannia Rules the Waves," "The Maple Leaf Forever," "O Canada," and other national and patriotic airs.

There was no thought save of victory, and while London has in the past at times born the reputation of strong anti-military leanings, sentiment was unanimously to the contrary.

On the afternoon of 4 August, the Public Utilities Commission fired Otto Becker.

He left town immediately.

1914 After years of controversy, London Street Railway begins operating on Sunday.

CHAPTER TEN

CRY HAVOC

Cry, "Havoc!" and let slip the dogs of war.
William Shakespeare, *Julius Caesar.*

The high contracting parties solemnly declare in the names of their respective peoples that
they condemn recourse to war for the solution of international controversies, and
renounce it as an instrument of national policy in their relations with one another.
Frank Billings Kellogg, Peace Pact, signed at Paris, 27 Aug. 1928.

The history of London now enters a period of which many present residents have personal knowledge. Human memory being the selective faculty that it is, it will prove impossible to offer a truly balanced picture of the years under review. One must try to avoid too narrow a focus. Events within one's special frame of knowledge will inevitably overshadow those within other parameters. The only approach that would seem to promise an impartial overview is that based on the importance given to various events by the public media.

In what our generation called "The Great War" the first concern of Londoners was with our own. The news of the great Canadian victory at Ypres, for instance, was of less interest than the answer to the urgent question "Is my boy all right?" Casualty lists were scanned with agonizing intensity. Only after the absence of the name of a dear one from the lists could the reader show an intelligent interest in the progress of the war.

It's difficult to recapture the mood of Canadians in the first year of the war. Patriotism was a fever that affected nearly everyone. A contagious enthusiasm informed every act. There was a supreme confidence in the outcome. The Germans would be taught a lesson. The fighting would be over by Christmas. The question came to be: *What* Christmas?

The war bogged down in the trenches in France and the general enthu-

1915 German submarine sinks Cunard Liner, *Lusitania*, 1, 198 lives lost.

siasm waned. The casualty lists grew longer. Life on the home front became more difficult. Coal, among other commodities, was rationed. People living along the main lines of the Grand Trunk Railway (the former Great Western) and the CPR sent their children out to scavenge the soft coal that fell from the engine tenders. Sometimes a friendly fireman would toss a shovelful on to the right of way. Ashes from domestic coal furnaces were raked over for bits of unburned fuel.

Rationing was a new experience for Londoners. On the whole they coped with it quite well. It was the troops stationed in the encampment on Carling Heights that caused the greatest disruption in the community's life-style. At one time (1916) more than 16,000 troops were receiving training at Wolseley Barracks. It was inevitable that there should be clashes between soldiers and citizens. In many ways it was a return to the uneasy relationships of the 1860s. The "dirty 33rd" were the worst. This was the 33rd Battalion of the Canadian Expeditionary Force. On one occasion they created a riot in downtown London.

They were dreary days; grey days as the dreadful fighting went on. The Edwardian generation had no previous experience in these matters to draw upon. Napoleon was a century gone; the Kaiser was a nightmare figure of daunting ferocity. Anything German became abhorrent to all right-thinking Canadians. By order of King George V the royal house of Saxe-Coburg-Gotha became the House of Windsor, and Berlin, Ontario, changed its name to Kitchener. The patriotic fervour that had hurled Canada into the European conflict within hours of the British declaration was beginning to ebb as the interminable battles resulted not in victory, but in longer and longer casualty lists. The cost to Canada in human lives was high: of 628,462 Canadians who served, 60,661 died.

New weapons appeared – the submarine, the tank, the aeroplane. Canadians made a name for themselves in all branches of the armed services, and by the end of the war it was apparent to the world that Canada was a country to be reckoned with. It has been said with much reason that Canada entered the conflict as a colony and emerged as an independent nation, a fact that was acknowledged when the British Parliament later passed the Statute of Westminster in 1931.

None of this was then apparent to the 20,000 war-weary Londoners who jammed Victoria Park on Monday, 11 November 1918, to celebrate the signing of the Armistice. The mood of the crowd verged on hysteria. A dummy representing Kaiser Wilhelm was strung up and burned. The celebration went on, in a lower key, for several days. Many of those who attended the spontaneous outburst of thanksgiving at the eleventh hour

---

1916 The Sinn Fein Easter Rebellion in Ireland: Sir Roger Casement arrested and executed.

of the eleventh day of the eleventh month carried within their own bodies a new and even more savage enemy.

Spanish influenza, so called because it was first identified in Spain, wrought havoc among the troops in the trenches in France, and from there spread around the world. Like all the earlier epidemics and pandemics it appeared in Canada first in Quebec City and from there spread westward. By the end of the year it was everywhere. The final global toll was more than twenty-two million dead, 30,000 of them in Canada.

The disease reached London in October and for three weeks raged with great severity. Schools, theatres, and all public places of assembly were closed for a time, and the streets of the city became deserted. One in every six persons contracted the plague, and those who hadn't walked in fear. Then, just as residents relaxed, feeling that the worst was past, the disease returned at the beginning of January 1919 in an even more severe form. Although fewer people were affected, the mortality rate was higher in the second outbreak.

At last it was over and London began to pick up the pace of normal city life again. In October 1919, Victoria Park again became the scene of a huge gathering of citizens as more than 20,000 Londoners turned out to greet the darling of the Empire, His Royal Highness Edward Albert Christian George Andrew Patrick David, the Prince of Wales. Men, women, and children lined up in orderly queues to shake the hand of the heir to the throne as Mayor Charles Ross Somerville looked on proudly. Those who were lucky enough to grasp the Imperial hand found themselves facing a slim young man of average height with a crooked, rather shy smile.

Such popularity as the Prince of Wales enjoyed has a price. That evening a former mayor of London, a physician, was called to the Tecumseh House Hotel by an equerry of the prince to treat an injured hand, grossly swollen by the overly-enthusiastic grip of hundreds of patriotic citizens.

The prince was well enough by the following morning to play a round of golf at the London Hunt and Country Club, where he was ambushed by a reporter from the London *Free Press*, Edmund J. Penny, and a photographer, Seward Lancaster. Penny got an exclusive interview. The prince met the mayor's son, Charles Ross (Sandy) Somerville, Junior, who was that year launching a career in tournament golf that would take him to the top rank of North American amateurs.

Ed Penny's newspaper suffered a grievous loss New Year's Day, Thursday, 1 January 1920, with the death of its publisher, Walter J. Blackburn, eldest son of Josiah Blackburn. Seven months later the paper lost its managing editor, Alfred E. Miller.

1918 Federal government introduced Daylight Saving Act in Canada.

These two deaths resulted in the arrival of a trio of interesting and important men in leading roles in the London drama. W.J. Blackburn's brother Arthur stepped into the management of the newspaper. The founding member of the Blackburn dynasty had been primarily a writer and a politician; the second was an astute businessman; the third was an amateur scientist. Arthur Blackburn had a keen interest in the fields of photography and wireless. Combined with a well-developed sporting instinct, his interest in photography led him to take the first action photograph ever published in the family's journal, a shot of the finish of the King's Plate race at Toronto in 1906. It was also he who introduced Linotype machines into the composing room of the *Free Press*.

Alf Miller died in August 1920. The search for a replacement resulted in the appointment of Arthur Rutherford Ford, a native of Point Edward, Ontario. Ford had been a member of the press gallery at the Parliament Buildings in Ottawa. He had covered the disastrous fire that destroyed the centre block on Thursday, 3 February 1916. During his Ottawa career Ford had met the *Free Press* correspondent there, Fred Landon. Landon left the field of journalism in 1916 to become city librarian. In the summer of 1920 Ford, while on his vacation, stopped off in London to see his old friend Landon. One thing led to another, and by October Arthur Ford was settled at the ancient walnut desk that had served his three predecessors as managing editor.

No one could call London a "hot" news town. During the 1920s it lived up to its reputation as "the biggest small town in Canada" – and one of the wealthiest. It's an exaggeration to say that everyone knew everyone else, unless one inserts the adverb "nearly" in both places. The population growth was almost infinitesimal. In 1920 there were 181 more people in the city than in 1919. In 1921, the gain was 503. The year 1922 saw a big jump of 1,585, but the following year there was in increase of only 498 persons, to a total of 61,867.

Socially, also, the community lagged behind the times. True, there was sin in London, but it was generally discreet and well concealed. At the top and bottom of the social scale, there were "fast" girls and boys and a rather startling number of hidden pregnancies and abortions. However, the great bulk of the population, the middle class, observed a Victorian rather than Edwardian code of morals. The majority of the girl children of this class were *not* rouged, short-skirted flappers, and the boy children wore short pants and long stockings until the magical age of sixteen, when these symbols of childhood were discarded (for long trousers with the fashion-ordained twenty-two-inch cuffs that flapped around the feet like the skirts London ladies wore in the 1880s.

1920 Earthquake in Kansu, China, kills 100,000 people.

In 1923 the citizens elected another of London's unusual, even eccentric, mayors. He was George A. Wenige, proprietor of Bicycle and Motor Sales Company, 425–427 Wellington Street, "phone 3182." George Wenige served in the mayor's chair for a total of nine terms, the most ever served by a chief magistrate in the city's history.

In spite of its slow growth the city had a town-planning commission as early as 1922. Its jurisdiction and that of the city stopped at Huron Street, which had been the city's northern boundary since the 1840s. The expected extension of the city's mercantile life in that direction had never happened.

On Monday, 18 June 1923, the Honourable Ernest Charles Drury, premier of Ontario, laid the cornerstones of the arts building and the natural science building of the University of Western Ontario. The site was the former "Bellevue Farm," owned by the Kingsmill family, north of the city on the west bank of the north branch of the Thames River.

There was much criticism of the university's choice. The site was considered to be a long way from the city centre and, furthermore, inaccessible.

Talbot Street Public School pupils, 1920. AUTHOR'S COLLECTION

HRH the Duke of Connaught, governor-general of Canada 1911–1916. As Prince Arthur he had visited London in 1869. UWO

A great deal of ribald comment was directed against "the college in Kingsmill's cowpasture," which, it was said scathingly, was "half way to Lucan."

However, with the financial support of the city and the province, a bridge across the Thames at the approach to the campus from Richmond Street was completed in November 1923, and the two new buildings were officially opened on Wednesday, 24 September, 1924.

In a corner of the arts building, Fred Landon, former Great Lakes sailor, newspaperman, and city librarian, took on a new job as librarian of the university. As late as 1908 the library of the Western University (as it was then called) contained no more than two hundred books. Ten years later Landon, himself a Western graduate (1906), secured for the university the private library of John Davis Barnett of Stratford, consisting of more than 40,000 volumes. The agreement was signed Saturday, 10 August 1918, the financial consideration being one dollar. Dr Barnett never got the dollar.

At the time of the acquisition the university was sharing the facilities of Huron College on St George Street. From its founding by Bishop Hellmuth in 1878 the university had led an extremely precarious existence. The medical school is the only faculty to have maintained an uninter-

1924 Olympic Games held in Paris.

Dundas Street looking west from Richmond Street, about 1925. UWO

rupted history, from 1881 to the present. A reorganization in 1908 withdrew the university from the control of the Church of England.

Now, at last, in 1924, the renamed University of Western Ontario had its own 225-acre campus, two handsome new Collegiate Gothic buildings, and more than 40,000 books. The cataloguing of the Barnett collection went on for years under Fred Landon and his immediate successor Dr James J. Talman.

1925 The United Church of Canada is founded.

For a season Londoners showed great pride in the addition to the city's educational mosaic, but they soon lost the first flush of hymeneal bliss. Despite the truly amazing growth of the university in the years since the opening of the new campus, London has never become a "university town" in the English sense. Town and gown have never made sweet music together.

Much more exciting to the average person than these fusty academic doings was the erection of the city's first traffic tower at the corner of Richmond and Dundas streets in 1925. There used to be a piece of motion-picture film comparing, in speeded-up motion, the haphazard movement of pedestrians and motor traffic before the installation and the orderly, almost military precision of cars and people afterwards.

All traffic on Richmond Street North came to a halt in mid-August 1925 as the funeral cortège of the "Hydro knight," Sir Adam Beck, moved south from his palatial residence, "Headley," through the heart of the city. It was probably the last such funeral to be seen in London. The procession consisted of dignitaries from near and far, top-hatted and frock-coated in the best nineteenth-century tradition. The men all wore black armbands.

Conspicuous among the formally-attired mourners was the mayor of London, dressed in a business suit and wearing a straw hat! Chided later for his lack of respect George Wenige denied the charge. It was his *best* suit, he declared, and the straw boater happened to be the only hat he owned.

Spectators by the thousands lined the route. Their reactions to the passing of the hearse were wildly mixed. There was no middle course where Adam Beck was concerned; in life he was either loved or hated. His coffin was greeted by both tears and snarls. Some men refused to remove their hats in tribute to the dead; women sobbed.

The city that Sir Adam Beck had helped to drag into the twentieth century marked the centennial of its founding in 1926. An Old Boys Reunion highlighted the celebration. Hundreds of old boys returned to the arena of their youth. "New boys" were scarce. Between January 1925 and January 1926 the population of London increased by only nineteen persons! The "biggest little town in Canada" was living up to its name.

The world (which included London) woke up with a start on Friday, 20 May 1927, to learn over the London *Free Press* radio station CJGC that a young man from St Louis, Missouri, Charles Augustus Lindbergh, was somewhere out over the stormy Atlantic in a single-engine monoplane, trying to win a $25,000 prize for the first non-stop flight from New York to Paris. All that day and into the next Londoners neglected work and

---

1925 First traffic lights installed in London, England.

study to strain after what little news was available. When the remarkable young man put his craft down at Paris after thirty-three hours and twenty-nine minutes aloft, France – and the world – went mad.

The tremendous surge of interest in the flight led to many imitative ventures, one of which originated in London. The Carling Brewing and Malting Company seized on the opportunity to publicize its product. After a decade of Prohibition Ontario had repealed the restrictive legislation passed during the Great War and the three major Canadian breweries – Molson's, Carling's, and Labatt's – were scrambling to get back into their pre-war markets.

Charles A. Burns, president of Carling's, came up with a natural. The company offered $25,000 for the first non-stop flight from London, Canada, to London, England. A call went out for flyers to undertake the hazardous adventure. Two veteran pilots took up the challenge. They were Captain Terence Tully and Lieutenant James Medcalf. They and their families needed the money.

Carling's bought a Stinson monoplane in Detroit and had it flown into the local airport, a dirt field on Highway 4, between London and Lambeth.

St James Court Apartments, one of a group of apartment buildings introduced into London after the First World War. UWO

Mr and Mrs G.A.P. Brickenden, members of the London Hunt Club, 1928. From the *London Free Press*. UWO

Hundreds of Londoners made the journey out to see the silver bird come in, the late afternoon sun flashing on her wings.

After several delays, the departure of the plane, the *Sir John Carling*, was set for the beginning of September 1927. It was a bad time of the year for an aerial crossing of the Atlantic. Tully and Medcalf knew it. Any Londoner who saw the two young men in the lobby of the new Hotel London prior to the take-off on Thursday, 1 September, will not soon forget the ashen faces and trembling fingers of the flyers.

The *Sir John Carling* took off from the new municipal airport at Crumlin, east of the city, and almost at once flew into bad weather. After a forced landing in Maine, they got as far as Harbour Grace, Newfoundland, before the flight was stalled again by weather conditions. The plane sat there for several days waiting for a break in the storms. Meanwhile the London public revealed some of its more unpleasant attitudes.

"They're just stalling" was a common comment, as was "They don't intend to go at all."

"It's just a promotion stunt" was another.

In the result, the two aviators took off from Newfoundland on Wednesday, 7 September, in spite of continued inclement conditions, and promptly

1927 15 millionth Model "T" Ford produced.

disappeared forever somewhere in the sullen grey swells of the Atlantic.

The episode of the *Sir John Carling* was soon over-shadowed by the train of news sensations that marked the "Roaring Twenties." Of special interest to local people was the investigation into fraud charges against Aimee Semple McPherson, the Oxford County native whose "Four-Square Evangelism" had profited her mightily in Los Angeles.

Many Londoners in search of profit "without benefit of clergy" were playing the stock market. "Margin buying" was the name of the game. An investor borrows money to buy stocks and then puts up the stock as collateral for the loan. If the stocks rise, the investor collects dividends. If they go down, he has to raise more cash to cover his investment. It's a socially-acceptable form of gambling, very popular with the middle class.

The castles in Spain proved to be built on quicksand. The disastrous slide in stock prices, which started on Thursday, 5 September 1929, hit bottom on "Black Tuesday," 29 October, when sixteen million shares were traded on Wall Street and losses reached the billions of dollars.

The collapse was complete. The American economy went into a sharp decline, dragging most of the economies of the western world along with it. The depression that followed – the Great Depression – was the longest and the most severe in North American history.

There were still a few Londoners around who remembered the savage depression of the 1850s. The parents of 1859 passed on well the lesson of those wicked times to their children and their children's children. It was lodged deep in London's community consciousness. As a result, the city emerged from the suffering of the Dirty Thirties in better financial condition than any other Canadian municipality.

The above statement must be examined carefully. It applies to the over-all picture, but not to specifics. The members of the financial establishment came out of the trauma of those years relatively unscathed. The middle classes endured much hardship; all were forced to retreat to a lower standard of living, some were wiped out. The poor, the single unemployed, and the unemployables suffered with great intensity.

Living tides of gaunt-faced men swept westward in summer, clinging by the thousands to wherever a handhold or a foothold offered on the freight trains, bound for harvest work in the wheatfields of the prairies – then ebbed again eastward as drought and despair reduced the western farmers to an equivalent state of indigent hopelessness.

By the mid-1930s the Canadian "dry bowl" was as bleak as the "dust bowl" of the United States, and the prevailing westerly winds were carrying tens of thousands of acres of prairie topsoil east to the sea. On a day in

---

1928 Olympic Games held in Amsterdam, Holland. Canada wins four gold medals.

The London Six, an automobile produced in London in 1923. The body was of aluminum over a wood frame. About ninety vehicles were produced in four body styles. UWO

May 1934, night came to London at noon as the sun was blotted out by a mammoth cloud of dust on its way to fertilize the Atlantic Ocean. God alone knew how many Western Canadian farms went to sea that day.

Attempts to recapture the impossible dream of economic stability came from two main sources, both political. Governments on the municipal, provincial, and federal levels strove to ameliorate the sufferings of the middle and lower classes by legislative measures. These measures were more designed to avoid future suffering than to treat present injury. The legislation passed into law at that time – family allowances, old age pensions, unemployment insurance, and the like – proved of inestimable value to generations to come, but did little to assuage the deep wounds of the Depression years.

1930 Adolf Hitler's Nazi Party wins majority in German elections.

ARMY AND NAVY VETERANS IN CANADA

IMPERIAL UNIT #229

252 King Street
September 6, 1935

Dear Sir:

It has been brought to our attention that a meeting of the Western
Fair Board of Directors will be held Monday, September 9th at 11:00 a.m.

We understand that at a former meeting of the Board of Directors
it was decided not to rent space to any organization wishing to place a
car inside the Grounds for the purpose of selling tickets.

We are totally in accord with this ruling in so far as outside
organizations are concerned, but at the same time feel that certain
exceptions could be made.

A visit to our present quarters at 252 King Street will show you
how necessary we need brighter and more sanitary club rooms.

May we, as Imperial War Veterans and Citizens of London, ask you
to support an application we are forwarding to the Secretary of the
Western Fair Board, Mr. W. D. Jackson, re renting sufficient space for
a car to stand during Fair Week.

Thanking you, we are,

Yours respectfully,

THE IMPERIAL VETERANS, UNIT #229

per T. J. Holmes, President

Army and Navy Veterans in Canada letterhead, 1930s. UWO

The second impetus to reform came from political parties not then in power. The politics of the left wing came into prominence at this time. The membership of the Communist Party reached its twentieth-century peak in the Depression period, attracting to its ranks many idealists of all ages and social backgrounds. The Canadian party was affiliated with the Third Communist International – the Comintern – founded in Moscow in 1919. For a time a member of the Comintern had his home in London, where he and his family lived under the constant surveillance of the RCMP.

The Communist Party, like all dissident groups, thrived on martyrdom and was aided greatly by the jailing of its leader Timothy (Tim) Buck, in 1931. This ill-judged action by the Conservative government of Prime Minister Richard Bedford Bennett played into the hands of the Canadian left wing. Small "l" liberals of all ages and classes reacted with anger to the government's use of the infamous Section 98 of the Criminal Code, which prohibited certain forms of public assembly.

Of the dissident political organizations that flourished in the dark thirties, only one made any lasting impact on the electorate. The Co-Operative Commonwealth Federation, founded on Monday, 1 August 1932, under the leadership of the Reverend James Shaver Woodsworth, met with an immediate and favourable response across the nation. The party's Regina Manifesto of 1933 made a clear statement of socialist intent. The party attracted to itself interest from all groups striving for political and economic reform, from the old style Fabian socialists to the communists. In 1934, the CCF, as it came to be called, found it necessary to purge itself of its far-left supporters, if it was ever to achieve widespread public acceptance as a reform, and not a revolutionary, party. Early that year a meeting of the members of the Woodsworth CCF Club of London continued halfway through the night before a majority succeeded in ejecting from the Club four of its members, including the secretary-treasurer, for espousing, or appearing to espouse, communist principles.

The average Londoner cared little for these political efforts, some of which in time came to benefit him through the introduction of social and economic reforms. The really big news of 1934, so far as this hypothetical human statistic was concerned, consisted of two blockbuster stories – the birth of the Dionne quintuplets on Monday, 28 May, and the kidnapping of John Sackville Labatt, president of the Labatt brewery, on Tuesday, 14 August.

The Labatt kidnapping and its confusing aftermath partially revealed the unsavoury underside of the Prohibition era. The kidnapping itself was bungled. Labatt was taken by his captors to a cottage in the Muskoka

---

1934 Mao Tse-tung leads the Chinese Red Army on its famous "Long March."

area. A note demanding a ransom of $150,000 was directed to the brewer's brother Hugh Labatt. The note was signed "Three-Fingered Abe." After three days the kidnappers apparently panicked and released John Labatt in Toronto.

The subsequent arrests and trials of three persons did little to clarify the issues. While public opinion has never been completely satisfied with the explanations given at that time, it is possible to draw some conclusions from the affair.

The two local breweries, Labatt's and Carling's, as well as the Hiram Walker distillery at Windsor, were involved in a "rum-running" operation across the Detroit River. This is not to say that the three companies were themselves actively engaging in illegal activities, but their products certainly were being shipped in quantity over the international border by persons who may or may not have been employed by those companies.

The border traffic was controlled by an organized-crime syndicate in Detroit. The group had decreed a levy on each bottle or case transported across the river from Canada. This "tax" was to be paid, directly or indirectly, by the producing companies. Both Labatt's and Carling's had refused to pay or to allow it to be paid. The Labatt kidnapping was apparently a means to enforce compliance.

Overlooked by the media in 1934 was an earlier, and successful, kidnapping directed at the Carling Brewery. Overlooked, because it was never officially reported.

Charles A. Burns, Carling's president, was the man who had organized the tragic flight of the *Sir John Carling*. His home was at 835 Richmond Street, at the southwest corner of Richmond Street and College Avenue (now the Ambassador Apartments). The Detroit gang kidnapped one of the Burns children, a little handicapped girl, and held her for a ransom of $25,000. The ransom was paid, the child was returned to her parents, and the London public was none the wiser.

By the mid-1930s everyone had become accustomed, perhaps inured is the better word, to the prolonged depression. Its effects were not all bad. People were driven in upon themselves and forced to rely upon their own resources, for entertainment, for instance. The cinema and the radio, as the wireless was now called, provided cheap amusement. The ornate picture palaces allowed all but the very poorest among us to pretend, briefly, that we "dwelt in marble halls," sipped champagne, and supped on caviar. The Gothic designs of such radio sets as the popular Philco helped us to dream that we lived amid mediaeval splendour as we listened

1935 First broadcast of a quiz programme in Canada.

to the clowns of the twentieth-century royal courts – Jack Benny, Fred Allen, Abe Burrows.

As the people of London struggled through the economic strictures of the Depression era, the future appeared to be an uncharted wilderness, with little hope of change. Only the past was certain. In this atmosphere local history came into its own. Nostalgia became organized. The London and Middlesex Historical Society had dwindled into obscurity as senility and death overtook its members. In 1936, a year that saw the Art Deco Dominion Public Building erected at the intersection of Richmond Street and Queens Avenue and a new Canadian National Railway station opened, was also marked by the reorganization and revitalization of the historical society. The people involved were Dr Edwin Seaborn, Fred Landon, and Orlo Miller. These three men were responsible for uncovering an immense mass of documentary material, long considered lost, in Middlesex, Huron, Norfolk, and Kent counties. These discoveries made possible a whole new approach to the social history of southwestern Ontario, based on contemporary records.

The dramatic history of the past was overtaken by the even more dramatic history of the twentieth century, when the tortured Thames River once more revenged itself on its tormentors. Heavy spring rains, falling on a still-frozen watershed, filled creeks and rivers to overflowing. In the late afternoon of Monday, 26 April 1937, floodwaters twenty-three feet above normal levels poured over the breakwater above the forks. With both north and south branches of the river in flood, all of London West, as well as low-lying sections to the north and south, was inundated. One life was lost and some thousand houses damaged. Total losses were estimated at slightly less than one million Depression dollars.

In spite of this renewed reminder of the power of the river and warnings from environmentalists like Edward G. Pleva, University of Western Ontario geographer, it took ten years and another flood threat (in 1947) before any practical steps were taken to control the capricious Thames.

As the bad times went on and on, London's poor and unemployed suffered ever more intensely. The long struggle against crushing odds took its toll on the mental and moral as well as the physical health of the victims. The most devastating effect was the loss of self-esteem. This in turn led to a decline in personal morals and a blurring of ethical standards generally.

An experiment in what would now be called "workfare" was launched at this time by the city administration, the university, and the London and

---

1936 Olympic Games held in Berlin. A black American wins four gold medals.

John D. Buchanan
ASSISTANT GENERAL MANAGER
AND ACTUARY

April 17, 1937

The Y.M.C.A. Campaign Canvassing Group –

Your excellent response to the call
for volunteers in the Y.M.C.A. Campaign is very much appreciated.
We are hoping to see you on Tuesday night at 6:15.

We hope that the Campaign this year
will be a success, so that Mr. Gauld and his staff, who are doing
a splendid job, will not be handicapped in their efforts. We
have every reason to believe that the results will be favourable
this year.

The plan of Campaign, it is hoped,
will save the time of the workers. We are having fewer meetings
and are concentrating the effort in two half days – Wednesday
and Thursday mornings, April 21st and 22nd. We have been
delighted with your willingness to devote these two half days
to promoting the success of the Y.M.C.A. for the next year.

We feel that the work can be covered
in the allotted time except for people who cannot be seen
because of absence from the city or on account of illness. These
cases will be cared for in a clean-up Campaign but this will
not involve the workers who are giving two full half days to the
canvass.

We believe that an enthusiastic
campaign, carried on over this short period, will make it
possible to reach the objective for the Y.M.C.A. this year. Be
sure to be with us on Tuesday night at 6:15 when we shall hear
from Mr. George McCullagh, who is returning to his home town to
help start the Campaign. Each team of four will meet together
at nine on Wednesday morning, and, after dividing up the cards
and making the plans for the morning work, we should be out on
the job in a few minutes.

Yours very truly

Chairman, Campaign Committee 1937

London Life Insurance Company letterhead, 1937. UWO

Middlesex Historical Society, acting cooperatively. A number of men on the city's welfare rolls, who had had previous clerical experience, were given an opportunity to "work out" their welfare cheques and make a little cash in addition by helping the Historical Society to sort and index some of the thousands of documents found in an attic at the Middlesex County Courthouse. The University and the Society between them provided the funds to employ a director for the project, who was paid the Depression wage of fifty cents an hour.

The outbreak of the Second World War gradually brought an end to the endeavour, but the indices are today a useful research tool in the Regional Collection of the University library.

On Wednesday, 7 June 1939, the city, no stranger to royal tourists, greeted its most important visitors of all – His Majesty King George VI and Her Majesty Queen Elizabeth. They were given an ecstatic welcome by an estimated 300,000 persons.

Many of those who lined Richmond Street in front of the offices of the London *Free Press* to see the royal cortège had stood at the same spot two and a half years earlier to listen to the abdication speech of King Edward VIII over the newspaper's radio station, now bearing the call letters CFPL.

On Sunday, 3 September 1939, Britain and France declared war on Germany. A week later Canada followed suit. For the second time in a generation, the youth of Canada were offered up a sacrifice on the altar of freedom.

Compared with the euphoria that gripped the city in August 1914, London's mood was sombre.

1939 German submarine sinks British passenger ship *Athenia*.

On 4 December 1939, the victorious mayoral candidate, J. Allan Johnston (seen answering the telephone) receives congratulations from exuberant campaign workers. UWO

CHAPTER ELEVEN

GROWING PAINS

Canadians who can think back to the Great War will recall the amazing difference in the reception of the news of the two conflicts. In 1914 Great Britain had not been engaged in a major struggle for over one hundred years. There had been so many years of peace that the world had come to believe that a war on a large scale was almost impossible. Only a few people imagined that Great Britain and Germany would come to blows – they were regarded as pure jingoists. ...

There are no illusions today as to what war means. Canada is just as determined and just as patriotic as in 1914, but Canadians of 1939 know the horrors of war. It is a more serious Canada which faces this crisis. ...
Arthur R. Ford in "Over the Week End," London *Free Press,* 4 September 1939.

At the beginning of the Second World War London was still recognizably the city to which the veterans of the First World War had returned. The corner of Dundas and Richmond streets was still the commercial hub, and the Smallman and Ingram department store still dominated the intersection. The cottage in which Sir James Alexander and his talented wife lived in the 1840s stood where it had for at least a century, at the southwest corner of Richmond and Horton streets, north of the framed house in which the artist Paul Peel was born in 1860.

Socially, London was still the tight little community where, it was said, "everyone knew everyone else," which was hyperbole, and "everyone knew his place," which was not. The lines between the classes, which had been established after the American Civil War and the oil boom, remained firm. Membership in the Establishment was based on money, rather than on church affiliation, as it had been earlier. There were two kinds of money – Old Money and New Money. Socially, the Old Money tended to practise philanthropy; the New Money practised expansion and development, which was called "progress."

1940 Germany invades Norway, Denmark, Holland, Belgium, and Luxembourg. British forces (430,000) evacuated from Dunkirk.

A military parade passes the pillared front of a branch of the Canadian Bank of Commerce at the northeast corner of Dundas and Richmond streets, during the Second World War. UWO

The most visible minority continued as before to be the black population, who were in equal measure tolerated and cherished. The invisible minority – London's Jewish community – continued to be respected in business and finance, but socially proscribed. Membership in the London Club, the London Hunt and Country Club, and the private golf courses continued to be the exclusive privilege of the city's accredited Gentiles.

Economically and physically London had stagnated during the years of the Depression. Since the major annexations at the turn of the century, there had been only small changes in the city's boundaries. In the ten-year period ending in 1940, the population had grown by less than 5,000.

1941 Germans invade Russia; the Japanese bomb Pearl Harbour.

Indeed, in 1938 and 1939 London actually lost 324 people, entering the first year of the war with a population of 76,099.

Income-tax statistics showed that London had many wealthy citizens, but records of bank clearings indicated little movement of entrenched capital. In 1925 the figure for the year was $136,640,609; in 1940 it was $137,393,049 – an increase of a little more than one half of 1 per cent.

All this changed in the six long years of the most terrible war in human history, but the changes were slow and subtle. The world was on fire, but the conflagration was too immense for comprehension. Today's students know far more about what happened in the Second World War than the civilians who lived through it. Tight censorship prevented the average Londoner from knowing how close to home it all was. The Holocaust was not even a rumour here, but there were families in London who lost relatives to Hitler's ovens. The war in the Pacific seemed far off, yet Japanese fire balloons landed in Michigan and Ontario, and native-born Japanese-Canadians were interned as though they were active enemies of the Canadian state. The war at sea reached Canadian territory on both east and west coasts.

In spite of the fact that the Second World War was longer, bloodier, and deadlier than the First, the effect of the conflict on London and Londoners was very different. The hysteria of the First War was missing. There were thousands of soldiers moving in and out of London; airmen of many Allied nations received their training at bases in and around the city; there were casualty lists and rationing – but in the main these things were taken in stride. People no longer believed everything they heard or read; the media reported to an audience that was more sophisticated, more cynical.

On Tuesday, 6 June 1944 – D-Day – Allied forces landed on the beaches of Normandy, and the push toward Berlin was on. Eleven months later, Germany surrendered. The articles of peace in Europe were signed on Tuesday, 8 May 1945, and cheering mobs went mad in all the major cities of the western world. A new phenomenon presented itself. It might be called "victory vandalism." Celebrants turned to violence and the destruction of property as a way of expressing their feelings. London escaped the vandals; Halifax did not.

With the change in the fortunes of war the media began to direct the attention of their audiences to the technological marvels that were to emerge from the womb of war. It is no coincidence that the years of the Second World War marked the rise to popularity of science fiction, in which the

---

1944 D-Day. Allied troops land in Normandy; US troops land in the Philippines.

A crowd gathers for an outdoor Victory Bond campaign sponsored by the "Kins-men Karnival" of the day. Place of honour goes to a Spitfire-fighter. *London Free Press*. UWO

scientific developments of the day were extrapolated into the wonders of tomorrow.

The prophecies achieved substance very quickly. A terrifying catalyst speeded up the technological machines. The atomic-bombing of Hiroshima and Nagasaki opened the gates of hell to the stunned gaze of a world that would never again know the benefits of an easy conscience. The A-bomb was the trigger that released the technological marvels that are still pouring into the markets of the world.

The physical and social face of London began to change, slowly at first. The city's street cars were abolished early in the war. Their rails were

1945 Hitler commits suicide: Victory in Europe (V-E Day), 8 May; US drops atomic bombs on Hiroshima and Nagasaki : Japan surrenders: End of Second World War 14 August.

ripped up and the steel was directed to Canada's war effort. Gasoline-powered omnibuses came into service. They are more efficient, more flexible in use than street cars, but they lack the charm. There was a camaraderie in the electric trolleys that has largely disappeared in the business-like buses. No one who ever rode the tiny "Toonerville Trolleys" of the North Belt Line will forget those monstrous little machines. The roadbed on Cheapside Street was an ill-kept one, and the little carriage or trolley that fed electricity to the cars would often bounce off the overhead wires. Usually the motorman or the conductor would manoeuvre the trolley or troller back on to the wire; sometimes one of the passengers would be allowed to do it.

The biggest crowd in London's history packs Dundas Street in front of city hall to celebrate V-J Day (Victory over Japan), on 16 August 1945. From the *London Free Press.* UWO

That was all a very long time ago, of course. In the last days of the trolley service the street cars were long, large affairs running smoothly on fine steel rails on a well-maintained roadbed, but they still retained much of the old neighbourhood feeling. In spite of the improvements in equipment and service, fewer people were travelling by public transportation systems. The automobile became the acceptable mode of moving from place to place for anyone who could afford one. Businessmen took to driving the family car to work, and little by little rush-hour traffic, morning, noon, and night, came to consist of a mass of automobiles, each often with only a single person inside – the driver. During the war "car pools" became the accepted thing, but we were all anxious to get back to our own chariots, our own enclosed living space.

A by-product of this changing pattern was the increasing isolation of the middle and the Establishment classes from their environment. A move to the suburbs by those people had began long before. Now the businessman and the industrialist moved between his house and his office in the privacy of his mobile carapace without coming into contact with the residents, permanent or temporary, of the core area. He did not meet them; therefore, for him, they did not exist.

Being thus insulated from reality, such people became increasingly difficult to convince of the existence of poverty and deprivation in London. On occasion they or their wives might shop in one of the prestigious luxury businesses on Dundas or Richmond Street without being aware that above the brilliantly-lighted storefronts, rabbit warrens of tiny drab rooms and sleazy apartments housed another London population of alcoholics, dope-users, drifters, prostitutes, and just plain poor people. The affluent Londoner picking out a gift of jewellery, lingerie, or furs for his wife or girlfriend would have been horrified to learn that the employees of the premises who put out the firm's garbage at night at the back of the building had best be equipped with a piece of wood or similar weapon to drive off the rats that had infested the downtown area for generations.

In this, of course, London differs scarcely at all from any North American community of more than village status. But London has generally preferred not to know of such conditions.

There have been exceptions to this purblind insularity. Many such exceptions have come from the old established families – the Carlings, Labatts, Cronyns, Bechers, and others. The late Edward E. Reid, vice-president and managing director of the London Life Insurance Company, used to walk daily to and from work from his home, as also did J. Allyn Taylor, then-president of the Canada Trust Company. The late Colonel

---

1946 Electronic brain built at Pennsylvania University.

London's perennial mayor, George Adelbert Wenige, with Barbara Ann Scott, figure-skating champion at the Winter Olympics of 1948. From the *London Free Press*. UWO

J. Innes Carling, descendant of Sir John, used to do likewise, as did the Ingrams (Gordon J. and Kenneth H.) of the Smallman and Ingram Department Store. These men and others like them knew their city in all its aspects, good and bad.

One of the first casualties of the war years in the business field was was the long-established department store Smallman and Ingram. Perhaps because there were no interested Smallmans or Ingrams prepared to carry on the tradition, or perhaps simply because the firm received an offer they could not refuse, the store was taken over by the Robert Simpson Company Limited of Toronto. Although this was a Hogtown takeover, local people could derive some satisfaction from the fact that the Burton family who controlled Simpson's had relatives in London and the surrounding area.

1946 Lillian Hellman, *Another Part of the Forest* play.

This was the first of the major changes to affect the London business community. Other changes in the immediate post-war years came more slowly and more subtly. A feature of London's business life for more than a century began to disappear – the independent grocery store. The Atlantic & Pacific Tea Company (A & P) was among the first of the big grocery chains to enter the competition for the shopper's dollar. Loblaw's, Dominion Stores, and Red and White stores quickly followed. In an effort to match the bulk buying-power of the big chains, many of the independents formed a cooperative organization, the Independent Grocers Association (IGA). The number of autonomous corner-grocery ventures steadily declined. In later years they metamorphosed into the so-called "convenience" or "variety" stores, many of which in their turn have been gobbled up by chains like Shaw's Diary stores, Mac's Milk, or Becker's.

In the past London had had little in the way of heavy industry aside from the two foundries, McClarys and Leonards. The Leonard foundry eventually closed (the London *Free Press* building now stands on the site of the foundry), and McClarys became General Steel Wares Limited. In 1950 the Diesel Division of General Motors of Canada located in London, on Oxford Street East, to engage in the glamourous business of building diesel-locomotive engines for use in Canada and abroad.

Romantics among us deplored the passing of the hugely beautiful steam railway locomotives and their never-to-be-forgotten whistles, whose mournful wail represented for generations the magic of travel and the lure of a world beyond. The raucous hoot of the diesel horn can never elicit the same nostaglia or evoke the dreams of Xanadu.

The diesels, they said, were more efficient. Efficiency became the new god of the market-place. Atomic energy was efficient as a killing device. Scientists were quick to point out the peaceable uses of atomic power, in medicine and in the production of electical energy.

It was in medicine that Londoners first saw the new energy source demonstrated. It had early been discovered that certain by-products of the atomic-bomb experiment could be useful in treatment of some forms of cancer. A radioactive isotope of cobalt was used in what the media dubbed the "cobalt bomb." The cancer clinic at London's Victoria Hospital installed one of the new treatment contrivances. Under the direction of the late Doctor Ivan H. Smith the clinic became famous throughout North and South America for its advanced method of treatment.

In fact it is in the field of medicine that London has long occupied a preeminent position among the cities of the western hemisphere. As instance, Doctor George Edward Hall, of the Royal Canadian Air Force,

1947 India becomes independent; partitioned into India and Pakistan.

The Ridout Street Restoration. After several years' campaigning by a group of heritage-minded citizens, John Labatt, Limited, took over the task of restoring these buildings, dating back to the 1830s and 1840s. Sketch by Bill McGrath, from *London Heritage* – second edition (London: Phelps Publishing 1979).

carried out special research in aviation medicine at the University of Western Ontario that earned him decorations from the Canadian and American governments. Dr Hall's pioneering study on the effects of gravity on the human body led to the development of "pressure suits" basic to the future of aeronautics and astronautics. In this work Dr Hall was associated with the late Sir Frederick Banting, who was a lecturer at Western's medical school when he made his initial discovery of insulin in 1921; and also with the late Walter J. Blackburn, publisher of the London *Free Press*.

After the war Dr Hall became dean of medicine at Western and, in 1947, president and vice-chancellor. Under this direction the University, and especially its medical faculty, greatly enhanced its reputation. The medical school became one of the top institutions on the continent, in the same league as McGill and Harvard.

In 1947 the Thames River once again reminded London of its presence and its threat to life and property. It was Sunday, 5 April, when the unruly river came a-knocking at the door. For two days the flood waters lapped at the London West breakwaters as they had ten years earlier. Londoners didn't need a house to fall in upon them – not quite. It had been ninety-five years since the first serious flood struck the city, in 1852.

Action was now taken, finally. The city moved with commendable speed. On Thursday, 8 April, a special meeting of city council authorized an expenditure of $134,999 for local-control measures. On Wednesday, 7 May, the Upper Thames Valley Conservation Authority was established at

1947 HRH Princess Elizabeth marries Philip Mountbatten, Duke of Edinburgh.

Woodstock. The first meeting of the authority was held at Stratford on Monday, 20 October. The Fanshawe Dam on the north branch of the river was the first stage of the flood control system. It was opened in 1953.

Two years later the city celebrated its hundredth birthday with great fanfare. Among the many special events was the play *This Was London,* staged at the Grand Theatre, directed by Roy Irving, formerly of the famous Abbey Theatre Players of Ireland. A Toronto newspaper reported that this was the first time a Canadian municipality had commissioned a stage play.

It was a time for centennial celebrations: the Roman Catholic Diocese of London celebrated its first hundred years in 1956. The Anglican Diocese of Huron had its centennial the year following.

The pace of development quickened in the 1950s and downtown landmarks began to disappear. The beautiful old Covent Garden Market building, once the subject of a sunny painting by Paul Peel, vanished and was replaced by a parking building and an enclosed market. The old firehall on King Street was razed and the site became still another parking lot. The city's first public library building was torn down and replaced by an architecturally uninspired combined YMCA/YWCA.

After much heated discussion a site was chosen for a new city hall. One proposal would have placed the municipal headquarters in Victoria Park, with a parking area underneath it among the tree roots. This, one of many such assaults, before and since, on the integrity of the city's cherished open space, aroused the anger of the citizenry. The proposal was hastily dropped and a site nearby was chosen, on Dufferin Avenue.

Another threat to London's heritage developed when a large-scale traffic study by A.D. Margison and Associates called for a twinning of the Dundas Street (Kensington) bridge. A block of buildings representing the earliest financial centre of the village would have to go. A campaign by a group of heritage-minded citizens over a period of years resulted in the Labatt Brewing Company rescuing and restoring three of the buildings, dating from the period 1835–1845. This development started a new trend in London. The three buildings were restored for commercial use, one being converted into a head office for Labatt's.

Local history was now beginning to find a place in London's social life. In 1958 the city established a temporary museum on Wellington Street opposite Victoria Park. This was a typical London achievement: such a museum had been proposed a mere fifty years earlier.

Further impetus was given to the promotion of the city's history when the Harris family, descendants of Captain John Harris, RN, one-time treas-

---

1952 King George VI dies and is succeeded by his daughter, Elizabeth.

urer of the old District of London, made a gift to the city of the family home, "Eldon House," together with much of its contents. This magnificent donation included the estate grounds and the river parkland below them.

These were matters of special interest to a relatively small group of citizens. Bigger fish were frying. Mercantile history was being made with the building of a one-block-square enclosed shopping mall and parking garage in the downtown area. Wellington Square, as it was called, was the first such structure to be built in a midtown setting in North America.

Simultaneously, the city was pushing its application to the Ontario Municipal Board for a massive annexation of land in the adjacent townships.

As a fitting climax to this year of frothy promise, London was host on Friday, 3 July 1959, to an official visit by the head of the Commonwealth of Nations, Her Majesty Queen Elizabeth II, and her consort, His Royal Highness Philip, Duke of Edinburgh. It had been a little over twenty years since the Queen's parents had visited the second London. There had been great changes in those two decades.

The year 1960 saw the formal ratification of the most significant of these changes. London was granted its annexation request on Monday, 9 May. It was to take effect on the first day of the new year. Wellington Square (now Eaton Square) was officially opened on Thursday, 11 August. His Excellency Major-General George Philias Vanier, governor-general of Canada, visited the city on Friday, 28 October, and the municipal elections for the "new, bigger and better" London were held on Monday, 12 December.

London was led into the new decade and its enlarged destiny by the second former policeman to be elected mayor. The first was Allan Rush, who entered the city police force as a second-class constable in 1931. He was mayor from Monday, 1 January 1951, to Tuesday, 29 March 1955, when he resigned to become superintendent of the newly-built Dr John Dearness Home for Elder Citizens. The home was named for one of the city's most distinguished educators. The job at the municipally-operated residence must have been an attractive one. When Mr Rush died suddenly on Tuesday, 9 July 1955, he was followed in that position by his successor as mayor, George Beedle. Mr Beedle was succeeded in turn by Alderman Ray Dennis, who thus became London's third mayor in one year, a record even for this city.

The new mayor of London in 1961 was F. Gordon Stronach, the pipe-smoking, sports-minded former chief of police for London Township.

1955 Blacks in Montgomery, Alabama, boycott segregated city bus lines.

Both Rush and Stronach floated into office on waves of sympathy for underdogs battling entrenched bureaucracy. Londoners have often been partial to anyone seen to be fighting city hall.

The new city broke, once and for all, the confining limits of the river valley, leaping the north branch of the Thames into London Township, and the main branch into Westminster Township. The population of the city increased by 63,072 to 165,815. As a means of guaging this increase, it may be sufficient to point out that the number of people absorbed by the annexation was almost equal to the total population of the city in 1924 (63,339). Even more startling however, was the physical size of the new metropolis of southwestern Ontario. Previous to the 1960 land-grab the city covered 12.37 square miles (32.03 square kilometres). On 1 January 1961, London's area ballooned to 66.37 square miles (171.89 square kilometres).

Lieutenant-Governor John Graves Simcoe would have been delighted at the progress of the city he had only dreamed of.

It is doubtful that he would have been so pleased with the orgy of planned obsolescence that infected the enlarged community. In Simcoe's day buildings, either public or private, were built to last for centuries. In the London of our times they are built to stand for decades only – and sometimes not that. As a case in point, the city's principal railway station, built in 1853–1854, was not replaced by a modern building until 1936, some eighty-two years later. That structure had hardly achieved voting age when it was torn down, to be replaced by the present, equally bland station, in 1963.

By way of contrast, London's river, on which its citizens had turned their backs for so many years, was slowly becoming, once again, a place of beauty. Without fanfare, the Public Utilities Commission transformed the banks of the river, wherever feasible, into parkland. The river flats below Eldon House became Harris Park. The old Dennisteel foundry was demolished, some aging and deteriorating buildings on Ridout Street were razed, and for the first time in more than a century, Londoners could see the forks of the Thames much as they had appeared to John Graves Simcoe and his staff in 1793. The development of parkland along the river continues to the present, a gracious presence, an antidote to the urban blight that threatens other parts of the city.

These were the years of the "flower children," of pot and LSD, of hippies and gurus, of meditation and demonstration, of protest, dissent, and anniversaries. Huron College had its centennial in 1963; the Canada Trust Company marked its first hundred years in 1964; Kingsmill's Department

---

1966 Race riots occur in slum areas of Chicago, Cleveland, and other US cities.

Store celebrated its centenary in 1965. There were no public festivities marking the centennial of the Fenian Raids in 1966; the 140th anniversary of the founding of London passed almost unnoticed in 1966, and the 110th birthday of the city's own railway, the London and Port Stanley Railway, was noted only by its sale to the Canadian National Railway system on Saturday, 1 January 1966 – to the great relief of all taxpayers.

The really big show, of course, was the centennial of Canadian Confederation in 1967. Every community in the nation pulled out all the stops, suitably to commemorate the occasion.

In retrospect it may be said that the effect of the celebrations on the Canadian public's perception of, and interest in, the history of the country and its communities, big and small, was beneficial. On the other hand, the attempts physically to cement the occasion in memory by buildings and memorials were not universally successful.

A small community in Alberta, with a large sense of humour, built a landing pad for visiting Unidentified Flying Objects (UFOs). London's project, Centennial Hall, is still looking for UFO's, or *anything* animate or inanimate, to land on its largely uninhabited formal plaza facing Victoria Park.

The new Canadian flag flapped proudly from every official flagpole as Centennial Year drew to a close, and a December twilight settled over a community of 206,000 people.

No longer could it be said of London, even half-truthfully, that "everyone knew everyone else"; nor could it be said, as it once was, that everyone knew his or her place.

The late Mrs Edna Cleghorn, daughter of William M. Gartshore, president of the McClary Manufacturing Company, once complained wistfully of the passing of those days as she sat beneath a portrait of herself as a young woman painted by Paul Peel. She told her visitors that she had gone uptown with her companion on a recent Friday night. Window-shopping on Dundas Street, she had not seen a single person whom she knew.

1967 Urban Renewal Report and Scheme filed with London City Council.

CHAPTER TWELVE

A City for Sale

[He] is brought as a lamb to the slaughter, and as a sheep before her shearers. ...
Isaiah 53:7

Young people tend to consider anything that happened five years ago as "away back then." Ten years ago is history; the events of twenty years ago are antediluvian.

Where the history of London is concerned, they may be right.

The pace of change in the city has accelerated to a blur since the centennial of Confederation was celebrated.

The annexation of 1960 merely whetted the city's appetite for more, more, and more. A new proposal at this present writing reaches out for additional parcels of land in the adjoining townships.

The face of London, especially in what is now called "the old city," has changed almost beyond recognition. Buildings that have benignly observed the passing scene for fifty, seventy-five, or a hundred and more years are being gobbled up by the developers' bulldozers, or starched, prettified, and "gentrified" like aging harlots, or propped up like Hollywood sets in the process called "preserving the façades."

Although the city has well-qualified architects, city-planners, artists, and specialists in all the multiple fields of design for human use and enjoyment, there is no concerted overall plan for the orderly development of its 43,000 acres of houses, stores, factories, trees, streets, avenues, and boulevards. What planning is done is all too often *ad hoc;* the zoning process is frequently laughable.

Years of discussion culminated in the building of new municipal offices on Dufferin Avenue, standing edge-on to Victoria Park. Its backside overlooks a handsome plaza named for a long-serving city clerk, Reginald H. Cooper. Facing the plaza and the park is one of the city's chief embar-

---

1970 Prime Minister Pierre Elliot Trudeau invokes War Measures Act.

rassments, Centennial Hall, a box-like structure incorporating most of the faults possible in such buildings. The plaza cannot be used for great public events, as originally intended, because the noise would disturb the occupants of an apartment building thoughtlessly built abutting Centennial Hall.

Two massive edifices hem in and trivialize the once-dominant Middlesex county courthouse, which now serves as the offices of the Middlesex county council. The new county courthouse is a monstrous concrete structure rather resembling an aborted egg-crate. On the northwest corner of Dundas and Ridout streets, where Dennis O'Brien built the city's first brick building, is the London Regional Art Gallery. The peculiar design, by Raymond Moriyama of Toronto, was once described by the late Edward Victor Buchanan, an associate of Sir Adam Beck, as "looking like a boiler factory." It appears that the architect had given London a scaled-down copy of an art gallery in Fort Worth, Texas. According to Don Smith, head of a London construction company, the principal difference between the two galleries is that "the Texas gallery is covered in Travertine marble, while ours is covered in grey tin."

"Tight money," as they called it a century ago, forced the University of Western Ontario to break its architectural tradition of Collegiate Gothic. In the main, the new buildings that crowd the once spacious campus are functionally adequate, but architecturally illiterate.

As in most North American cities, the needs of the automobile and its symbiotic driver have led to the development of massive shopping malls in London's suburbs, where shoppers may dawdle in a protected environment after parking their vehicles free on huge, paved prairies. These gigantic bazaars, strategically located at all the major points of the compass, have siphoned off a good deal of the trade traditionally attracted to the city's core. An alarmed downtown merchant-community and a concerned city council have sprung, belatedly, to the defence of "downtown," in a series of uncoordinated panic leaps of unfettered civic plagiarism. Attempting to copy the architectural renaissance of such old rivals as Hamilton and Kitchener, civic authorities have offered themselves as willing sacrifices to lustful developers both within and without the city's limits.

The sharks have risen to the bait. Two giant developers, Campeau Corporation and Cambridge Leaseholds, are at present snarling at one another over the bones of downtown London. Cambridge has been talking up a planned $400 million development at the western end of Dundas Street. The talk has been going on for some time. The only result so far has been the razing of most of the properties in the block bounded by

1973 A natural-gas explosion destroys or damages 24 homes in London, Ontario.

Dundas, Talbot, King, and Ridout streets, and the deliberate abandonment to the elements of a surviving Victorian era streetscape.

Meanwhile the Campeau firm has stolen a march on its rival and made a start on a somewhat smaller ($175 million) development to the east of the main intersection, in an area roughly bounded by Dundas, Clarence, King, and Wellington streets.

Around the works, projected and actual, of the two major developers, a clutch of smaller fry is hatching its own plans for the destruction of the rest of London's nineteenth- and early-twentieth-century streetscapes. One bizarre result has been the erection of a luxury hotel within the skeleton of the 1905 Armory building. The effect is rather like an Art Deco candle rising out of a regimental birthday cake.

Other projects, if fully realized, may turn the streets of the core area into canyons of high-rise steel, concrete, and glass mediocrities. This is highly unfortunate since many of the older structures are capable of being turned into attractive retail shops and boutiques of the kind that in other communities have charmed and attracted not only visitors but suburban shoppers as well.

Many United States cities are discovering and restoring the lavish cinematic palaces of the golden age of films to great effect – and profit. The fine old Loew's Theatre on Dundas Street would make an excellent arts centre, with facilities already in place for the production of theatrical and musical events. It will be a very great shame if this potential showpiece is allowed to be razed.

London, of course, is not alone among North American cities in falling victim to the financial pressures exerted by major developers. In many cities in California, residents are ruefully admitting that they were all for "progress" – until they saw what it looked like.

It is not just the physical face of the city that has changed since Canada celebrated its centennial. The human make-up of the city has changed even more dramatically.

In Centennial Year there was much talk of such things as national identity, multiculturalism, the Canadian mosaic, the two founding nations, and similar concepts. London's eggheads spoke learnedly and polysyllabically about such stimulating ideas, but aside from the university community, few had little direct contact with exotic individual examples.

With the advent of television in 1953 Londoners for the first time found themselves suffering with the suffering of other people, half a world away, in person. There they were, on the little screen. We saw them die, in black and white. It was even worse in colour.

1974 Margaret Lawrence: *The Diviners* (novel).

Bell tower of the Dundas Street Congregational Church, an imaginative piece of heritage preservation. The church was destroyed by fire in 1967. Only the tower survived; it was preserved as a monument to the past by the owner of an adjacent apartment block. EDWARD PHELPS

Then they were among us, the refugees. The Hungarians, the Czechs, the Vietnamese, the young Americans fleeing their country's participation in what they saw as an unjust war. Then, in the 1980s, the starving Africans. It seemed that half the world was in flight from political systems, from oppression, from poverty and malnutrition.

London received its share of the globe's shifting populations with commendable compassion, for the times were reasonably good. It is usually when jobs are scarce and the newcomers are seen as competitors for one's daily bread that skin-colour and language-difference become a source of friction.

Increasingly after 1967 the long-established White Anglo-Saxon Protestant (WASP) majority in London became diluted by the number of these exotic ethnic minorities. The number of black people rose, as an instance, but the voices were different now; the accents were African or Caribbean instead of American. There were dark-complected Pakistanis and sari-clad Indian women. There were Sikhs, with their beards and distinctive turbans. There was a Moslem community with its own mosque.

An important change was also taking place in the economic structure of the city. Top management of the principal industries remained, to a large extent, in the hands of the old Establishment. The Labatt, Cronyn, Ivey, Blackburn, Jeffery, and McClary clans continued to control much of the city's financial life. However, the "new men" who filled the active working positions – the chief executive officers (CEOs), the second-in-command men, the comptrollers, the various grades of vice-president, from the nominal to the active – these were very largely imports, men on the rise in regional offices of London firms. These men, depending on their importance to their companies, joined the London Club or the Hunt Club, or both. Their object, socially, was to get a quick "handle" on London, for their own benefit and that of their company. The handle had to be quick and superficial, for if they succeeded in their positions, London was merely a way-station to business stardom. If they failed, they were soon relegated to the minor leagues in Oshawa, Kingston, or even Montreal.

The tests these "growth executives" had to undergo were really quite simple. How well could they hold their liquor? How well could they raise money for charity? The testing-grounds for the first were, of course, the two clubs. The testing-ground for the second was the annual fund drive for what has been called variously the Community Chest, the United Appeal, the United Fund, and now the United Way. This second challenge was the acid test and remains so today.

1976 Parti Québecois wins majority in Quebec legislature. René Levesque becomes premier.

The Simcoe Elm. In March 1969, ravaged by the Dutch elm disease, the last living relic of Lieutenant-Governor Simcoe's visit to the site of London in 1793 fell to the saws of a team of workmen from the Public Utilities Commission. From the *London Free Press.* UWO

"Wharton's Folly": a 1988 luxury hotel rises from the gutted interior of the 1905 Armory building. Only an eccentric eighteenth-century peer could have bettered this impish confection. EDWARD PHELPS

It is not automatically to be assumed that the 2-I-Cs who headed up the various appeals for funds were passionately addicted to the cause of the poor, sick, and disadvantaged. Some few actually were. For the others, though, it was, and is, a game of numbers that they must win or their bosses will look elsewhere for someone to inherit the key to the executive washroom.

Regardless of motive, these efforts have benefited London. There is no real need for anyone to suffer in London in 1988. If all other sources of governmental or charitable aid fail, the media can always be depended upon to pluck at the heart-strings of the public.

There was much talk in the 1960s about the so-called "generation gap." That gap has become a chasm. The pace of events since 1967 has become so fast that every new generation is in danger of losing its way altogether, having lost its knowledge of its roots. This acknowledged fear has led to a great increase in the number of amateur and professional genealogists.

Lance Morrow, writing in *Time* (11 January, 1988), has called 1968 "the knife blade that severed past from future." The events of that watershed year, with its bitter conflicts between the generations, traumatized American youth. It was not, however, a purely American phenomenon. The whole world was suffering, not from the Vietnam War, but from a new disease of the soul for which there is no known cure. The buzzword is "alienation." We are in danger of becoming alienated, not only from our past but from one another. It has been discovered that high-rise apartment buildings do not breed neighbourhoods; quite the contrary. Walls separate people more than lawns. The whine of the lawnmower tells us that our neighbours are alive and well. Apartment dwellers have been known to die alone in their rooms, unnoticed by those in adjacent cubicles.

London learned this chilling fact in 1977. In April of that year a young woman, Louella Jeanne George, was found strangled to death in her top-floor apartment in a high-rise building on Grand Avenue. In July the body of a twenty-two-year-old woman, Donna Veldbloom, was discovered strangled and stabbed in an apartment on Orchard Street. Intensive police investigation tied the two murders together and linked them to a thirty-year-old automobile-plant worker, Russell Maurice Johnson. On Thursday, 28 July, Inspector Bob Young and Detective Larry Ross went to Johnson's apartment. As Frank Jones tells it in his study of Canadian murder cases *Trail of Blood* (Toronto: 1981), this is what they saw:

Facing them, Russell Johnson, 30, was not a sight soon forgotten. Six foot one, 190 pounds, a trim figure in jeans and white shirt, biceps bulging, he had the

---

1977 Guy Lombardo, London-born bandleader, dies.

Russell Maurice Johnson, "Canada's most frightening serial murderer." From Frank Jones, *Trail of Blood* (Toronto: *Mc Graw-Hill Ryerson,* 1981).

aquiline good looks of a Greek god. Behind him the apartment was as neat as a pin, the floors gleaming.

Johnson's confession, which he volunteered immediately following his arrest, was a grim account of seven murders and ten assaults on young women in London and Guelph, Ontario, over a period of eight years. Jones calls Johnson "the most frightening killer this country has ever seen." Strikingly handsome, compulsively neat in his personal habits, he was quite, quite mad. When the blood-hunger stirred in him he was capable of scaling high-rise buildings like a human fly. As he himself described his frenzy:

All of a sudden I am climbing balconies. I have strength way beyond me. I've got no regard for caution or danger. My mind is racing at a terrible speed. I am going hand over hand up the balconies and if I lose my grip it doesn't matter. Or if I grab something and it isn't safe, it doesn't matter. One time I was up fifteen floors. The door was locked. The next day I went by and looked up and shuddered to see where I'd been.

At his trial in 1978 Johnson was found not guilty by reason of insanity and committed to the maximum security wing of the Ontario Mental Health Centre at Penetanguishene, where he remains at this present writing.

By the mid-1970s high-rise office and apartment buildings like the fifteen-storey building that Russell Johnson climbed, were proliferating like the trees that once presented little but a blanket of green to high-flying birds and airmen.

1978 One of the greatest winter storms on record hits London, Ontario, 26 January.

To serve these widespread "people barracks" big business circled the city outskirts with suburban shopping malls, to the number of about thirty by this year, 1988.

To return to the problem outlined at the beginning of this chapter, the city's administrators and elected representatives finally realized what was happening and began to look for a *deus ex machina* to save the inner city. At once London became a Mecca for architects, city planners, and dreamers with multiple degrees and little knowledge of people and their legitimate needs.

Treading hard on the heels of the academics came the heavy-footed major developers from the Outlands, clutching bundles of someone else's

Modern ziggurats. The architecture of the future? EDWARD PHELPS

money in their hands, shouldering one another aside in their eagerness to claim the city and all who dwell therein as their own profitable vineyard.

The perils of Chaos-on-the-Thames were foreseen long ago. It is not London's custom to proceed precipitately. It takes at least twenty-five years for a simple idea to be accepted and adopted. A more complicated concept like flood-control can take up to a century.

As Frederick H. Armstrong puts it in his *The Forest City* (Windsor Publications: 1986): "Although downtown problems have been regularly discussed over the last quarter of a century, a cohesive, overall strategy has yet to emerge."

Leaving aside at this point the ravaged bones of the old city of London, what can one say of the broader picture? What of London's economic future?

London is still the "fat cat" city all Ontario knows and some hate. Its top rating on Wall Street is the envy of all other Canadian municipalities. However, a subtle change is taking place. Many, but not all, of the great companies of the past proudly maintain their "head offices" in London – Canada Trust, London Life, Emco, Lawson and Jones, among others. But the real power in these companies has moved elsewhere. The giant multinational corporations have gobbled up the assets; the big decisions are being made in lush boardrooms in Toronto or Montreal or New York or London. The City at the Forks, despite the billions of dollars in the vaults of its financial establishment, has become that thing most dreaded by Canadian nationalists – a home to branch plants.

A kind of unstructured frenzy has seized upon the business community. None of them seem to know where they're going.

That's probably because they don't know where they've been.

This last chapter, rather than being a chronicle of the events of the last twenty-five years, has been an attempt to help us understand what the heritage of that quarter of a century has been. London can never again be what it once was in the days of the "Great Queen across the Waters," as the Amerindians called Queen Victoria, but it can certainly be better than it is and threatens to become.

This book, it is hoped, may provide some answers. The mistakes of the past can be avoided in the present and in the future only by knowing what they were.

London, Canada, is a proud city. It has been a beautiful city.

Its pride and its beauty can be secured and maintained only by constant, unremitting vigilance.

1985 David Peterson of London, Ontario, becomes premier of Ontario.

BIBLIOGRAPHY

I BOOKS

Addington, Charles *A History of the London Police Force* London, Ont.: Phelps Publishing, 1980.

Armstrong, Frederick H. *The Forest City: An Illustrated History of London, Canada* Northridge, California: Windsor Publications, 1986.

Barr. Murray L. *A Century of Medicine at Western* London, Ont.: University of Western Ontario, 1977.

Bremner, Archie *Illustrated London, Ontario, Canada* London, Ont.: n. pub. 1897.

Brock, Daniel J. *Dan Brock's Historical Almanack of London* London, Ont.: Applegarth Follies, 1975, 3 vols.: Spring, summer and autumn 1975.

Brown, Ron *Ghost Towns of Ontario* Vol. I. Toronto: Cannonbooks, 1984.

Cahn, Julius *Julius Cahn's Official Theatrical Guide, 1905-1906* New York: n. pub., 1905.

Campbell, Clarence T. *1826-1926 Milestones, London, Canada* London, Ont.: n. pub., 1926.

— *Pioneer Days in London* London, Ont.: Advertiser, 1921.

Carty, Arthur C., ed. *A Thousand Arrows: Biographical Memoir of the Hon. Henry Edward Dormer* London, Ont.: n. pub., 1970.

Collins, Robert *The Age of Innocence 1870/1880* Toronto: Natural Science of Canada, 1977.

Cronyn, Verschoyle P. *Other Days*. London, Ont.: n. pub., 1976.

Crowfoot, A. H. *This Dreamer: Life of Isaac Hellmuth, second Bishop of Huron* Toronto: Copp Clark, 1963.

Dodds, Philip, ed. *The Story of Ontario Agricultural Fairs and Exhibitions 1792-1967* Picton, Ont.: Picton Gazette, 1967.

Dod's Peerage, Baronetage and Knightage of Great Britain and Ireland Vol. 66. London: Whittaker, 1906.

Drew, Benjamin, ed. *The Refugee; or the Narratives of Fugitive Slaves in Canada* Boston: n. pub., 1856; facsimile ed., Toronto: Coles, 1972.

Fuller, Robert M. and Mrs. Kathleen Bowley *Barclays of Pickering* Windsor, Ont.: The author, 1977.

Graham, Percy W. *Sir Adam Beck* London, Ont.: The Carl Smith Publishing Co., 1925.

Guillet, Edwin C. *The Lives and Times of the Patriots* Toronto: University of Toronto, 1938.

Hamil, Fred Coyne *Lake Erie Baron: The Story of Colonel Thomas Talbot* Toronto: Macmillan, 1955.

Hamil, Fred Coyne *The Valley of the Lower Thames: 1640 to 1850* Toronto: University of Toronto, 1951.

Hill, Nicholas and Ted Halwa *London Downtown Façade Study* London: Corporation of the City of London, 1986.

Hill, Pearl M. *Index to the London Free Press "Looking over Western Ontario" pages, Oct. 8, 1921 to Aug. 20, 1949.* London, Ont.: London Free Press, 1951.

Honey, Terrence W., ed. *London Heritage* London, Ont.: London Free Press, 1972.

Innis, Mary Quayle, ed. *Mrs. Simcoe's Diary* Toronto: Macmillan, 1965.

Kilbourn, William *The Firebrand* Toronto: Clarke, Irwin, 1956.

Landon, Fred *An Exile from Canada to VanDiemen's Land: being the Story of Elijah Woodman* Toronto: Longmans Green, 1960.

__ *Western Ontario and the American Frontier.* Toronto: Ryerson, 1941.

Lutman, John H. *The Historic Heart of London* London, Ont.: Corporation of the City of London, 1977.

Lutman, John H. and Christopher L. Hives *The North and the East of London* London, Ont.: Corporation of the City of London, 1982.

Miller, Orlo *A Century of Western Ontario* Toronto: Ryerson, 1949 (also Westport, Conn.: Greenwood Press, 1972).

__ *Gargoyles and Gentlemen* Toronto: Ryerson, 1966.

__ *The London Club; An Irreverent History* London, Ont.: 1954.

__ *Twenty Mortal Murders* Toronto: Macmillan, 1978.

Miller, Orlo and A. Brandon Conron *The London Club: a century in light-hearted retrospect* London, Ont., 1980.

Miller, Warren Cron, ed. *Vignettes of Early St. Thomas* St. Thomas, Ont.: Sutherland Press, 1967.

Owen E. A. *Pioneer Sketches of Long Point Settlement* 1st. ed. 1898; facsimile ed. Belleville, Ont.: Mika, 1972.

Paddon, Wayne *The Story of the Talbot Settlement, 1803-1840* St. Thomas: The author, 1975.

Poole, Nancy Geddes *The Art of London 1830-1980* London, Ont.: Blackpool Press, 1984.

Purdom, Thomas H. *London and its Men of Affairs* London, Ont.: 1915.

Read, Colin *The Rising in Western Upper Canada 1837-8* Toronto: University of Toronto Press, 1982.

Rosser, Frederick T. *London Township Pioneers* Belleville, Ont.: Mika, 1975.

Seaborn, Edwin *The March of Medicine in Western Ontario* Toronto: Ryerson, 1944.

Smith, Heman C. and Frederick M. Smith *Nauvoo the Beautiful: The City of the Saints* Lamoni: Iowa, 1910.

Spicer, Elizabeth *Descriptions of London and its Environs, 1793-1847* Western Ontario History Nuggets, 31. London, Ont.: Lawson Memorial Library, University of Western Ontario 1964.

Stevens, George Roy *The Incompleat Canadian* Toronto: T. Eaton Co., 1965.

Stimson, Elam, MD. *The Cholera Beacon* Dundas, Upper Canada: G. H. Hackstaff, 1835. Reprinted in *Transactions* of the London and Middlesex Historical Society, part XV, 1937.

Stott, Glenn *Witness to History: Tales of Southwestern Ontario* Arkona, Ont.: The author, 1985.

Talman, James J. and Ruth Davis Talman *Western 1878-1953* London, Ont.: University of Western Ontario, 1953.

Tausky, Nancy Z. and Lynne D. DiStefano. *Victorian Architecture in London and Southwestern Ontario: Symbols of Aspiration* Toronto: University of Toronto, 1986.

Tiffany, Orrin Edward *The Relations of the United States to the Canadian Rebellion of 1837-1838* Buffalo, N.Y.: Buffalo Historical Society, 1905.

II PERIODICALS, ORIGINAL SOURCES, ETC.

Armstrong, Frederick H. and Daniel J. Brock "The Rise of London: A Study of Urban Evolution in Nineteenth-Century Southwestern Ontario" in F. H. Armstrong *et al.*, ed. *Aspects of nineteenth century Ontario: essays presented to James J. Talman.* Toronto: University of Toronto P, 1974. Pp. 80-100.

"The Gallows Tree; Over Half a Century of Hangings in This City: The Culprits and Their Crimes" London *Free Press* (26 November 1885), pp. 2-3.

Landon, Fred. "London and its vicinity 1837-38" Ontario Historical Society, *Papers and Records*, XXIV, (1927), 410-438.

London, Ontario *Charter of the City of London* 1854. (Reprint of the proclamation of Lord Elgin, Governor-General of British North America, issued at Quebec City, 21 September 1854; in *By-laws of the City of London*, 1908, pp. 3-5.)

Malone, Mary "Imperial Beginnings" *London Magazine* (December 1986), 115-118.

Miller, Orlo "The Bratton Kidnapping" *Canadian Science Digest*, (London, Ont.), 1, 3 (April 1938), 166-169.

— "The History of the Newspaper Press in London, 1830-1875" Ontario Historical Society, *Papers and Records*, XXXII (1937), 114-139.

— "The Letters of Rebels and Loyalists" *Canadian Science Digest* (London, Ont.), 1, 1 (January 1938), 70-78.

— "Topics of the Town," London *Free Press*, various issues, 1934. Scrapbook, Orlo Miller Papers, Regional Collection, University of Western Ontario Library.

Miller, Orlo and Godfrey Ridout *The Saint – A Chamber Opera* London, Ont., 1955. Unpublished script, Orlo Miller Papers, Regional Collection, (University of Western Ontario Library.)

Morrow, Lance "1968," *Time*, 131, 2 (11 January 1988).

Proudfoot, William "The Proudfoot Papers, 1832-1848," London and Middlesex Historical Society, *Transactions*, various parts between 1915 and 1938.

Railton, George "London in the Forties; Reminiscences." Unpublished manuscript transcribed in the *Edwin Seaborn Collection: Diaries*, pp. 1074-1081, London Room, London Public Library.

Strong, George Templeton "The Panic of 1837" in vol. 6 (1833-1840) of *The annals of America.* Chicago: Britannica, 1968.

CHIEF OFFICERS OF
THE LONDON COMMUNITY
1840–1988

From the first settlement of the site in 1826 until 1840, London was officially a part of the Township of London. In the latter year London was granted the status of a "police village." The Board of Police consisted of one representative from each of the four wards, plus an additional representative at large, commonly called the "fifth member." From among themselves the five members of the Board chose their chief officer, known as President.

Since the first Boards of Police contained many prominent pioneer residents, the complete roster for the village period, 1840-1847, is here given.

1840 *George Jervis Goodhue, President*
St Patrick's Ward   Dennis O'Brien
St George's Ward   George Jervis Goodhue
St Andrew's Ward   Simeon Morrill
St David's Ward   John Balkwill
Member-at-large   James Givens

1841 *James Givens, President*
St Patrick's Ward   Dennis O'Brien
St George's Ward   John Jennings
St Andrew's Ward   Simeon Morrill
St David's Ward   John Balkwill
Member-at-large   James Givens

1842 *Edward Matthews, President*
St Patrick's Ward   John O'Neil
St George's Ward   John Claris
St Andrew's Ward   H. Van Buskirk
St David's Ward   John Balkwill
Member-at-large   Edward Matthews

1843 *Edward Matthews, President*
St Patrick's Ward   Edward Matthews
St George's Ward   John Claris
St Andrew's Ward   Richard Frank
St David's Ward   John Balkwill
Member-at-large   John O'Neal

1844 *James Farley, President* J. Cruikshank
    St Patrick's Ward John Jennings
    St George's Ward John Talbot
    St Andrew's Ward John Balkwill
    St David's Ward James Farley
    Member-at-large

1845 *John Balkwill, President* J. Cruikshank
    St Patrick's Ward John Jennings
    St George's Ward John Balkwill
    St Andrew's Ward John Blair
    St David's Ward John O'Flynn
    Member-at-large

1846 *T. W. Shepherd, President* William Balkwill
    St Patrick's Ward T.W. Shepherd
    St George's Ward Simeon Morrill
    St Andrew's Ward John O'Flynn
    St David's Ward George Thomas
    Member-at-large

1847 *Dr Hiram Davis Lee, President* H.S. Robinson
    St Patrick's Ward William Barker
    St George's Ward Philo Bennett
    St Andrew's Ward James Graham
    St David's Ward Dr Hiram Davis Lee
    Member-at-large

The Clerks of the Village Board of Police, as given by Goodspeed (1889), were:

1840	Alexander Robertson
1841	David J. Hughes
1842-1843	Dr William King Cornish
1844	George Railton
1845-1846	Thomas Scatcherd
1847	Henry Hamilton

No complete set of records from the village period survive today. An Assessment Roll for 1844, sporadic newspaper accounts of the proceedings of the Board, and tantalizing references in Goodspeed to documents that were apparently still in existence in 1889, are all we have left. On page 231 of the *History of Middlesex,* the Goodspeeds note that there was "no record antedating April, 1843, when clerk W. K. Cornish was instructed to obtain a minute book and the necessary stationery for the use of the Police Board." No trace can be found of this Minute Book.

London was incorporated as a town, effective Saturday, 1 January 1848. The mayors of the town from that date until its incorporation as a city in 1855 were as follows:

1848	Simeon Morrill
1849	Thomas C. Dixon
1850	Simeon Morrill
1851	Simeon Morrill
1852	Edward Adams
1853	Edward Adams
1854	Marcus Holmes

The principal paid officer of the Town Council was the Clerk. Alfred Carter served in 1848; he was succeeded by James Farley, who served from 1849 until London's incorporation as a city.

The complete record of the mayors of the City of London since incorporation follows:

1855	Murray Anderson
1856	William Barker
1857	Elijah Leonard
1858	David Glass
1859	William McBride
1860	James Moffatt
1861-1864	Francis Evans Cornish
1865-1866	David Glass
1867	Frank Smith
1868	W. Simpson Smith
1869	John Christie (resigned after one month); Simpson H. Graydon
1870	Simpson H. Graydon
1871	James M. Cousins
1872	John Campbell
1873	Andrew McCormick
1874-1875	Benjamin Cronyn
1876	D.C. McDonald
1877	Robert Pritchard
1878-1879	Robert Lewis
1880-1881	John Campbell
1882-1883	Edmund Meredith
1884	Charles Smith Hyman
1885	Henry Becher
1886	T.H. Hodgens
1887-1888	James Cowan
1889-1891	George Taylor
1892	W.M. Spencer
1893-1894	Emanuel T. Essery
1895-1897	John W. Little
1898-1899	John D. Wilson, MD

1900-1901	Frederick Rumball
1902-1904	Adam Beck
1905	Clarence T. Campbell, MD
1906-1907	Joseph C. Judd
1908-1909	Samuel Stevely
1910-1911	J.H.A. Beattie
1912-1914	C.M.R. Graham
1915	H.A. Stevenson, MD
1916	William M. Gartshore
	H.A. Stevenson, MD
	(At the election of 1 January 1916, Mr Gartshore received 3,887 votes, Dr Stevenson, 3,873. On recount, each man received 3,887 votes. The City Clerk, Samuel Baker, cast the deciding vote in favour of Dr Stevenson.)
1917	H.A. Stevenson, MD
1918-1919	Charles R. Somerville
1920-1921	Edgar Sydney Little
1922	J. Cameron Wilson, MD
1923-1925	George A. Wenige
1926-1927	John M. Moore
1928	George A. Wenige
1929-1930	W.J. Kilpatrick
1931-1932	George Hayman
1933	F.B. Kilbourne
1934-1935	George A. Wenige
1936-1938	T.F. Kingsmill, Jr.
1939-1940	Joseph Allan Johnston
1940	William J. Heaman
	(Mr Heaman was appointed by Council on 8 September 1940 to act as presiding officer in the absence of Mayor Johnston on active military service.)
1941-1945	William J. Heaman
1946	Frederick George McAllister
1947-1948	George A. Wenige
1949	Ray A. Dennis
1950	George A. Wenige
1951-1954	Allan J. Rush
1955	Allan J. Rush
	George Ernest Beedle
	Ray A. Dennis
	(Mayor Rush resigned 29 March 1955. On 1 April Alderman Beedle

was elected by Council to serve for
the balance of the term. On
8 August Mayor Beedle resigned
and Alderman Ray A. Dennis was
chosen by Council to serve the
balance of the term.)

1956-1957	Ray A. Dennis
1958-1960	Joseph Allan Johnston
1961-1967	Frank Gordon Stronach
1968	Herbert J. McClure

(Mayor Stronach died in office 1
January 1968. Controller McClure
was elected by Council to fill out
the balance of the term.)

1969-1971	Herbert J. McClure
1972	J. Frederick Gosnell
	Jane Elizabeth Bigelow

(Mayor Gosnell resigned 6 March
1972. Controller Bigelow was
elected by Council to serve the
balance of the term.)

1973-1978	Jane Elizabeth Bigelow
1979-1985	Martin Al Gleeson
1986-1988	Thomas Charles Gosnell

In the City of London's 133 years of corporate existence, it has been served by
ten City Clerks. The dates given below are in each case the year of their appointments. Two clerks, Samuel Baker and Reginald Cooper, between them served a
total of fifty-four years.

1855	John Doyle
1858	Alexander S. Abbott
1891	C.A. Kingston
1902	C.B. Edwards
1904	Samuel Baker
1933	Kenneth Grant Crawford
1944	Nora Toll
1946	Reginald H. Cooper
1971	William S. Ross
1981	Kenneth Walter Sadler

INDEX